U0165548

智慧財產權法專論
——科技時代新思維

曾勝珍 | 著

序

　　我喜歡寫學術論文，尤其是針對某個議題的專業論文，從蒐集資料、整理初稿、完稿修飾乃至投稿成功，心血躍然為學報期刊的鉛字時，彷彿歷經一場從無到有的建設，很有挑戰性與成就感。然而這樣自我成長的喜悅，若無嶺東科技大學張台生總執行長與蔡寶倫董事長二十餘年的支持，加上行政同仁楊永列院長與馨瑱、安裕的鼎力相助，我絕對不會有目前的餘裕度，能醉心並遨遊於學術瀚海。

　　這本專書的出版，首先感謝五南法政編輯振煌學弟與奇蓁的催生與完成，並借重嶺東科技大學財經法律研究所研究生祥維與維拓協助校稿。郭振恭院長與師母對我的提攜，恩師陳文吟老師對我的栽培，我只能用謙卑與進修的努力來回報；新興議題往往使我沉迷，而國際交流的經驗，更使我有師事

SHIGENORI MATSUI教授的機會，加拿大英屬哥倫比亞大學法學院（The University of British Columbia）這些年的互動，增長我更宏觀的視野，而這一切都在我持續不斷的研究中，和世界各地的讀者分享。

　　我最愛的先生和孩子們！僅以此書獻給你們對我的包容與照顧。

曾勝珍

謹誌於溫哥華英屬哥倫比亞大學

2011.6.22

目　錄

第一章　智慧財產權售出與購入之探討

曾勝珍

■摘要 SUMMARY

　　知識、技術和新發明帶來嶄新的經濟收益，智慧財產權的所有成了經濟收益的利器，在法律上有所保障，可以拉開競爭者的追趕，也可以遏止仿冒侵權的發生，讓智慧財產權擁有者具有絕對的經濟利益。然而智慧財產權的取得向來是自我研發、創作，需要時間的積累才能有所成就、甚至沒有成就，這也產生了智慧財產權的買賣發生，就像人類交易行為一樣，無法自產的物品便以金錢或勞務換取，智慧財產權的售出與購入也是如此。如何買賣智慧財產權，是近年來的熱門話題，操作此種資產的除了鎖定特定買賣標的的企業、仲介團體外，還包括基金經理人、投資客等，智慧財產權被視為有別於傳統金融產品的投資利器，無形資產的買賣形成新興的經濟勢力，正確的資產估價與流通方式，將能更週全的保障買賣雙方與整體交易市場。

關鍵詞

▣ 智慧財產權	▣ 專利授權公司	▣ 估價
▣ 網際網路	▣ 專利	

Abstract

　　"New Economy" based on knowledge, innovation and other intangible assets. This paper tries to understand of intellectual property law and particular IP transactions. Secondly, it hopes to advise opinions on both the practical and strategic aspects of buying and selling IP, especially about why, what and how to purchase intellectual property. The valuation of IP assets is a vexing endeavor, and as a result keeps many cautious banks and investors out of the IP marketplace.

Keywords：Intellectual Property Rights, Internet, Non-Practicing Entities, Patent, Assessment.

壹、導　論

　　知識、技術和新發明帶來嶄新的經濟收益，無體財產權的價值形成「新型經濟」（new economy）[1]的蓬勃成長，如何買賣智慧財產權，是近年來的熱門話題。買方希望得到價格低廉、所有權完整且取得容易的商品[2]，因協調與使用智慧財產權的費率節節升高，如專利授權公司（non-practicing entities, NPEs），也能以種種名目向大型公司收取使用費用，以2009年為例，超過225個項目的收取費用高達美金30億[3]。操作此種資產的除了鎖定特定買賣標的的企業、仲介團體外，還包括基金經理人、投資客等，智慧財產權被視為有別於傳統金融產品的投資利器[4]。

---

[1]　Peter C. Schechter, Buying and Selling Intellectual Property: Why, What & How, 992 PLI/Pat 85(2010).

[2]　Lew Zaretzki and Kent Richardson, The Patent Transaction Market at a Crossroads, Intellectual Asset Management, March/April 2009, at 25-29, last visited: http://www.iam-magazine.com/issues/article.ashx?g=714f853e-b68c-4d88-a0bb-00d70d5f0302&q=Lew+Zaretzki+and+Kent+Richardson#search=%22Lew+Zaretzki+and+Kent+Richardson%22(2010/9/11); IP Valuation, IP Auctions and IP Licensing Roundtable, FICPI World Congress, June 8, 2009, last visited: http://www.ficpi.org/library/09WashingtonCONGRESS/session-summaries.html#8(2010/9/10).

[3]　John Amster, CEO, RPX Corp., IP Aggregators and Intermediaries, Monetization 2009 PLI Presentation, May 13, 2009 (San Francisco); NPE指自己不生產產品，但是藉由控告其他公司侵權而取得損害賠償金，或是透過授權取得權利金之公司為專利流氓（Patent Troll）主要以購買或取得重要專利控告大公司而取得利益，將本屬於無形資產的智慧財產權或是專利，轉換成現金，皆為NPE的營運模式。David，誰是Patent Troll眼中大肥羊？科技產業資訊室，財團法人國家實驗研究院科技政策與資訊中心，2008年12月5日，http://iknow.stpi.org.tw/Post/Read.aspx?PostID=3361 (上網日期:2010/9/12)。

[4]　Jennifer Hughes, Morgan Stanley Unveils $250 million Securitization, Financial Times, July 13 2009.

貳、購買智慧財產權的理由

　　通常購買智慧財產權的理由不外希望據此權利生產相關產品銷售，或純粹只為取得先機超越競爭對手，或如德州儀器（Texas Instruments）購買DSL專利，或微軟（Microsoft）購買網路電視（Web TV）專利，以維持其市場競爭力及專屬性；以下說明現今市場中可能出現的原因。

一、進入銷售市場的捷徑

　　直接購買智慧財產權是絕佳的市場發展武器，因為不需經由冗長的研發試驗程序，也相對節省了生產成本，而購買人要留意購買的智慧財產權是否權益完整，出售人擁有合法的所有權，該項權利的聲譽與評價，其他如藉由此項權利開發成商品後進入市場的人脈管道，與社會關係的連結都是決定的關鍵；買方同時要確保該權利的授權契約有效，及製造商、經銷商、當地顧問間的關係和睦，以維持市場的活絡與價值，此外，還須在產品被公開前保持保密性，避免商品化的過程不如預期影響公司商譽。

二、獨佔市場的利器

　　買方也有可能純為佔有市場，防止競爭對手搶得先機瓜分市場，根本沒有製造成商品進軍銷售市場的計畫，也就是購買智慧財產權的目的，只為防堵競爭對手能創新產品的機會，而終極目標仍為獨佔市場避免流失客戶，買方甚至可能買下競爭對手取得授權的公司，以斷絕其取得授權的來源，然而此種斬草除根的做法，在交互授權頻繁的資訊業中並不值得推崇，不但造成爭訟的來源，更無益於事業的永續發展和良性互動；當訴訟發生時，也有可能被控侵權的被告成為買方，即買下對造的智慧財產權結束訟爭，取代昂貴的訴訟費用及冗長的權利攻防過程。

　　無論基於何種理由，買方於買下智慧財產權時，都應對維持、執行及保障該權利付出心力，以維持該資產的價值，因而，買方於買受時亦應慎重思考該當維護費用，該費用有可能還超過買方當時購買的權利價值，因此買方是以何種心態買受該權利值得慎思。

參、如何決定

　　智慧財產權的價值往往和其鄰接權有關，如何包裝及開發智慧財產權，使其成為有利潤的商品，建議如下。

一、首先確認欲購買的智慧財產權其核心價值

　　如新發明的藥品搭配單一專利權即可，但如其他工業產業則不然，一種產品可能伴隨多種專利或商標、營業秘密等權利，買方在此種情形購買某一種專利，無法滿足其獨占市場壟斷顧客來源的目的，亦無助益經濟效能的提升，因此，本文建議當買方不是為了開發新商品的目的而購買智慧財產權時，要確認其價值是否符合買方想像，若是要開發新產品的情形，還要考慮與其他權利的關聯性，避免買到的智慧財產權實質效益無法發揮。

二、智慧財產權估價的重點

　　智慧財產權的價值仰賴許多和傳統資產不盡相同的因素，買方的購買意願影響智慧財產權的買賣價格，如專利的獨特及稀有性，或法院對相關案件的見解看法，都會對智慧財產權的價格產生影響，舉例而言，商標估價遠比專利容易，因為商標價值往往依附在其商譽（good will）上，並和實際的商品相結合，以市場上對此商品的評價很容易估算出該商標的價值。此外以下有三種方式檢測智慧財產權的價值[5]，1.市場價格，2.取代或重新建立此智慧財產權的費用，3.此智慧財產權能創造的收益現值；1及2兩種估算方式都不容易，一般傾向於第三種計算方式，即以一個智慧財產權的價值乘上未來授權費用的總額，目前估價的程式及計算方式都有既定的標準存在[6]。

肆、如何購買

　　當買方在做決定會衡量的因素有下列幾項。

一、是否也一併購買智慧財產權所附著的事業體

　　買方即使取得智慧財產權，但無法擁有經營團隊或後台管理甚至技藝精湛的員工，智慧財產權本身無法擴展生產線或業務，而原擁有

---

[5]　Keith Bergelt, head of the Open Invention Network, as quoted in the Roundtable discussion appearing in Mergers & Acquisitions, October 2008.

[6]　可參考http://www.gathering2.com/# 及https://www.patentfreedom.com/index.html兩個網站。

權利的公司與其他機構搭配的人脈或關係，並不會隨著權利移轉而由買受人承接[7]，買受人是基於防範他人獨占或壟斷市場的原因時，則必須排除購買固定資產或公司企業體的想法，一則花費更大，二則還須背負未在預期之中的經營責任。

　　買方還要慎重考慮產品的生命週期，美國USPTO對專利的使用有明文規定[8]，當事人必須對USPTO出具申請書（the Amendment to Allege Use）後，才能主張使用（intent-to-use），否則當此專利與原先之事業體有一定的相關連時，專利轉讓不一定順利；其他配套的契約也須留意對買方的保障，如果買方買到的權利受限於非獨家（non-exclusive），將大大減損其預期利益。

二、經由公開拍賣

　　智慧財產權的公開銷售市場是買賣的重要場所，2006年4月Ocean Tomo公司在美國舊金山進行2.5小時的拍賣會，當日銷售比例達百分之44的專利，金額達850萬美金[9]，到2009年3月最後一場拍賣會金額僅270萬美金[10]。公開拍賣使一般人皆有機會接觸到智慧財產權的買賣，然而因為拍賣場的時間限制，買方必須在極短時間內做決定，加上場內還有純觀望的買家及投資客等，對真正有意購買的買方不見得有利。

---

[7]　Karen N. Ballack, Acquisitions and Spin-Offs, Handling IP Issues in Business Transactions 2009 PLI Presentation, February 9, 2009 (San Francisco).

[8]　15 U.S.C. 1060.

[9]　James A. Malackowski, Keith Cardoza, Cameron Gray and Rick Conroy, The Intellectual Property Marketplace: Emerging Transaction and Investment Vehicles, The Licensing Journal, February 2007, Volume 27, Number 2, at 1-11.

[10]　Zusha Elinson, Ocean Tomo IP Auction Unite Draws Low Bid, IP Law & Business, June 17, 2009.

三、經由法院執行

因為經濟衰退使得公司無法經營時，會出售其擁有的智慧財產權，近年最有名的例子是Nortel Networks Corp.一案[11]，Ericsson AB公司以11億3千萬美金買下破產的Nortel Networks Corp公司，通常因賣方缺乏資金急於求現，亦無法給買方任何保證，此買賣必須經由法院進行，最好在賣方宣告破產前完成，破產公司在被正式宣告前九十天的交易都會被檢查，避免其藉由此種方式脫產。

四、經由網路交換

如Yet2.com（www.yet2.com）及Patentbidask（www.patentbidask.com）都是網路上進行智慧財產權競價與拍賣的網站[12]，尤其是Yet2.com標榜是世上最大的智慧財產權交換網站。

五、經由授權方式

經由授權契約取得使用權，但因權利人不見得願意授權他人使用，即使授權後也可能在期限屆至時拒絕延展，且取得授權有時遠比直接買下權利還難，因為授權人會以種種理由限縮被授權人的使用，對急於使用權利的買方而言，經由授權方式獲得使用權，也是變通的一種方式。

---

[11] Suzanne Stevens, Distress Continues Driving Patent Deals, The Deal, July 27, 2009.

[12] Yet2.com: About Us, available at http://www.yet2.com (last visited October 28, 2009).

伍、如何出售

一、為何要出售

　　當維護智慧財產權的費用過高，或公司進行合併時所買入的智慧財產權，甚至是為了研發或實驗所添購的項目，未料表現不如預期，或如商標所有人不再使用該商標，或已結束該產業之營運，都有可能是出售智慧財產權的原因，為避免被競爭對手使用或藉由有信譽的買方重新對該權利附著之商品，注入新生命以延續該產品之商品命脈，也可能是所有人考慮出售的原因，賣方可以得到出賣的對價，又能延續該智財權所維繫的商品週期；而對買方而言，直接購入一個優良的品牌，不但可以吸引原有顧客群，減少廣告支出與開發客源的時間[13]，對買賣雙方都是很好的機會。

二、出售內容

　　閒置未用的智慧財產權可能被權利人遺忘，因此，權利人應固定檢視本身所擁有的權利內涵，也許目前對該等權利沒有任何使用計畫，也沒有產生獲利，但權利人應在出售前仔細檢測，是否確定不再使用或未來仍有使用的機會，賣方在買賣契約中加入「買回條款」，也是一項可行的建議方式。

---

[13] David S. Ruder, New Strategies for Owners of Discontinued Brands, Northwestern Journal of Technology and IP, Fall 2004, Vol. 3, No. 1., at 73.

三、如何出售

　　權利首重包裝其出售的智慧財產權以吸引買家，仰賴仲介人士也是一種做法，賣方為了避免其權利被競爭對手買入，通常不會使用公開拍賣而採用私下交易的模式，賣方主導所有的買賣契約內容及願意揭露的資訊部分，除非賣方希望用快速競價且吸引眾多買家時，才會採取公開拍賣的做法。此外出售予專利授權公司亦是一種途徑[14]。權利人也可以將智慧財產權資產交由仲介團體，當繳交仲介費用後經由仲介團體的服務取得售出的機會，如科技、電子、資訊等產業往往使用此類途徑將其資產市場化，如2008年6月成立「Allied資產信託」（AlliedSecurity Trust）；同年秋天，另成立「Rational 專利交換」（Rational Patent Exchange）[15]。

四、保密義務

　　買賣雙方對保密義務的遵行能維護智慧財產權資產的交易，尤其是涉及專利的部分，建議賣方至最後成交階段才對買方提供核心資

---

[14] 專利授權公司並不進行生產製造或產品銷售，但經由獨立研發或專利轉讓取得專利權，以授權談判及專利訴訟為主要手段，向從事生產或製造公司收取權利金或賠償金為營利目標，根據PatentFreedom資料庫統計，自1985年以來，截至2008年12月31日，已確定專利授權公司超過220家（這數字仍在增加）。這群NPEs向3500家正常營運公司興訟案件超過2200件，且這些訴訟活動也在日益增多之中。2008年NPEs參與的專利訴訟案件約350件，約佔全年專利訴訟案件之13%，相較2004年以前年平均不到5%，已成長一倍多。May，專利授權公司（NPEs）參與的美國專利訴訟案件約佔13%，科技產業資訊室，財團法人國家實驗研究院科技政策與資訊中心，2009年7月6日，http://iknow.stpi.org.tw/Post/Read.aspx?PostID=3421（上網日期：2010/9/12）。

[15] Hewlett-Packard Co., Nokia Corp., Cisco Systems Inc., IBM Corp., Panasonic, Samsung and TiVo Inc.等公司組成，見www.rpxcorp.com 網站。Peter C. Schechter, Buying and Selling Intellectual Property: Why, What & How, 992 PLI/Pat 98(2010).

訊，或聘請第三人撰寫契約，徹底防範秘密資訊被外洩的可能。

五、不出售的替代方案

將無形資產證券化是不出售智慧財產權但仍可獲利的方式，2006年5月，在無形資產證券化中資產來自因智慧財產權而產生的現金流量，而非實際出售該智慧財產權的對價，因使用商標、著作權、專利而付出的授權費用，能製造出另一種資產價值，由特殊目的機構或公司購買及包裝資產後（Special Purpose Vehicle, SPV），發行證券並能隔絕破產時被債權人求償，是一種高度信用化與資產證券化的核心，買受人則能享有從SPV產生的授權金利潤。

無形資產證券化最大的缺點來自金額的門檻過高，在美國至少需要美元2,500萬的資金，因此，另一種對權利人有利的方式是經由仲介團體，獲取對其所有的智慧財產權的利益；或將權利經由授權方式取得對價，皆比直接出售還能保有所有權。

陸、結　論

在知識經濟的時代下，經濟活動中擁有智慧財產權是進行經濟行為有力武器，大家都想要擁有別人沒有的創意、無形資產，在經濟活動中有更好的競爭力，而智慧財產權的買賣過程若能更加周全，便能夠使整體市場更活躍、更健全。買賣的行為的產生，自人類有經濟活動以來都是以相同的目的在進行，都是為了彼此的利益在做交換行為，從遠古時代以物易物，到金錢貨幣的交易，都是為了滿足雙方最大的需求，讓雙方可以心滿意足獲取最大效用，而智慧財產權等無形資產亦是如此，智慧財產權所有者、提供者與智慧財產權需求者，雙方若能夠透過良好的交易方式進行，便可使整體知識經濟的發展更好。無形資產的買賣形成新興的經濟勢力，正確的資產估價與流通方式，將能更週全的保障買賣雙方與整體交易市場。

參考文獻

中文

David，(2008)，誰是Patent Troll眼中大肥羊？，*科技產業資訊室，財團法人國家實驗研究院科技政策與資訊中心*，http://iknow.stpi.org.tw/Post/Read.aspx?PostID=3361（上網日期：2010/9/12）。

May，(2009)，專利授權公司（NPEs）參與的美國專利訴訟案件約佔13%，*科技產業資訊室，財團法人國家實驗研究院科技政策與資訊中心*，http://iknow.stpi.org.tw/Post/Read.aspx?PostID=3421（上網日期：2010/9/12）。

英文

David S. Ruder, (2004), New Strategies for Owners of Discontinued Brands, *Northwestern Journal of Technology and IP*, 3(1), 73.

IP Valuation, IP Auctions and IP Licensing Roundtable, FICPI World Congress,(2009), last visited: http://www.ficpi.org/library/09WashingtonCONGRESS/session-summaries.html#8(2010/9/10).

Karen N. Ballack,(2009),Acquisitions and Spin-Offs, Handling IP Issues in Business Transactions PLI Presentation, (San Francisco).

Lew Zaretzki and Kent Richardson,(2009),The Patent Transaction Market at a Crossroads, *Intellectual Asset Management*, 25-29,

last visited:
http://www.iam-magazine.com/issues/article.ashx?g=714f853e-b68c-4d88-a0bb-00d70d5f0302&q=Lew+Zaretzki+and+Kent+Richardson#search=%22Lew+Zaretzki+and+Kent+Richardson%22(2010/9/11).

Peter C. Schechter, (2010), Buying and Selling Intellectual Property: Why, What & How, **992 PLI/Pat 85**.

Jennifer Hughes, July 13 2009, Morgan Stanley Unveils $250 million Securitization, **Financial Times**.

James A. Malackowski, Keith Cardoza, Cameron Gray and Rick Conroy, (2007), The Intellectual Property Marketplace: Emerging Transaction and Investment Vehicles, **The Licensing Journal**, 27(2), 1-11.

Zusha Elinson, (2009),Ocean Tomo IP Auction Unite Draws Low Bid, **IP Law & Business**.

Suzanne Stevens, Distress Continues Driving Patent Deals, The Deal, July 27, 2009.

IP Valuation, IP Auctions and IP Licensing Roundtable, *FICPI World Congress*,(2009), last visited: http://www.ficpi.org/library/09WashingtonCONGRESS/session-summaries.html#8(2010/9/10).

James A. Malackowski, Keith Cardoza, Cameron Gray and Rick Conroy, (2007), The Intellectual Property Marketplace: Emerging Transaction and Investment Vehicles, *The Licensing Journal*, 27(2), 1-11.

Jennifer Hughes, July 13 2009, Morgan Stanley Unveils $250 million Securitization, *Financial Times*.

Karen N. Ballack,(2009),Acquisitions and Spin-Offs, *Handling IP Issues in Business Transactions 2009 PLI Presentation*, (San

Francisco).

Lew Zaretzki and Kent Richardson,(2009),The Patent Transaction Market at a Crossroads, *Intellectual Asset Management*, 25-29, last visited: http://www.iam-magazine.com/issues/article. ashx?g=714f853e-b68c-4d88-a0bb-00d70d5f0302&q=Lew+Zaret zki+and+Kent+Richardson#search=%22Lew+Zaretzki+and+Kent +Richardson%22(2010/9/11).

Peter C. Schechter, (2010), Buying and Selling Intellectual Property: Why, What & How, *992 PLI/Pat 85*.

Suzanne Stevens, (2009), Distress Continues Driving Patent Deals, *The Deal*.

Zusha Elinson, (2009),Ocean Tomo IP Auction Unite Draws Low Bid, *IP Law & Business*.

第二章　An Analysis of P2P Copyright Infringement

曾勝珍

目次

Abstract

June 2005, U.S. Supreme Court made a judgment on MGM v. Grokster, the Court held that Grokster must take the secondary liability, and this case was used to clarify and correct some legal opinions before from the lower courts. As network technology develops rapidly, even the United States Congress wants to cover the shortage of existing regulations and practices on P2P Infringement of internet copyright through legislation, the following explored related legal norms in US Copyright Law on the application of P2P technology, hoped to develop better business models for recording industry, so that users could afford the cost of software to solve legal issues arising from above, reducing the current infringement situation, and allowed real creators access to the best interests; apart from reference to the experience of the United States, reflection and suggestions of related issues in Taiwan were also covered.

Keywords: copyright infringement, copyright law, internet, p2p, music file download, intellectual property right, Computer Law, Digital Millennium Copyright Act (DMCA)

Ⅰ. Introduction

As the gap between Internet and the real world, the theoretical uncertainties in academia and judicial circles are formed, from the paper contract to network contract, from the physical store to E-Shops, the Internet world and e-commerce increase more possibilities for commercial operations or trades; the world of network is a space full of expectance and imagination, resembling such as site establishment, document exchange and system functions expand users' demand and dependence on the network greatly[1].

However, unsound environment would encourage and drive the prevalence of pirates, although the low-cost or even free of charge is the incentive for users, the motivation of creators' creation is injured greatly; if excessive restrictions on users and short-term protection of the author, in the long run, the circulation speed and popularity of works are impacted, which is even adversely to promote in the market. Since the Supreme Court of the United States issued a verdict on the Sony[2] case in 1984, the inducement doctrine theory from Grokster case in 2005 was different from the secondary liability in the aforementioned traditional cases; the U.S. Congress passed the Digital Millennium Copyright Act (DMCA) in 1998, and it actively encourage other countries to comply with DMCA when signing a bilateral treaty of trade[3].

On June 27, 2005, the Supreme Court of the United States issued a verdict on Merto-Goldwyn-Mayer Studios, Inc. V. Grokster, Ltd.[4]: when somene distributes or installs certain equipment for the purpose of copyright infringement, he should still take the responsibility of the

---

[1] See Steven a. Heath, Contracts, Copyright, and Confusion Revisiting the Enforceability of 'shrinkwrap' licenses, 5 Chi.--Kent J. Intell. Prop 12 (2005).

[2] Sony Corp. of Am. v. Universal City Studios, Inc., 464 U.S. 417, 442 (1984).

[3] Matthew Rimmer, Hail to the Thief: A Tribute to Kazaa, 2. U. Ottawa L. & Tech. J. 173 (2005).

[4] Metro-Goldwyn-Mayer Studios, Inc. v. Grokster, Ltd., 125 S. Ct. 2764, 2775 (2005).

results[5]. Since the popularity of the Internet, the Supreme Court of the United States' decision in Grokster not only can produce the effect of an injunction, but also can promote audio-visual industries, such as Stream Case and Sharman Networks to set up tort liability, as the standard for general public to determine.

The MP3 case of National Cheng Gung University[6] happened in April 2001 in Taiwan, which had a significant impact on Taiwan's Copyright Law and relevant norms; on September 9, 2005, Taipei District Court also declared Kuro violation of copyright[7], different from the judgment of another case on June 30 in the same year: Shilin District Court declared ezPeer not establish tort[8], not responsible for tort and criminal liability, but also first determined that users had to bear criminal liability[9].

---

[5] eth. A. Miller, P2P File Distribution: An Analysis of Design, Liability, Litigation, And Potential Solutions, 25 Rev. Litig. 183 (winter, 2006).5

[6] On May 23, 2006, IFPI formally sued 14 students involved in MP3 download from National Cheng Gung University to Tainan District Prosecutors Office, accused them of illegally setting up website for others to download copyrighted music, in violation of copyright law. After the accusation reception, Tainan District Prosecutors Office changed case file "Ta" to case file "Cheng", which was investigated by Kun-ting Chen, inquisitor responsible for the case of students download MP3 (Article 228 Code of Criminal Procedure). IFPI pointed out that, one student were suspected of setting up their own private website illegally, from which other people can download copyright music, it seriously infringed the rights of the record industry; As regards the other 13 students involved in the case, simply download copyright music, copyright infringement was less serious, so they were not sued. The inquisitor even searched into that student's dormitory. Chuan Ping Law Network, Apr. 2001, www.cyberlawyer.com.tw (search date: Nov. 15, 2005).

[7] Judgement (2003) Su-2146.

[8] Judgment (2003) Su-728.

[9] "IFPI vs Kuro", IS Law Network, http://www.angle.com.tw/focus/focus117.htm (search date: Nov. 23, 2005).

This paper focused on P2P infringement of copyright in the United States[10], based on the opinions from Supreme Court of the United States in Grokster, compared with Taiwan court's reason of decision in related cases, first of all, the application of P2P transmission technology was introduced - mainly centralized management and distributed management directory systems, followed the opinions from Napster,

---

[10] P2P is called Peer-to-Peer, some are translated as "point-to-point", "end-to-end", the so-called "Peer" is to be as the server and client at the same time. Its scope of application contains the sharing of information resources, distributed computing (be multiple paralleled in P2P environment, assembling many computers scattered in the network, combined and become a supercomputer with powerful computing. In the network computer formed by network link, its idle CPU and storage space can be fully utilized), cooperative work, real-time communication technologies and search engines; Peer originally refers to "A person who has equal standing with another or others, as in rank, class, or age"; and the significance of Peer to Peer can be known: "two persons of equal status" contact and interact, so Peer to Peer itself means two linking points are on an equal footing, rather than a common master-slave architecture in Internet. This is the "distributed server" concept, a PC is transformed and have dual functions, breaking the original network structure, which used one or more servers to provide content, data is directly transmitted between two points. See Yeh, YB, P2P concepts and their practical significance of society, Information Society Journal of the Institute of Sociology, Nanhua University, Issue 7, pp.223, July 2004; because the author of P2P opened the source code, so currently a number of well-known download software are resulted from, including eMULE, eDONKEY, BT, Kuro and ezPeer software, which all use P2P technology; even the prevalent real-time messaging software, such as MSN and ICQ and so on are also the deformation of this technology; one is the centralized type, operator stores clients' directory which can be downloaded together in a server, so the client can access to it rapidly, Kuro and ezPeer have used centralized technology; another is distributed type, eMULE and eDONKEY have used it; due to slower, the user has to search for other users' download resources through the server. Ke, HY, P2P, Section A7, United Daily News, Jan. 3, 2006. For the subject of this paper, see Tzeng, SC, Hsu, YH, related questions analysis on online music – take P2P technology of MP3 music download as the core, 2006 the second seminar of information management and project management practices, pp.33-1, School of Informatics, Kainan University, May 5, 2006.

Aimster and Grokster[11] cases by the courts were explained, which formed different types of tort liability; and then recommendations and conclusions were made to existing federal regulations and new acts, hoping to provide other kinds of thinking and observation for Taiwan.

Ⅱ. P2P Technology

P2P file-sharing program enables fast and cheap e-document reproduction and distribution, which can reach the hands of many recipients in a very short time; however, author's exclusive right granted by Copyright Law needs to prove that infringer has the intent of profit, then the infringement is established, and author's exclusive rights to reproduce and spread are also ensured; the rapid spread and replication also give wealth and reputation to copyright holder; however, the use of P2P system has a great impact on traditional copyright law, although it has a significant contribution to upgrading Internet technology, the models for distribution and dissemination of copyright re-establish.

In P2P application cases, opinions from the case of Sony were first applied, the defendant Napster used the first generation of P2P network architecture, and the central directory server systems[12], each user or customer of the system is connected to the network, forming a node, the central directory server maintained complete content details

---

[11] This case was presented in Part Section 2 of this paper

[12] See Jesse M. Feder, Is Betamax Obsolete?: Sony Corp. of America v. Universal City Studios, Inc. in the Age of Napster, 37 Creighton L. Rev. 859, 864-65 (2004).

available to browse at each node, and each node had its own unique web site[13]; in order to maintain the function and control, users had to register each log-in for the latest document directory index, the central server could receive and send all of the search data and instructions, when the supply corresponded with demand, the requesting customer would receive another corresponding computer web site to meet his needs[14].

To view from the copyright holder's standpoint, musicians, lawyers, including some professional movement groups have also expressed their views, they firmly believed that the Grokster case was decisive[15], many pop music singers[16], which have also expressed support[17] for the outcome of the case. As to the consumer, Grokster

---

[13] Id. at 864.

[14] Advantages of this system lies in the central directory contains a complete list, and search quickly and effectively, Id. at 865. By virtue of the functions of a central server, it can also avoid the users to share files between them, Id. Also because of this, P2P file-sharing of non-centralized management was developed as technological developments. See Tim Wu, When Code Isn't Law, 89 Va. L. Rev. 679, 726-36 (2003).

[15] E.g. Jim Backlin, vice president of the legal department for the Christian Coalition, considered it was important to protect children from inappropriate network information, as well as the protection of its industries, so as to avoid litigation-ridden; therefore proper planning is very important to the legislation on Internet file transfer. Penny Nace, Ernie Allen & Chuck Canterbury, P2P Pressure: A Copyright Case Has Implications for Tracking Down Child-Porn Brokers, Nat.Rev. Online, Feb. 17, 2005, http://www.nationalreview.com/script/printpage.p?ref=/comment/nance200502170751.asp.

[16] Alex Veiga, Unlikely Alliances From in File-Sharing Case, Associated Press, Feb. 27, 2005, http://www.post-gazette.com/pg/05058/463051.stm.

[17] All music workers, creators with intellectual property right and consumer groups supported Grokster and P2P technology, for fear that the freedom of speech will be subject to restrictions, such as Jeff. Tweedy was a rock band's lead singer, who still supported the position of Grokster: artists should be protected; however, the use of P2P makes the

case's decision led and accelerated the upgrading of new technology. After the Supreme Court's judgment, consumers wanted download only for file sharing, not resulting in copyright infringement; for fear of being treated as an individual copyright infringement, users hoped to ascertain its area of responsibility when downloading; in entertainment industry, the Hollywood believed that the outcome of Grokster case hit its basic and the future structure, there was a loss of 240m U.S. dollars in the music industry in 2003, the movie industry lost 300m U.S. dollars[18], enterprises considered that illegal download were the main cause of loss, if the Supreme Court did not agree with the views of the entertainment industry, Hollywood must change their business approach, that is, reconstruct another successful business model.

1. Applications of P2P technology

As to the applications of traditional non-P2P Internet, users gather or contact businessmen through the Internet[19], information should be

---

Internet as audio-visual library. Other artists such as Steve Winwood, Chuck D, and Heart thought that, Grokster and Kazaa should provide a legal and important channel, so their works could be best-selling outside the world of general sales channel. Musicians Break Ranks in Grokster Case, Wash. Times, Mar. 1, 2005, http://washingtontimes.com/upi-breaking/20050301-1222226-6223r.htm. Once famous or not famous musicians consider P2P can introduce new listeners, their creativity and talent are shown on another stage, attracting more audience. Lorraine Woellert, Hobbling Grokster—and Innovation, Too, Bus. Week, Mar. 24, 2005, http://www.businessweek.com/print/technology/content/mar2005/tc20050324_0001.htm.

[18] Anna E. Engelman & Dale A. Scott, Arrgh! Hollywood Targets Internet Piracy, 11 Rich. J.L.&Tech. 3 (2004).

[19] Metro-Goldwyn-Mayer Studios, Inc. v. Grokster, Ltd., 380 F.3d 1154, 1158 (9th Cir. 2004) [hereinafter Grokster II].

transferred through a server between users to the recipient, that is, transmission of data through the server. Normal circumstances, direct transmission between users will not happen, the most important thing is the server will leave the web site and user name of the two sides, and it is absolutely impossible to happen this phenomenon in P2P system. Usually, non-P2P technology application has a number of problems: 1. so frequent links will increase the burden on the server and reduce its speed, as server has to handle queries far and near and respond them[20]. 2. Vulnerable to hacking, so when there are political or legal considerations, dissemination or transmission of content will be terminated through technology[21]. In contrast, through various terminal points, P2P technology can make the points and points be freely links, P2P computer system requires intensive and ever-linking links, so more users willing to exchange files, and make it even more rapidly.

In addition, P2P system does not store information in a central server, on the contrary, it uses many computers to simultaneously play the function of the customer and the server, P2P software is used in the following directions: 1) client, server and directory client sides as the network searcher, so that users can search for and collect information; 2) the server interprets and fulfill the requests from each side of Internet; 3) directory is full of a wide range of appropriate information and detectable Web sites, the client side and server operate with respective P2P transmission; the court found that the largest difference between Napster and Grokster cases was the distributed or centralized

---

[20] Andrew Kantor, File-Sharing Is a Lot More than Stolen Music, USA Today, Mar. 29, 2005, http://www.usatoday.com/tech/columnist/andrewkantor/2005-03-16-kantor_x.htm.

[21] Id.

management directory system, which is described below.

If the Supreme Court's opinion is in contrast, the overall technology industry will have a tremendous impact, which will also be a major constraint on technology and industry for innovation, if not trying to get consumers response in the market before, P2P technology may be regarded as an offense and worry about the impact of technology update[22]. What's worse, it is more likely to cause only big companies or enterprises can engage in technology update, smaller companies or inventors may be not satisfied by the entertainment industry, in the face of long-term or large-scale proceedings, who simply can not put up any defense[23].

In the face of the secondary liability under the decision by Supreme Court, measuring the costs of legal proceedings, including the cost of money and time appealing to the Supreme Court of the United States, when the product or the design has not yet been formed, and the company must first probe whether there is a possibility of litigation between entertainment or audio-visual industry[24], which is a major depletion and obstacles to R&D time or cost[25]. In other words, the overall entertainment industry or the copyright holder attempts to control technology R&D innovation, consumer choice will inevitably

---

[22] All of Mark Cuban, NBA's Dallas Mavericks are the co-founder of HDNet, which is high-speed software of DIRECTV. Mark Cuban, Grokster and America's Future, CNT News, Feb. 2, 2005, http://news.com.com/2102-1028_3-5559340.html.

[23] Martyn Williams, Mark Cuban to Finance Grokster's Fight, PC World, Mar. 28, 2005, http://www.pcworld.co/resource/printable/article/0,aid,120198,00.asp.

[24] Grant Gross, P-to-P Case May Have Far-Reaching Impact, PC World, Mar. 25, 2005, http://www.pcworld.com/resource/printable/article/0,aid,120189,00.asp.

[25] Id.

be limited, so the multi-application products are no longer, and the price will be difficult to change, new distribution methods are reduced, resulting in increasing more restrictions on technology improvements.

2. Centralized management directory systems

In the case, Sony Corp. Of America v. Universal City Studios, Inc. in 1984[26], which was about the TV program copyright holder sued Video tape manufacturers, the Supreme Court of the United States found that, although copyright law granted the copyright holder of certain exclusive rights, "fair use" was not included[27], the Court held that VCR machine was instantaneous shift programs, it was substantial non-infringing use, even if customers used the VCR to copy other Video Tape with copyrights[28]; the opinions from Sony case have far-reaching impact on the subsequent ruling, as to the substantial non-infringing use defended by Sony Corporation, the Seventh and Ninth Circuit Court of Appeal developed different views on joint tort liability.

On February 12, 2001, the Ninth Circuit Court of Appeal handed down Napster[29] case involving copyright infringement; the collegiate bench endorsed district judge Patel's decision to allow a preliminary injunction, that is, the record companies proposed that Napster should stop online music exchange[30]. Based on the "contributory copyright

---

[26] 464 U.S. 417, 419-20 (1984).

[27] Id. at 433.

[28] Id. at 446,456.

[29] A&M Records, Inc. v. Napster, Inc., 239 F.3d 1004-1029 (9th Cir. 2001).

[30] Id. at 1001.

infringement" and "vicarious copyright infringement" two principles, the collegiate bench maintained the judgment that Napster had to be responsible for direct copyright infringement, but it considered District Court's preliminary injunction was too broad in scope, the San Francisco federal appeals court also held that, so that injunction must be amended.

On March 6, 2001, district judge Marilyn Patel amended the original injunction, requiring Napster must build an internal screening mechanism, blocking copyright-protected songs from the server, and then carry out any action to exchange and access; RIAA also must provide a list of records, helping Napster to screening and identifying[31], the amended injunction was: only when knowing that a particular file is music or sound recording with copyright infringement, that is, know or have reason to know, and the file is stored in the Napster system, but could not prevent it from spread, Napster have to take copyright infringement responsibility. In addition, when failing to effectively supervise, Napster[32] will also have the responsibility of vicarious

---

[31] Chuan Ping Law Network, http://www.cyberlawyer.com.tw/alan4-1201.html, search date: Nov. 23, 2005.

[32] Napster's network architecture is of centralized type, this network would have two elements: a central index server, and the user endpoint. The architecture has a very large weakness: highly rely on a central index server. This weakness impacts the development of follow-up P2P applications. For the legality, safety, reliability, anonymity and other reasons, more and more P2P procedures use distributed architecture, which is the trend. The node replacing the central server is known as ultrapeer (also known as Super-node). Each one is selected from normal user nodes, and each Super-node is responsible for the maintenance of a group of users. Super-nodes will communicate with each other to form a mixed and distributed architecture. See Lin, CM, Uncovered P2P thieves through analysis of network traffic, pp.108-109, Information and Computer, Issue 306, Jan. 2006.

copyright infringement.

Although Napster demurred it was a network service provider with exemption protected by Digital Millennium Copyright Act of 1998, as it did not directly transfer audio works[33], only ways to link for Internet users to access, itself not covered reproduce works; the court held that Napster transmitted MP3 file sharer's IP to users, although links between users and share were though the Internet, rather than through the Napster system, while users' Napster browser constituted part of the system, files spread from one part of system to another part, it was also not transmitted through the system, therefore Napster was not the ISP provided by Digital Millennium Copyright Act, it could not ask for exemption[34].

The court also examined the discussion whether the Napster case constituted a substantial non-infringing use[35]. What level of infringement is the so-called "informed" infringement? If the use of product not constitutes the non-substantial infringement, it can presume that the copyright holder is informed of the infringement (the copyright holder has low burden of proof); if the use of product constitutes non-substantial infringement, then the copyright holder must prove that the defendant knowingly and negligently avoid the infringement (the copyright holder has high burden of proof). The Court found in the case that the software did not provide substantial infringing use, and then determined whether Grokster had a valid

---

[33] 512(a).

[34] Id.

[35] Grokster, 380 F.3d at 1161.

reason aware of the infringement[36], because Grokster using P2P, rather than directory management system of non-concentrated central server, to make users share files, Grokster could not be informed of the existence of infringement[37].

Ninth Circuit Court of Appeals applied the theory from Sony case in P2P case for the first time, A & M Records, Inc. V. Napster, Inc.[38], Napster enabled the users use and search their required electronic documents as long as download the necessary software in public[39]; the Court used the theory from Gershwin case to make Napster shoulder joint copyright infringement[40], Napster was informed of the infringement; re-applied the theory from Sony case - substantial non-infringing use[41], whether it constituted a substantial infringement should not be limited by the present using state, but should be compared with the status and the future parts not constitutes infringement[42]. To this end, the Court developed a two-part knowledge test, if the defendant's product did not constitute a substantial infringement, he would not be inferred to have the knowledge and to assume tort liability; but he should assume the liability if he had the knowledge, that is, measure off the responsibilities based on the

[36] Id. at 1161-62.

[37] Id. at 1163.

[38] 239 F. 3d 1004 (9th Cir. 2001).

[39] Id. at 1010-11.

[40] Id. at 1019 (quoting Gershwin Publ'g Corp. v. Columbia Artists Mgmt., Inc., 443 F.2d 1159, 1162 (2d Cir. 1971)).

[41] Elizabeth Miles, Note, In Re Aimster & MGM, Inc. v. Grokster, Ltd. : Peer-to-Peer and the Sony Doctrine, 19 Berkeley Tech.L.J. 21, 27-28 (2004).

[42] Napster, 239 F.3d at 1021.

defendant's practical situation.

Besides the discussion on whether the defendant has the knowledge or not, in substantial infringing, the District Court held that there was no services provided by the defendant, Napster's users could not search and download information related in issue[43], therefore determined Napster was compliance with "contributory infringement," which was supported by the Ninth Circuit Court of Appeals, holding that Napster has vicariously infringed plaintiff's copyright[44]; In addition, the Ninth Court also endorsed the view by the District Court that, Napster had authority and ability to monitor the activities of infringement and to reap profits[45], Napster's future expected revenue had much to the number of registered members directly, increase in the number had considerable relevance with the quality of music programs provided[46]; Napster had the right to monitor the structure of document uploaded in its system, and the right to terminate the user's track, so it was considered as had meet the infringement liability[47].

In Napster system, if a user logs in with passwords and account numbers, collect other users' data of files through the directory, when accessing to file data, it must be back to a central server; when the user searches for a particular document, the server downloads data from other's database, IPs of (web site) user and provider are through Napster's central server, Napster can understand the source of

---

[43] A&M Records, Inc. v. Napster, Inc., 114 F. Supp. 2d 896, 920 (N.D. Cal. 2000).

[44] Napster, 239 F.3d at 1022.

[45] Id. (quoting Gershwin Publ'g Corp. v. Columbia Artists Mgmt., Inc., 443 F.2d 1159, 1162 (2d Cir. 1971)).

[46] A&M Records, 114 F.Supp. 2d at 902.

[47] Napster, 239 F.3d at 1024.

information through the collecting user's information, so the situation that Napster uses users' information is informed[48]. Napster has the right to and take the initiative to remove the content with copyright, or freeze of bulk users' accounts, but it did not do its oversight responsibilities[49].

Napster claimed and defended based on following laws and regulations, the Audio Home Recording Act of 1992 (AHRA)[50], and the Digital Millennium Copyright Act of 1998 (DMCA)[51]; when it was in the defense quoting AHRA, Napster advocated the nature of using MP3 was not for commercial purposes[52], the court rejected this claim, considered the download act involving MP3 did not apply to the AHRA. Napster also advocated the normative content of DMCA could protect network services, without the application of joint copyright infringement[53]. This case was the first one involving P2P applications, it is expected to have more related cases in the future, whether or not using DMCA to resolve such questions, it depends on the opinion and treatment of the court in each case[54].

As for the main product sales theory, it was seen as the proof Napster was "informed" by the Ninth Circuit Court of Appeals, because when Napster sold its products, it must first know products may constitute a normal non-infringing and infringing use; when

---

[48] Napster II, 239 F. 3d at 1021-22.

[49] Id. at 1022.

[50] 17 U.S.C § 1008 (2000).

[51] 17 U.S.C § 512(2000).

[52] Id. at 1024.

[53] Digital Millennium Copyright Act, 17 U.S.C § 512(2000); Napster II, 239 F. 3d at 1025.

[54] Napster II, 239 F.3d at 1025.

investigating evidence, the District Court found that Napster did inform of infringement and constitute participation, so that even the Court of Appeal had considered whether the case should be verdict as to contributory copyright infringement, but then considering Napster "informed" of the elements, it remained the decision by the District Court. The "centralized directory system" provided by Napster was also the major cause that the user could easily download and rapidly exchange, it was also the proof that the court decided Napster had to take the contributory copyright infringement[55].

Napster centralized server management system enabled the defendant not only informed of the infringement of its system software, but can not be exempt from infringement that showing a huge number of files and documents in the web directory[56], advocating that RIAA alleged there were at least 12,000 infringing files document[57]; in conclusion, the Court adopted the following opinions in this case: 1. When the product design was the substantial non-infringing use, it should not deduce that the dependant was informed of the infringement just because products had the behavior of infringing use; however, 2. in this case, the judge found enough evidence to show that the defendant was informed of the system provided infringing use[58].

3. Distributed Management Directory System

Later in the case of Metro-Goldwyn-Mayer Studios, Inc. V.

---

[55] Napster II, 239 F.3d at 1021-22. quoting the district court, 114 F. Supp. 2d at 919-20.

[56] Id. at 1011-13.

[57] Napster, 239 F.3d at 1022 n.6.

[58] Id. at 1020-22.

Grokster Ltd.[59], the Ninth Circuit Court of Appeals re-examined the Sony case's theory and the secondary liablility. The court examined three P2P architectures[60]: 1) the directory system concentrated in all central servers of the company, with the list of all music or video files available for download, such as the system owned by Napster[61]; 2) the one non-concentrated in the company's central server, the company only maintains directory lists in its network can be managed[62]; 3) There is no directory list, document files are recorded by links of personal computer[63]. (Grokster's model)

Grokster's model was a normal operation P2P model, the users were free and mutually connected, not through a central server; distributed server system is the main point of dispute by majority of the Court telling tort liability of P2P[64].As to the system works of Grokster, all users separately operate with the highest speed not through a central server but through one after another point connections, such procedure is to make the search process more smoothly, and it is more quickly to obtain Grokster's network information. Grokster provides free software so that computer users online through P2P networks, sharing computer files, and do not have to through the central server.

Grokster did not provide substantial equipment and network

---

[59] 380 F. 3d 1154 (9th Cir. 2004).

[60] Id. at 1158-59.

[61] Id.

[62] Id.

[63] Id.

[64] See, e.g., In re Aimster Copyright Litig., 334 F.3d 643, 646-47 (7th Cir. 2003). [hereinafter Aimster II] (holding that Aimster was not a direct infringer because the actual copies of the songs were located on the user's computers rather than on Aimster's servers).

location for infringing, but its users with software system to link
and create network meanings and provide relevant channels, finally,
the Ninth Circuit Court of Appeals didn't determined Grokster's
contributory copyright infringement[65]; As for whether Grokster should
take the duty of supervision, the court held that it did not have the
right to terminate or to turn off the user's access and links between
them[66], the plaintiff cited the "willful blindness" said by the Seventh
Circuit Court of Appeals, however, the Ninth Circuit Court of Appeals
in this case held that Grokster had no way to monitor and manage
users' indirect infringement, so it had not duty for monitoring; finally,
it was hoped to apply by the secondary liablility based on the Inducing
Infringement of Copyrights Act[67].

III. Infringement Liability

Important points from above cases were consolidated in this
chapter, such as Napster case was the first well-known one of
P2P, Grokster case also triggered a major response, the types and
responsibilities of copyright infringement were introduced as follows:

---

[65] Grokster, 380 F.3d at 1164.

[66] Id. at 1165.

[67] This bill was explained at the end in particular.

1. Direct infringement liability

As to the rational use advocated by Napster, including copy the samples provided, share the space, allocation and use of authorization[68], the court held that the users involved in this case only had copied, rather than creation of a new conversion result[69]; In other words, such infringing use had commercial purposes, but the higher court disagreed with the Court of First Instance's opinion, namely "commercial use" did not exist, there was no direct economic interests from that act[70]; the Court of Appeal held that "even it was not sold after copying, duplicating and abuse of the copy also constituted a commercial use[71]"; Napster system users did illegal copying through such way to avoid purchase original products, which made Napster's defenses no longer exist, also, free software provided by Napster affected the sale capacity of the market[72].

The court found that illegal download and sharing would make buyers not buy the CD, or not only download one song or one part; on the contrary, they would copy the entire contents, and so must result in a threat to record sales. The Ninth Circuit Court of Appeals had different opinions in Napster and Sony cases, even Napster itself had no intention against audio-visual industry, but because of their

---

[68] A&M Records, Inc. v. Napster, Inc., 239 F.3d 1004, 1012 (9th Cir. 2001) [hereinafter Napster II].

[69] Id. at 1015.

[70] Id.

[71] Id.

[72] Opinions in this case: 1. Napster harms trading market as the number of CD sale by students was declined. 2. Napster made sales of online music decline. A & M Records, Inc. V. Napster, Inc., 114F. Supp. 2d 896, 913 (ND Cal. 2000) [hereinafter Napster I].

knowledge and had the right to remove or delete the infringing files and it did that, so that it was asserted that the Napster did not do its oversight responsibilities properly[73]; Secondly, Napster enjoyed the direct benefits of this tort, because more people used the Napster system for the convenience of the free download and cost reducing, making Napster's returns in the future be even more impressive.

In Napster case, the Ninth Circuit Court of Appeals also held that the person involved had " implied knowledge " of the infringement, so it had rights and capacity to manage the cases, which were different from the elements of contributory copyright infringement - not necessarily to have direct benefit circumstances, however, the doer of contributory infringement must know the facts, so he had a chance to assist or encourage; take the " bad intention " of person involved as the standards to assess as following reasons: (1) in agent relations of limit application, the person involved must have the right and ability to supervise agents' elements; (2) reduce the scope of indirect infringement from vicarious infringement to contributory infringement at the same time.

The "direct economic benefits" and "right and ability to supervise" two elements in Napster case were in compliance with vicarious copyright infringement, which is not like the contributory copyright infringement, the defendant must be informed of the situation of infringing use, as whether the user knows that, which is not within the scope of contributory copyright infringement; but the users may deliberately turned a blind eye to it (deliberately ignored), so there are two types of responsibility together sometimes when the court tries

---

[73] Napster II, 239 F. 3d at 1022-1023.

cases, so as to make it easier to set up the case.

Although the doer of vicarious copyright infringement has not criminal intent, he has the knowledge but overlooks it, or even deliberately disregards it happens, which makes different responsibilities on the defendant, that is, to prove that the defendant does not have the knowledge but with illicit-intent. However, in recent years because the development of P2P technology, particularly the far-reaching impact in the case of Napster, the court judged the defendant defeat based on vicarious copyright infringement, not complying with the principle of the judge "whether the defendant has the right and ability to supervise ", Therefore, in the present cases, how to comply with the elements of this copyright infringement, whether there are different responses and measures, which were discussed later.

2. Indirect infringement liability

According to the decision of Napster case by the Ninth Circuit Court of Appeals, the court considered that Napster prohibit infringer to contact a particular website, which was the evidence it had the right and ability to supervise, Napster had the right and ability to manage and maintain its network system, and find infringing data in its search directory, as well as to terminate user access to its system, but it didn't use that, so it should bear the vicarious copyright infringement[74]; it was obvious that software provided by Grokster or even free software would not be controlled by any individual or company, the court held

---

[74] Hsiao, BG, The impact of Peer-to-Peer software on the network copyright in post-Napster time . Http://www.apipa.org.tw/Area/Article-ViewAdA.asp?intAreaType=2&intAdAArticleI D=149, search date: Nov. 23, 2005.

that there was no evidence that the defendant enjoyed the right and ability to supervise and control, so the defendant did not have to bear that responsibility[75]. The Seventhe Circuit Court of Appeals did not agree with the Ninth Circuit Court of Appeal's "informed" theory[76]. However, Aimster was willfully blind, which was still in line with "informed" element, so it was the contributory copyright infringer[77].

In 2003, the Seventh Circuit Court of Appeals gave a judgment to Aimster case[78]. Aimste provided AIM, so that users could freely communicate and share information[79]; Aimster server did not save any files, so it was away from direct infringement liability[80]; the court looked into its Secondary Liability but did not use the principle of Sony case, whether the substantial use of non-infringing technology constitute contributory copyright infringing[81], that is, examine the use of products to determine whether there was an infringement; the judge Poster proposed that the principle of Sony case lied infringing use of products[82]; in this case, the copyrighted content was infringed through Aimster system, based on the decision of the case, devices, technology and meanings involved in the infringing use could also inflict criminal liability to infringement.

In addition, different from the Napster case, in which the

---

[75]　Id.

[76]　Id. at 649.

[77]　Id. at 650.

[78]　In re Aimster Copyright Litig., 334 F. 3d 643, 645 (7th Cir. 2003) [hereinafter Aimster].

[79]　Id. at 646.

[80]　Id. at 646-47.

[81]　Id. at 649.

[82]　Aimster, 334 F. 3d at 648.

defendant should be informed of user's infringing behavior; in this case, the judge didn't take the defendant informed as the element[83]; if Aimster's R & D department and procedure designer were fully aware that user would infringe through the system, they should not design related procedures or should make every effort to prevent the violations; in this case, the trial judge adopted more rigorous identification standards on the Aimster company, so whether it interrupted the technology and R & D upgrading? The court determined that Aimster was "willful blindness" for the norms of copyright law, that is, the defendant attempted to avoid the fact that it was aware of the existence of a crime in criminal law; the defendant knew of the existence of the crime, but it evade its responsibilities, therefore Aimster was unable to assert impunity[84], the court took it as accessory and abettor. Whether it was related to the loss of economy and revenue was not the essential point of this case, as long as the copyright holder asserted his copyright infringement, he didn't need to prove that he suffered physical damage on the economy. Aimster quoted fair use from DMCA to defense, because Aimster didn't make any effect to make system users stop repeated infringing, the Seventh Circuit Court of Appeals approved an injunction, so that Aimster system ceased to function.

As the Seventh Circuit Court of Appeals granted the injunction to the defendant Aimster in this case, thinking it's the contributory infringer[85]; just like Napster service, as required operators to provide

---

[83] Id. at 649.

[84] Aimster, 334 F.3d at 650-51.

[85] 334 F. 3d 643, 653, 656 (7th Cir. 2003).

specific download software to enable registered members upload information and obtain electronic documents[86]. Aimster provided related services and prevented users from infringement, so that the Circuit was not easy to determine whether it had "substantial non-infringing use", to judge whether it had sufficient ability to prevent its users from violations, based on which to decide whether Aimster was the contributory infringer; if requested to avoid user's infringing use, it was easy to lie burden on Aimster. Moreover, this case applied balancing test, that is, to see whether the expenditure costs and benefits can reach a balance, so as to prove the proportion of the non-infringing use, and ultimately Aimster was unable to prove it[87], and it should still have to shoulder the responsibility of copyright infringement.

Based on the decisions of Napster case and this case by US court, due to technical differences in two years, the court made entirely different judgments network download copyright infringements. In 1709, UK pioneered the world's first copyright law, "Annie Act", which was because of the rise of printing, making the copyright protection become necessary. Looking at the development of copyright law, it is indeed because the rapid development of new technology; copyright law has to keep expanding the scope of protection, updating the protection subject, in response to the impact of technological innovation on copyright holder. In face of legal strategies taken by IT industry in the enforcement aspects, the representative of copyright holder has taken counter-measures.

---

[86] Id. at 646.

[87] Aimster, 334 F. 3d at 653.

In the P2P-related cases of Grokster in US, no matter Aimster[88] or Napster[89] case, the medium industry hoped to promote P2P software system provider to take the responsibility for copyright infringement due to P2P, but the contributory infringement should have two elements: (1) informed of the infringing; (2) directly or partially constitute an infringing, lead to damage to the copyright holder[90]. Therefore, the plaintiff (such as record or entertainment industry) must prove that software service provider was informed of or have reason to know user's infringing, as to whether the defendant gets profit from it or not, which is not the necessary condition of infringement liability.

Grokster case and Sony case showed different verdict benchmarks; the majority of Grokster users effectively used its software to engage in infringement, that is, Grokster defense that its users were lawful use, as it was the use for commercial purpose, so the court considered Grokster should not take the user's responsibility of infringement[91]. In Grokster system, even if user's infringing was informed, the defendant was still difficult to stop it effectively, even Grokster was turned off, the users were still able to share files, and therefore the defendant would not know its infringing, the plaintiff could not prove that the defendant's informed of, so not to set up contributory infringement[92].

---

[88] In re Aimster Copyright Litig., 334F.3d 643 (7th Cir. 2003).

[89] A&M Records, Inc. v. Napster, Inc., 239 F.3d 1004, 1022 (9th Cir. 2001).

[90] Gershwin Pub. Corp. v. Columbia Artists Mgmt., Inc., 443 F.2d 1159, 1162 (2d Cir. 1971).

[91] Related cases in recent years were followed by Sony (1984) to Napster (Napster Ⅰ, 2000; Napster II 2001); Aimster case (2003); to Grokster (Grokster Ⅰ, 2003; Grokster II, 2004; Grokster Ⅲ, 2005). Grokster II, 380 F. 3d at 1160-62.

[92] See Grokster II, 380 F. 3d at 1163, and Metro-Goldwyn-Mayer Studios, Inc. V. Grokster, Ltd., 259F. Supp.2d 1029, 1041 (CD Cal. 2003) . California District Court's decision

The Ninth Circuit Court of Appeals continued to look at whether Grokster was informed of users infringing or not, the result was not. Compared with Napster case, Aimster case's largest difference was it had measures to track whether the copyrighted contents has been assigned or sold not, but the Grokster distributor didn't have this authority, nor could it trace the user account[93]. Grokster did not provide information relevant to the infringed content, the system users formed access and online through their respective links on Internet, Grokster could not provide or arrange for any files, distributors also could not freeze the user account, the court did not find any adequate proof against Grokster to participate in or provide infringing[94]. Take Napster case as an example, the plaintiff adduce evidence that the defendant expressed it had the right to terminate any user's access in writing[95], however, Grokster case did not exist such state, because Grokster didn't use central management server system, members obtain user-based approach without registering; the Ninth Circuit Court of Appeals supported District Court's opinions, not giving Grokster criminal responsibility, which was to encourage technological innovation in existing market competition[96]; but finally to the Supreme Court, it still held that Grokster should bear the Inducing infringement[97].

---

described in 2003: even if the defendant (Grokster) closed its system and controlled the linked computers, users could still share files with very little interference or little disturbance.

[93] Grokster II, 380 F. 3d at 1163 (citing Grokster I, 259 F. Supp. 2d at 1037, 1039-41).

[94] Grokster II, 380 F. 3d at 1164.

[95] Id. at 1165.

[96] Id. at 1167.

[97] See the latter for the details

3. Inducement copyright Infringement

In this case, the copyright holder, including the music and lyrics creators, music publishers and animation audio-visual operator unitedly accused P2P file-sharing software distributors. District Court's judgment supported the defendant, therefore the plaintiff appealed against, but the Ninth Circuit Court of Appeals affirmed the judgment of first instance[98]; the plaintiffs continued to appeal to the U.S. Supreme Court[99], which concluded that the defendant should bear the responsibility for copyright infringement. This judgment was given in the summer of 2005, which not only wanted to clarify the fuzzy zone before in Sony case[100], but also re-inspected the principles of for infringement liability, which have been followed more than two decades.

Internet grows rapidly today, opinions[101] as the Ninth Circuit Court of Appeals in 2004 are no longer applicable to Internet all-around; take Grokster case as an example, new technological inventor or copyright

---

[98] 380 F.3d 1154.

[99] Metro-goldwyn-mayer studios inc.,v. Grokster, Ltd.,125 S.Ct.2764,162 L.Ed.2d 781.

[100] The opinion from Sony case "substantially prove non-infringing use" was pursued by later court sentence, in the case of Matthew Bender & Co. V. West Publ'g Co., 158 F. 3d 693, 706-07 (2d Cir. 1998), the defendant alleged that the asterisks system marking the page was not against the plaintiff's copyright, and in the case of Ga. Television Co. v. TV News Clips, Inc., 718 F. Supp. 939, 948 (ND Ga. 1989), considered that when the defendant used radio content for-profit, it did not constitute infringement, which was not in line with Sony's case theory. Jesse M. Feder, Is Betamax Obsolete? Sony Corp. of Am. v. Universal City Studios, Inc. in the Age of Napster, 37 Creighton L. Rev. 859, 863-68 (2003).

[101] MGM Studios Inc. v. Grokster, Ltd., 380 F.3d 1154, 1162n.9 (9th Cir. 2004), vacates, 125 S.Ct.2764 (2005).

holder[102] no longer used Sony principles[103], namely, exclude the new technology allocated by the inventor, if one is set for the destruction of other's copyright, such as infringement by means of the various steps, only when he has to bear the responsibility[104]; as to " causing principle"[105], the court must prove that new technology's main topic[106] or goal[107] is to damage other's copyright mainly.

US Supreme Court's principles in the Grokster case were: although the file-swapping software was a neutral technology, which should not be blamed or prohibited, the behavior using or providing such software or services might not necessarily be exempt, it still depended on whether or not doer's behavior had induced, assisted, caused other's copyright infringement[108]. Copyright infringement liability did not targeted at direct infringer only, but also indirect infringer; so US record and video industries were dissatisfied with the company developing P2P system, as it made them lose their most direct profits, causing a major economic damage; it was easier to require the company for compensation than millions of users[109]; it must first have a direct copyright infringement, then have the indirectly copyright

---

[102] Grokster, 125 S. Ct. at 2770.

[103] Based on the principles set up in the Sony case by Supreme Court in 1984, video technology can have a reasonable use, which should not be prohibited only because someone takes infringing use.

[104] Id. at 2780.

[105] Id.

[106] Id. at 2774.

[107] Id. at 2781.

[108] Chang, C.H., http://www.copyrightnote.org/, search date: Nov. 23, 2005.

[109] Peter Katz, Copyright Infringement: The Perils of Indirect Liability, 16 J. Proprietary Rts.1 (2004).

infringement[110]; it one directly shares and copies files and documents, resulting in the sale of pirated CD, the direct infringer may take the burden of indirect responsibility[111].

On June 27, 2005, US Supreme Court gave the decision to Grokster case, it was a new milestone[112] for the new body, technology, software development, music, videos, intellectual property laws and so on. The Supreme Court considered that the Ninth Circuit Court of Appeals wrongly interpreted Sony case's opinion, that is, it was based on Grokster's software was not designed for infringing use, excluding its joint copyright infringement[113]; the defendant was keen to promote its products through the infringing use, the point in question about the case lied in "under what circumstances will distributors shoulder joint copyright infringement for the third person's damage when facing legal and illegal use?[114]" Eventually, it held that if product-related device, technology were involved in tort, even one has tried to take the necessary measures, it should still be responsible for the damage of the third person[115].

Grokster's software products enhanced user's infringing

---

[110] Llewellyn Joseph Gibbons, Entrepreneurial Copyright Fair Use: Let the Independent Contractor Stand in the Shoes of the Fair User, 57 Ark. L. Rev. 539, 547 (2004).

[111] Fonovisa, Inc.v. Cherry Auction, Inc., 76F. 3d 259 (9th Cir. 1996). In this case, as the defendant failed to prevent the sale of infringing articles, he should also take the responsibility for indirect infringement.

[112] Metro-Goldwyn-Mayer Studios, Inc. v. Grokster, Ltd., 125 S. Ct. 2764 (2005).

[113] At 2778. (Justice Breyer thought the Sony principles could be applied to this case - companyproducts' substancial or comercial purpose was non-infringing use, but Grokster didn't apply to this principle).

[114] Id. At 2770. This is the trial judge's infringement opinion of the case.

[115] Id.

technology, so no matter it was informed of or have reason to know, the infringement was caused by; on the other hand, the principle applied to the Sony case, this case eventually constituted willful or intended an infringement when Supreme Court cited Patent Law[116]; this theory required the plaintiff to prove that the defendant was informed of and wanted to help or abet other's direct infringing[117], the plaintiff presented evidences were as follows: 1. Grokster knowingly and with intent to spread its software to enable users spread copyrighted contents (90% of works owned by Grokster were copyrighted). 2. Grokster was certain users using its product for downloading copyrighted information, such as Grokster receiving e-mail was related to ask how to play copyrighted movies[118]. Take the case of Oak Industries v. Zemith Electronics[119] as an example, to determine from the nature of a product, if there was nature of infringement, then it was possible to lead to infringement[120]. Finally, the Court firmly believed Grokster should assume liability for tort based on the following three points.

The defendant tried to absorb previous Napster users, besides Grokster and Napster names were similar, both provided contents were much similar[121], and the defendant was slack to prevent and restrict infringing, but reap profits.

The court found that the defendant did not attempt or try to

---

[116] 35 U.S.C. § 271 (b).

[117] Grokster III, 125 S. Ct. at 2776.

[118] Grokster III, 125 S. Ct. at 2772.

[119] Oak Indus., Inc. v. Zenith Elec. Corp., 697 F. Supp. 988-992 (N.D I11. 1988).

[120] Grokster III, 125 S. Ct. at 2779.

[121] Id. at 2881.

develop, filter or use other tools and technologies, so as to terminate the infringing due to the use of its software[122], the Ninth Circuit Court of Appeals did not consider this point, but the Supreme Court was more positive that the defendant intended to make users more easily engaged in infringing based on that.

More people used the software of the defendant, which got more advertising revenue. Verdict in this case did not reach a positive help ot technological innovation and the allocation of resources, because the internal or public sharing will all lead to infringing, therefore the results may lead to new inventions; but regardless of this judgment, the file-sharing on Internet increases with time, if not through the aforementioned system, only through e-mail or real-time messages (MSN) is also OK.

IV. Relevant Laws

Internet has been seen as a condition where the files free exchange, for copyright holders, there are still a considerable number of disputes in the future; to revise, enlarge or modify the federal and state legislations was one of the directions to settle disputes. Currently, there is Digital Millennium Copyright Act[123], Audio Home Recording Act[124], The Inducing Infringement of Copyright Act of 2004 (Induce

---

[122] Id. at 2781.

[123] 17 U.S.C. § 512 (K)(1)(A) (2000).

[124] 17 U.S.C. §§ 1001-1010.

Act)[125], The Family Entertainment and Copyright Act of 2004[126]; may be electronics industry operators were busy with R&D of new products and procedures, and strived to maintain market competitiveness and improved the international consumer market, overlooked in the proposals and legislative efforts, a sound system of regulation was more useful for fair market competition, so that consumers have more authority to select, the electronics industry operators should increase the interaction with the federal government, so that the public sector had a better understanding of the needs of the private sector.

In September 1999, the number of Napster users in the consumer market increased doubly every 5-6 weeks[127], till February 2001, there were 80 million users[128]; as illegal music download was too serious, then including the well-known singers such as Don Henley, Garth Brooks, Art Alexakis of Everclear Elton John, Puff Daddy[129] etc lodged a protest; in December 1999, the Recording Industry Association of American (RIAA) filed a complaint against Napster. In March 2000, Metallica and Dr. Dre also sued Napster personally[130]; after that, the Motion Picture Association of America (MPAA), the Music Producers

---

[125] S. 2560, 108th Cong. (2004).

[126] 18 USCS § 2379B. Digital Media Consumers' Rights Act of 2005, HR1201, 109th Cong. (2005). Republican senator, Rep. Rick Boucher's proposal Electronics Consumer Law of 2005 -- Digital Media Consumers, Rights Act of 2005, HR 1201, 109th Cong. (2005).

[127] Matthew Green, Note, Napster Opens Pandora's Box : Examining How File-Sharing Services Threaten the Enforcement of Copyright on the Internet, 63 Ohio St. L.J. 799, 801 (2002).

[128] Id. at 802.

[129] Id. at 803.

[130] Reuters, Metallica Raps Napster, Mar. 29, 2001, http://www.cbsnews.com/ stories/2001/03/29/archive/technology/main282384.shtml.

Guild (MPG), the Business Software Alliance (BSA) jointed RIAA to sue Napsterr, so how to solve the problem of illegal P2P use , which is instructed by following the legislative process, the application and operation of business models.

P2P Privacy Prevention Bill is not the first legislation on copyright infringement of illegal download. In 1998, Internet Service Providers (ISPs) worried about its users direct infringed copyright, so Congress enacted and passed Digital Millennium Copyright Act (DMCA)[131], this Act also set up a safe haven for ISPs, there were very few regulations trying to resolve copyright infringement of P2P technology; until 2002, Congressman Howard Berman was in support of "P2P Privacy Prevention Bill"[132], standardizing the copyright holder, which can use any technology to effectively prevent and avoid any unauthorized use without harming the users.

Although this Bill was supported by copyright holders, it also suffered from the network user's complaints. In January 2003, there was another bill, "the Digital Media Consumer's Rights Act"[133], the contents were about protecting the legitimate CD so that trade of pirated CD was illegal; it is argued that to consider the people rights on Constitution, which should neither lose sight of consumers' property rights (such as through network function), nor want to reduce the chance for the growth of R & D[134]; moreover, these two bills were not

[131] Elliot M. Zimmerman, P2P File Sharing: Direct and Indirect Copyright Infringement, Fla. B.J., at 40, 41 (May 2004) ; See Digital Millennium Copyright Act, Pub. L. No. 105-304,112 Stat. 2860 (1998).

[132] H.R. 5211 pmbl., 107th Cong. (2002).

[133] H.R. 107, 108th Cong. (2003).

[134] Rebekah O'Hara, You Say You Want a Revolution : Music & Technology-Evolution or

passed.

In September 2004, California passed State Law Proposition No. 1506, which penalized the one spread P2P and developed copyrighted content[135], including system operators, if not with reasonable diligence to prevent their users from spreading copyrighted information, fined U.S. dollars 2,500 and a year in prison; the one wanted to use P2P software must first register at the state, otherwise there would be criminal penalties[136].

State Laws (such as California part) were still unable to properly solve the overall problem of copyright infringement, but with the updating and rapid progress of electronic technology, the law language and norms should not be too broad or specific, although there were DMCA and AHRH, it was very important to reach all human consensus[137], rather than simply restricting the user and penalty, if audio-visual industry operators accepted a wide range of new technologies, considering more orientations, such disputes could be resolved.

Online music is a business model with profit, but it is worth noting that Taiwan's market economy is small-scale, coupled with content providers charging excessive royalties, online music store owners are very hard to be profitable; moreover, there are industry operators with P2P model platform, making online music store owners are currently

---

Destruction?, 39 Gonz. L. Rev. 247, 288 (2004).

[135] Cal. Penal Code § 653aa.

[136] Id.

[137] Redefining the Debate Over Protecting Intellectual Property, Ecoustics. Com, (Mar. 19,2005), http://news.ecoustics.com/bbs/messages/10381/127979.html.

faced with prospects, but the challenge of hard profit[138]; to date, lots of P2P users are legitimate, SKY, NTL and Warner Brothers have also promoted P2P services, millions of users make free phone on Internet through Skype, the academic circles can also make use of P2P to search and share data[139], so the updating and creation of this technology really benefit human society largely.

1. Federal regulations

Traditional copyright law and other legislations are not sufficient to resolve the current problems encountered in practice, so the following described the existing regulations to know whether there is the need to enact new laws.

(I) DMCA

Under the protection of the Digital Millennium Copyright Act (DMCA), file-sharing can only be limited through turning off the

---

[138] He, YW, online music services are network killer application, but the industry operator generally has not yet been profitable, http://www.digitalcontent.org.tw/e/files/94/0511/940511-2.htm, search date : Dec. 23, 2005.

[139] On February 23, 2006, EITO and OECD teams made a research briefing to the legislators in Brussels, Beijing, claiming that P2P technology was to create job opportunities and pushing hands for economic growth, and appealing the Government to open up and develop P2P application business. In addition, the original creator of file-sharing software BitTorrent also discussed with movie producers, recording industry, and network service providers, plan to introduce online download services. BitTorrent launched Visual inquiry portal NTL, some UK areas began to enjoy this service 3 months later, through its download software to download authorized program. Edited by Li, JH of Epoch Times, P2P file-sharing has unlimited prospects, http : // www.epochtimes.com/b5/6/3/30/n1271944.htm, search date: April 14, 2006

system, so as to avoid copyright infringement[140]; the younger generation use the Internet to share and exchange copyrighted documents, files or other information, which is regarded as an offense[141]; however, if a total ban on sharing, public use is impeded, the resources with common good purpose or agreed to share by copyright holder are blocked, which will hinder innovation[142].

Restrictions on the use of the Internet, ISPs must take adaptive strategy to infringing users, such as to notice account user to stop improper conduct or terminate his account[143]; but ISPs must not hinder copyright holder to protect his rights and interests[144]; according to DMCA Article 512 (a) to (d), four ISPs impunity situations are standardized[145], described as follows: communicate with temporary electron net, such as the situation that user simply shares information[146]; storage systems, user short-term stores system data and work[147]; system or network information controlled by the user, when user operates system, ISPs as a bona fide third person, knew nothing about the user's infringing, and did not obtain any benefits, therefore, once informed, immediately cease and remove the above-

---

[140] A&M Recs., Inc. v. Napster, Inc.,239 F.3d1004,1021(9th Cir. 2001); Metro-Glodwyn-Mayer Studios Inc. v. Grokster, Ltd., 380 F. 3d 1154(9th Cir. 2004).

[141] Wendy M. Pollack, Note, Tuning In: The Future of Copyright Protection for Online Music in the Digital Millennium, 68 Fordham L. Rev. 2445(2000).

[142] Itza Wilson, Online Music Distribution Compromise: Protecting the Artist's Copyright While Not Stifling Digital Development, 2001 Syracuse L. & Tech. J. 3(2001).

[143] § 17 U.S.C.§512(i)(1)(A)(2005).

[144] § 512(i)(1)(B).

[145] § 512(a)- (d).

[146] § 512(a).

[147] § 512(b).

mentioned data against copyrigh[148]; tools marking the location of data, the impunity situation of ISP using information location tools includes the use of directory, guidelines, network links, keywords and so on.

In Verizon case, RIAA invoked "terms on service of summons" of DMCA in July 2002 and February 2003, accused Verizon network services company, suspected of two cases using the Kazaa P2P software[149]; Verizon argued that the above-mentioned infringements only used transmission channels provided by it, absence of any storage, and therefore not within the Article 512 h[150], the District Court allowed the request of RIAA, Verizon's defense was rejected[151]; However, the Supreme Court of the United States thought service of summons involving the relevant ISP copyrighted information was only for communication, if it was the user's behavior, the information was not stored in the ISP's server[152]; and in the individual computer[153], remove or disable access provided in DMCA Article 512 C Paragraph (3) (A) could not apply; when DMCA enacted legislation, not yet had P2P

---

[148] §512(c).

[149] In Re Verizon Internet Servs., Inc., 257 F. Supp. 2d 244, 246-247 (D.D.C. 2003); Alice Kao, RIAA v. Verizon: Applying the Subpoena Provision of the DMCA, 19 Berkeley Tech. L.J.405(2004); see also, Jordana Boag, The Battle of Piracy versus Privacy: How the Recording Industry Association of America (RIAA) is Using the Digital Millennium Copyright Act (DMCA) as its Weapon Against Internet Users' Privacy Rights, 41 Cal.W.L. Rev. 241(2004).

[150] Verizon Internet Servs., Inc., 240 F. Supp. 2d at 24, 26.(D.D.C. 2003).

[151] Id. at 45.

[152] Recording Indus. Assn. of Am., Inc.v. Verizon Internet Servs., Inc., 351F.3d 1229, 1233(D.C. 2003).

[153] Id. at 1235.

mode of operation, nor did Congress consider such behavior patterns[154], and ultimately the court considered including P2P was not the legislative intent of Congress, so the court did not consider expanding the DMCA scope to protect the copyright[155].

According to Article 512 of "The One-Line Copyright Liability Limitation Act" in DMCA, it requires ISPs to stop providing link services to specific Internet, and to hand over user data which links the website and downloads copyrighted files. In this case, the court was based on this provision, issuing summonses to request ISP Verizon exchanged user data through Kazza website, Verizon said it only passively provided a conduit to the user to transmit data, rather than belong to a real web server against copyright; it also questioned the court the constitutionality of provision. The Court did not adopt Verizon's view, as the provision given the copyright holder the right to apply summons from the court, which was applicable to all ISPs, including Verizon also.

The Eighth Circuit Court of Appeals had the same opinion on Charter case[156], if RIAA wanted to invoke DMCA Article 512 (h) for service of summons, similar to Verizon case, ISP Charter only had conduction function, did not store any relevant data posing infringement[157], the Eighth Circuit Court of Appeals recognized District Court's opinion, ISP only had conduction function between users[158], it

---

[154] Id. at 1238.

[155] Id.

[156] Recording Indus. Assn. of Am. v. Charter Commun. Inc., 393 F.3d 771(8th Cir. 2005).

[157] Id. at 775.

[158] Id. at 777.

also considered that expanding the legal scope of P2P was DMCA's legislative duty; this paper thought that the legislature should solve the problem DMCA could not standardize P2P presently, rather than epanding the interpretation of laws and regulations for individual cases, therefore considering ISP illegal. The District Court and the Eighth Circuit Court of Appeals did not want to expand legal interpretation for Internet copyright infringement[159], they held that whether ISPs should be responsible for network users against copyright violations or not, depending on whether they "know" or "have reason to know"[160].

(II) AHRA

It was passed in 1992, advocated for the protection of the artist's job[161]; AHRA allows music to be copied by electronic way, mainly for the digital audio tape recorder (DAT), not including the home computer; even DATs were replaced by computer with mass memory and large spread speed, AHRA still protects the copyright holders, its biggest disadvantage is not including the home computer.

(III) DPRSA[162]

It was announced in 1995 by President of the United States, aimed at the emerging e-commerce markets rising as Internet, empowering

---

[159] David Gorski, The Future of the Digital Millennium Copyright Act (DMCA) Subpoena Power on the Internet in Light of the Verizon Cases, 24 Rev. Litig. 166(2005).

[160] Religious Technology Center v. Netcome On-Line Communications Services, Inc., 907 F.Supp.1361 (N.D. 1995).

[161] Tom Graves, Picking Up the Pieces of Grokster: A New Approach to File Sharing, 27 Hastings Comm. & Ent. L.J. 165-66 (2004).

[162] Digital Performance Right in Sound Recordings Act (DPRSA), Pub. L. No. 10439, 109 Stat. 336 (1995) (codified at 17 U.S.C. 106 (6), 114.

music record's copyright holder to get some option money when digital transmission, so as to obtain a certain degree of compensation.

(IV) NETA[163]

In 1997, the U.S. Congress enacted the No Electronic Theft Act, and its purpose was to constrain the non-significant for-profit copyright infringement through penalty, so as to fill the loophole of previous copyright law in 1997, which only punished for-profit one.

Since 2005, RIAA has cited the terms of DMAC as the legal basis for the summons strategy, which compelled ISPs to hand over the identity of anonymous download. The way RIAA confirming download music through P2P was different from the general court summons, such a summons was applied by NGO, which were not attached to the lawsuit in the future. Verizon, first receiving summons issued by RIAA, considered it was in unconstitutional danger. In April 2006, the Federal Court of Appeal determined the practice that RIAA tracked down P2P users and indicted was illegal. Washington, DC court said that, the US Copyright Law did not allow any organization to issue a summons to the ISP asking for publication of the ID of file exchanger without the permission of a judge[164].

It was passed in 1998, of which the Article 512 sentenced the responsibility of network operators; in the K (1), providing the five elements of ISP, which may be exempt if they satisfy the requirements: (1) should not participate in any infringing; (2) select information; (3)

---

[163] No Electronic Theft Act (NETA), Pub. L. No. 105-147, 111 Stat. 2678(1997)(codified in scattered sections of 17-18 U.S.C.).

[164] The US and Dutch court stroke two serious blows at RIAA, http://taiwan.cent.com/news/ ce/0, 2000062982,20086544,00. Htm, search date: April 11, 2006.

select the recipients; (4) store the information to specific people; (5) add the contents of information[165]. In the Napster case, the defendant argued that the PMCA through it eluded its responsibilities; however, as there was not clear enactment, whether P2P systems can be regarded as ISP has yet to be deliberated.

2. To enact new laws

On June 22, 2004, Senator (Sen. Hatch) raised the Induce Act, which was the latest legislative proposals adopted by the Federal Supreme Court in Grokster Ⅲ; this Act has not yet passed legislation, it attempted to terminate the Grokster's behavior, although it is argued that it will harm the development of technology R&D[166], however, this Act provides that copyright infringer must be responsible for its voilation.

(I) Original proposal

Hatch put forward in its draft legislation: enable children offenses are illegal without morality, artistic creators firmly believe that the destruction of children's innocence is adults' biggest sin[167]; Senator Leahy also supported this, considering this draft against the P2P software provider to give P2P service, technical R&D, electrical products designers or network service provider needed not worry about

---

[165] Michael Suppappola, Note, The End of the World as We Know It? The State of Decentralized Peer-to-Peer Technologies in the Wake of Metro-Goldwyn-Mayer Studios v. Grokster, 4 Conn. Pub. Int. L.J. 133-34 (2004).

[166] Katie Dean, Techies Talk Tough in D.C., Wired, Jan. 20, 2005, http://www.wired.com/news/politics/0,1283,66329,00.html.

[167] 150 Cong. Rec. S7189 (daily ed. June 22, 2004) (statement of Sen. Hatch).

its establishment[168]; this draft includes following parts[169].

(1)This draft applies the definition of "Intentional Inducement" from the Patent Law, it means intentionally help or induce doer to infringe other's copyright[170]; the Federal Supreme Court explained the substancial infringing based on Patent Law in the Sony case, legislative congressman recommended to apply this definition in P2P problems[171].

(2)Whether it will cause an increase in the litigation; the definition of this draft based on a third reasonable person's standard; any person who willfully impacts on commercial benefits is penalized by the provisions of it; the court will give the plaintiff an opportunity, although on the surface of this draft, the standards of "intentional inducement" seem too high; however, the plaintiff needs not prove that the defendant actually engaged in or aware of, as long as there is a clue in the defendant's any documents, so the plaintiff can make the infringer bear the responsibility based on this draft[172].

(3)Does not change the existing legal norms, only including the meaning of existing sentences; an overly broad definition of

---

[168] 150 Cong. Rec. S7193 June 22, 2004.

[169] Inducing Infringement of Copyrights Act of 2004, S. 2560, 108th Cong. (2004).

[170] Id. at § 2.

[171] Id. Andrew Greenberg also permitted such views representing electrical and electronic machinery department as congressional testimony; Andrew Greenberg, Institute of Electrical and Electronics Engineers, in his congressional testimony before the Senate Judiciary Committee.

[172] Hearings on S. 2560(statement of Kevin McGuiness).

inducement would cause the application difficult[173].

(4)This draft attempts to overthrow the Sony case, which had a tendency to protect capitalists' opinion, encouraging them to invest at ease without being accused, this draft is trying to change this point[174].

(II) Copyright Office's proposal

After the public hearing of the foregoing draft, Copyright Office widened the scope of radiocast, modifying another proposal of it[175], which insisted it was technology-neutral to increase the part of technological use[176]; the terms used in the draft will enable the users can not escape from responsibility, because the judgment of Grokster case by the Ninth Circuit Court of Appeals urged the copyright holder to promote this draft[177]. The draft re-emphasized the scope of technology application, if the public had illegal behavior through it, people should not lay too much blame on scientific and technological inventors, this proposal attempted to improve shortcomings of aforementioned draft, the terms of which were too wide, which are described as below.

---

[173] The Intentional Inducement of Copyrights Act of 2004: Hearing on S. 2560 Before the S. Comm. on the Judiciary, 108th Cong. (2004) [hereinafter Hearings on S. 2560] (statement of Andrew Greenberg, Vice-Chairman, Intellectual Property Committee of the Institute of Electrical and Electronics Engineers- United State of America).

[174] Steve Seidenberg, Senate Bill Puts Power in Hands of Copyright Owners, Corp. Legal Times, Sept. 2004, at 16 (quoting Michael Petricone, vice president of technology policy for the Consumer Electronics Association).

[175] See Gigi B. Sohn, Radical Act Would Induce Big Chill, Legal Times, at 19 (Oct. 11, 2004).

[176] Id.

[177] Id.

Elements of the one penalized to have responsibility. No matter who manufactures, offers to the public any product or service, such as computer programs, technology, device or component, constituting violations, he/she: 1) involving the use of commercial distribution in the general public; 2) thus obtain the main proceeds; 3) has the main purpose to attract individuals accountable for their products and services[178]. For the completion of this draft, the Copyright Office paid special attention to science and technology industry business models, pay attention to the extent of infringement caused by such products or services, looking carefully the damage to the object of copyright, and thus generating the percentage of the revenue to determine, and giving up partial vague or ambiguous language of foregoing draft.

Such as the definition of "public dissemination" and other terms are related to compensation, damages and an injunction promulgated of this proposal; the provided damages only occur when the doer has "intentional" acts and some cases, including damage and reduced interest caused by fault behavior, though it is not deliberate, one should also compensate. An injunction is against the possible violations, of course excluding the unintentional violations. This proposal was not passed as the views of the two (the copyright holder and IT industry operator) can not reach an agreement[179].

---

[178] See Explanatory Memorandum from Copyright Office, http://www.copyright.gov/docs/S2560.pdf (last visited, Apr. 24, 2006).

[179] The definition of terms has different views, Senator Hatch's provision terms left some leeway to the two sides, as expected they were still unable to reach a consensus. Sarah Lai Stirland, Talks Collapse in Effort to Reach Deal on File-Sharing Bill, CongressDailyAm (Oct. 7 , 2004).

V. Cases

In the use of P2P file transmission system, as to Napster, Aimster and Grokster cases, the court's major consideration was whether the defendants had the right and ability to supervise user's behavior; on the contrary, the court did not ascertain the requirements for direct significant economic interests[180]. In the comparison on Grokster and Aimster cases, it seemed to agree the standard of "knowingly" element since the case of Sony, that is, to be "actual" knowledge, the activities of specific infringing[181]. However, the actual inquiry found the two were still different in determining extent and the proportion, the Seventh and Ninth Circuit Court of Appeals took different views, impacting the use of standards, they were described as below.

1. Definitions of Actual Knowledge Are Different

As to what was the special knowingly element, these two courts excluded that the defendant must have actual knowledge - that is, the cognitive and producing purposes of a merchandise were to infringe

---

[180] In Grokster case of Ninth Circuit Court of Appeals in 2004, after discovering that the defendant had no right and ability to monitor the user, it could not infer the defendant obtained direct economic benefits, Metro-Goldwyn-Mayer Studios, Inc. V. Grokster Ltd., 380 F. 3d 1154, 1146-66 (9th Cir. 2004); in Aimster case of the Seventh Circuit Court of Appeals in 2003,it was unable to comply with elements in "direct economic interest" of copyright infringement, In re Aimster Copyright Litig., 334 F. 3d 643, 654-55 (7th Cir. 2003); while Napster case recognized the requirements for direct economic benefits by District Court, because there were proofs that user's infringement made the defendant obtain benefits, Napster, 239 F. 3d at 1023.

[181] See Grokster, 380 F. 3d at 1161. Aimster, 334 F. 3d at 649.

others' right[182]; but according to opinion of Sony case, the merchandise VCR could have both infringing use and non-infringing use, which was accepted by 25% customers, who regarded their cognition as "actual knowledge of violations[183]"; This opinion was the same with that of the Ninth Circuit Court of Appeals in the Grokster case, it held that the actual knowledge was "know the existence of specific file under reasonable circumstances[184]"; and Aimster case used the condition that knowing the file-sharing was sufficient to form the defendant's "actual knowledge"[185]; there may be differences in standards of different courts, therefore, how to find a fair and reasonable boundary between the taking responsibility and impunity by the defendant, which affords for thought is in the United States, where the case leads laws and regulations.

Such as Sony case, which only applied contributory copyright infringement, or the use of consumer; vicarious copyright infringement was also applied in Sony case, earlier, the Supreme Court admitted that it was difficult to judge direct, contributory and vicarious copyright infringements in Sony case[186]; in fact Sony did not apply vicarious copyright infringement, only using this term to explain the principle of

---

[182] See Aimster, 334 F. 3d at 649; see also Grokster, 380 F. 3d at 1161.

[183] Aimster, 334 F. 3d at 649.

[184] In Sony case, the defendant was not judged to have the secondary liability, because when the defendant sold machinery and equipment, he could only infer with" as informed "that, his customers may have infringing use after buying. Sony Corp. of Am. v., Universal City Studios, Inc., 464 US 417, 439 (1984).

[185] Aimster, 334 F. 3d at 649.

[186] Sony, 464 R.S. at 435 n.17 (quoting Universal City Studios, Inc. v. Sony Corp. of Am., 480 F. Supp. 429, 457-58 (C.D. Cal. 1979)).

respondent superior; until in Napster case, which shown that Sony case used vicarious copyright infringement as a general infringement[187]; even in the Grokster case, the court had not a clear definition and distinction between the two, only expressing whether the infringer was intentionally induced or encouraged in written judgment; and because of their violations for profit but without stopping, it must take the responsibility for the secondary liability[188].

2. Elements of Knowledge Are Different

Only in the face of knowledge there are different views on the following discussion to distinguish whether there is contributory copyright infringement or not. Such as P2P systems, after the computer company sells electronic reproduction or distribution system, it no longer has a direct link to users in violations, such as Grokster case, even if the computer company shut down its system, the user could still continue to use and not be affected[189]; while, the Napster case was different, Napster and its users maintained the continuous relationship of consultancy services[190]; therefore whether have the knowledge that merchandise will be used in infringement is a key. Its extent and timing are also the keys in determining responsibility, take the opinion of Grokster case as the benchmark for judging - the time points when had the knowledge was the key to judge its contributory copyright

---

[187] See Napster, 239 F. 3d at 1022-23.

[188] Grokster, 125 S. Ct. at 2776.

[189] See Metro-Goldwayn-Mayer Studios, Inc. v. Grokster Ltd., 380 F. 3d 1154, 1163 (9th Cir. 2004).

[190] A&M Records, Inc. v. Napster, Inc., 239 F. 3d 1004, 1011-12 (9th Cir. 2001).

infringement, only when the defendant knew the infringement and could control it[191].

Even though when and how did the defendant know are not easy to ascertain, the court still need to measure whether the general or specific knowledge is enough to prove that the defendant's supporting acts constitute a violation; the most important is the defendant knew his violation for benefits, the court should pay attention to whether it provides clear criteria to the future behavior - need to have unlawful intentions, or have special knowledge, or prior knowledge, or even covering all of them will constitute infringement liability.

Sometimes, it is difficult to have clear boundary to determine constructive knowledge and actual knowledge; according to Gershwin case's opinion on this[192], the judgment that the defendant "had knowledge" was based on his subjective standard, actually the defendant must had it; and the court held that "reason to know" was to adopt an objective standard[193], which was known by general people; in Grokster case, if the merchandise was proved that it was substantial infringing use, namely there was a possibility of infringement, the plaintiff (copyright holder) only had to prove that the defendant was prepared by knowledge[194], that is, the court would select a certain standard depending on the case.

---

[191] See Grokster, 259 F. Supp. 2d at 1035-38, aff'd, 380 F. 3d 1154 (9th Cir. 2004), rev'd, 125 S. ct. 2764 (2005).

[192] Gershwin, 44.3 F. 2d at 1162 (citing Screen Gems-Columbia Music, Inc. v. Mark Fi Records, Inc., 256 F. Sup. 399, 403 (S.D.N.Y. 1966)).

[193] Casella v. Morris, 820 F. 2d 362, 365 (11th Cir. 1987).

[194] Grokster, 380 F. 3d at 1161.

3. Interpretations of Infringement Are Different

After Grokster case, copyright infringement had a new interpretation; the elements of inducement copyright infringement, contributory and vicarious copyright infringement are significantly different, and their applicable cases are also different; vicarious copyright infringement applies to a more broad scope of principal and agent relationship, as it requires no criminal intent elements or knowledge element; contributory and inducement copyright infringements apply to similar cases, the former requires only knowledge not criminal intent, it is difficult to find general principle in the past cases; inducement copyright infringement had sought another way of relief for copyright holders.

As to the analysis on the secondary liability, among the opinions from Federal Circuit Courts, the Ninth Circuit Court of Appeals' opinion in Fonovisa identified vicarious copyright infringement, which could also be inferred inducement copyright infringement; in this case, the defendant operated second-hand barter market, it provided parking facilities and ads to attract lessees lease its booth, and it could be arbitrarily refused to lease to the lessee, but also permitted the sale of counterfeit goods on leasing stalls, ignoring repeated warnings from the police. The court held that the defendant violated both contributory and vicarious copyright infringements[195]. Having the knowledge should not be considered the only element of inducement copyright infringement, such as Fonovisa case was penalized as guilty for vicarious copyright infringement, and inducement copyright infringement was developed in Grokster case; it was obvious that there were different views on

---

[195] Fonovisa, Inc. v. Cherry Auction, Inc., 76 F. 3d 259, 264 (9th Cir. 1996).

requirements and judgment of liability elements in 1996 and 2005.

Generally speaking, the court often penalizes contributory copyright infringement in related copyright infringement cases; but the Internet-based cases do not comply with the elements of inducement infringement in Grokster case, but constituting the responsibility of "informed of document be spread[196]", that is in line with the elements of contributory copyright infringement; Additionally, when involved in "the sales principle of main merchandise" from Sony case, the defendant will be penalized if he "knew the infringing" and contributed to direct violations; this is more standard than the inducement infringement penalized in Grokster case, the defendant had a special intent (malicious) to inducement infringement, therefore contributory and inducement copyright infringement can complement each other, forming complementary rights and remedies.

As for the cases prior to the Grokster case, the related theory about contributory and vicarious copyright infringements was not clear; as required by case law, the lower court's opinions were modified or corrected based on the representative cases. In 2005, US Supreme Court tried bravely in Grokster case, which gave copyright holders more protections and supports, when seeking for rights and remedies, they could both sue direct infringer and distributors, companies and manufacturers related; relatively, of course the inducement copyright infringement gave considerable help in provision of legal basis and cases, because this was decided by the Supreme Court of the United States in the near future, the impact on the practical or the lower court was major naturally.

---

[196] Universal City Studios, Inc. v. Reimerdes, 111 F. Supp. 2d 294, 316-19 (S.D.N.Y. 2000).

Reviewing the theory of copyright infringement, responsibility and case studies in US Copyright Law, especially the "inducement copyright infringement" deduced by the Supreme Court of the United States at Grokster case in 2005, it expanded the basis of claim for copyright infringement; but at substantive decision, especially in the exploration of intendment to determine whether there is criminal intent and inducing others to infringe. As to determine whether there is direct economic benefit or participate in, assist, encourage, or even ignore the infringing, or "intentionally blind" leads to violations, it depends on practical situation and process of different cases; there is a jury trial and a court verdict, which are taken as the thread of thought and tracks.

VI. Cases in Taiwan

Whether MP3 music is legally depends on the "re-produce" behavior accompanied with download, whether or not it belongs to the scope of fair use in the Copyright Law[197]. As to the fair use of copyrighted works, including reproduction or recording or other way for comment, review, news reporting, teaching (including the majority reproduce materials used for school), academic or research purposes, which are non-infringement of a copyright, the decision whether it is fair use or not is made in the particular case[198]. Furthermore, according

---

[197] Lai, W.C., Chen, C.L., Yan, Y.L., Liu, C.C., "IS Law-web", p. 53, July 2002.

[198] Shen, YC, Brief discussion on copyright and privacy rights issues in information society, Journal of the Institute of Sociology, Nanhua University, Issue 39, May 15, 2004, http://mail.

to Taiwan's Copyright Law Article 65, Paragraph 2: "whether the use complies with Article 44 to 63 or other circumstances of fair use or not, which depends on all the situations[199]. 1. The purpose and nature of use, including the purpose of commercial use, or for the non-profit educational purposes. 2. The nature of works. 3. Quality and its proportion in the entire works. 4. The impact of use on potential market and present value of works.

If others' music files, such as works of music or sound recording, are compressed in MP3 standards, such a conversion action, that is, in fact a kind of "re-produce" behavior. And compressed music works of others, the act itself includes reproduction are compression two procedures, therefore "visibly re-produce through other methods" of Copyright Law in Taiwan belongs to the alleged acts of reproduction[200]. And in accordance with the Copyright Law Article 22[201], the right to reproduce belongs to property rights of copyright holder, so if users download copyrighted music without reasonable use and lawful

nhu.edu.tw/ ~ society / ej / 39/39-04.htm (search date: Jan. 3, 2006).

[199] Chao, J.M., Tsai, K.C., Chou, H.F., Hsieh, M.H., Chang, K.N., "Introduction to Intellectual Property Rights", p.15, Feb. 2004.

[200] Yu, D.C., "Criminal responsibility of illegal use of the Internet", master's thesis, Department of Law, Tung Hai University, p.151, 2000.

[201] Copyright Law Article 22: An author has the exclusive right to reproduce his/her works unless otherwise provided. A performer has the exclusive right to record, video-record or film his/ her performance. The two front provisions are not applicable, as they are adoptive transfer, or through legal writing, which is the necessary transition in technical operating process, it is incidental without the temporality of an independent economic significance. But computer program is not included in this scope. Temporary lawful reproduction in the preceding paragraph, including web browser, quick access, or other technically inevitable phenomenon to reach transmission. See Wu, SK, "Network Living with the law", p. 123, January 2005.

authority, it would constitute an infringement of Reproduction Right[202].

When exchanging music through the software provided by the software company, apart from a "download" (reproduction) circumstance, it also includes the "provide to general public" behavior, which share with others the copyrighted music files stored in their computers and available to other users download , they are also the "public transmission" behaviors provided in the Copyright Law[203].

In June 2003, Taiwan added the content of Public Transmission Rights[204], which was in Article 3, paragraph 1 and paragraph 10 of new Copyright Law, defined as follows: " Public Transmission Rights: refers to the right to provide or transmit copyrighted contents with sound or images through electric cable, radio network or other communication methods, including making the public obtain it in chosen time or place." Article 26, paragraph 1 states: "Except as otherwise stipulated (by this law), the authors have the exclusive right of public transmission." Therefore if network users record CD into MP3 file without the author's consent, it is not the fair use according to Article 65 of the Copyright Law, and the infringer must bear civil liability[205].

When reading the file in a computer, it is necessary first read the

---

[202] Liu, C.B., "Case Analysis on Law and Management of Intellectual Property(1)", p.124, Oct. 2003.

[203] National Tsing Hua University Life Information, Copyright of music downloaded by users through network exchange software, Mar. 2005, http://www.nthu.edu.tw/Hot-New/property/property.htm (Dec. 23, 2003).

[204] Wu, S.K., "Network Living and the Law", p.125, Jan. 2005.

[205] Chen, C.S., Chung, L.F., Evaluation in copyright law on transmission and reproduction of P2P resource-sharing architecture, p.11, http://www.ntpu.edu.tw/law/paper/07/2003/79271202c.pdf (search date: Jan, 4, 2006).

file stored in the media into the computer's Random Access Memory (RAM[206]), so as to see the contents on the screen, and this action is a kind of reproduction. As to the action searching or reading data on internet, which involves downloading data from the network to the host personal computer, which also is a kind of reproduction.

When exchanging MP3 on MP3 platform, the MP3 files in members' computers provide other users to download through the software, which is the "public transmission" of the new Copyright Law; on September 1, 2004, Article 91, Paragraph 2 of the new Copyright Law, the penalty of "five pieces" or "damages below $ 30000 NTD" had been deleted, making the "non-intent to profit-seeking" behavior have copyright infringement and criminal liability. As for whether or not there are invalidation action and punishment, still reserves the prosecutors and judges to be case-by-case investigation, depending on whether it is a "Not indict petty criminality" or "Not punish petty criminality" (reference to the new Copyright Law, Article 91 to 93), otherwise they would be considered as infringing other's copyright and property rights through reproduction, be liable to three years imprisonment, or fined up to $ 750000 NTD.

---

[206] RAM is computer's internal memory, used to store computer's instructions or data immediately to use. It is variable with quick access, so it is applied to computing and in the process of enforcement procedures; the current data used is store in RAM. This phenomenon, which loads applications in RAM for execution, is necessary in general PC when implement procedures; if a computer program without a load in RAM, it can not communicate with the computer. See Intellectual Property Office, Ministry of Economic Affairs, Lee & Li Attorneys at Law, June 6, 2003] Legislative Yuan passed case study on "attached resolution of the new amended Copyright Law", pp.180-181, May 2004. Chen, CC, Copyright issues of temporary storage in RAM (I) - talking about from MAI v. Peak case - And the disscusion of the impact on network environment, intellectual property, pp.101-103, Jan. 2000.

In 2001, as The United States judged Napster's P2P services company sentencing as infringement, there are several international P2P infringement cases succeed; on September 5, 2005, after Australia determined Kazaa, global famous P2P industry operator, as infringement, on the 9th in the same month at Taipei District Court, Kuro was also declared in violation of copyright[207]; different from June 30 in the same year at Shihlin District Court, which declared ezPeer not established tort[208], did not assume tort and criminal liability, and also first held that users had to bear criminal liability[209]. In the above-mentioned Taiwan cases, the courts have confirmed that the file-swapping software is neutral technology and should not be blamed or prohibited, but it depends on whether or not the behavior providing or using such software induces, assists, or causes copyright infringement of others. As to Kuro and ezPeer cases, the former was judged that the provider and users were partners in crime, shall be guilty; as for the latter, the users were considered to bear criminal liability of copyright infringement, but the provider only had civil liability, without criminal liability[210].

1. EzPeer Case

The industry operator providing users with "ezPeer" P2P file download platform, Shihlin District Court acquitted; legislators may

---

[207] Verdict (2003) Su-2146.

[208] Verdict (2003)Su-728.

[209] "IFPI vs Kuro", according to Angle Law Network, http://www.angle.com.tw/focus/focus117. htm (search date: Nov. 23, 2005).

[210] Chang, C.H., "Analysis on Kurocase", last updated Nov. 4, 2005. http://www.copyrightnote. org/crnote/bbs.php?board=6&act=read&id=58 (search date: Nov. 25, 2005).

mediate it based on norms of administrative law, even in the general consensus against ezPeer, legislators can also legislate to regulate as required, such as the Penal Code. Before there is no express provision, the judiciary must be strict comply with the absolute boundaries in "principle of legality", so the copyright loopholes could not be analogized or supplemented by extensive interpretation, which should be interpreted strictly. Collegiate bench said that, recently, a number of foreign verdicts on P2P infringement are tort cases, such as Napster case in the United States, the main purpose was confirming wealth damage and the distribution; and these foreign case elements of tort were different from the ones in Taiwan.

The foundation of ezPeer verdict: ezPeer itself neither engaged in illegal public transmission and reproduce, nor set up a "complicity" relationship, based on the "last resort of Criminal Code" and "legality" principles[211], it was sued by the Prosecutor ((2002) Cheng-Tze-Di # 10786, 4559), the judgment was: ezPeer company's representative Wu Yida was acquitted, Global Digital Technology Co., Ltd. was impunity[212]. In ezPeer verdict, for such new lifestyle due to network technology, which was different from the scope of existing copyright law, the court wanted to solve new social conflict or for a specific development goal, the court adopted a serious attitude to it[213].

---

[211] Chian, R.C., When P2P meets the Copyright Law, http://taiwan.cnet.com/enterprise/column /0,2000062893,20101695,00.htm (search date: Jan. 13, 2006 日).

[212] Taiwan Shilin District Court Criminal Case Verdict (2003) Su-Tze-Di#728.

[213] Wu, CY, Liao, WJ, "Discussion on problems in network download music copyright based on the decision of Kuro copyright infringement case (2)", Nov. 10, 2005, the article also pointed out that P2P operator had commissioned legislator in the Fifth Legislative Yuan Fourth session to propose "copyright compensation system," hopefully to set up new rules

2. Kuro Case

Kuro, Taiwan's largest MP3 download platform website, due to setting up file exchange website to support MP3 download without authorized, it's accused by Rolling Stone, Sony and Taiwan's 11 major record companies, as it legally provided members pop music, data files to unlimited download freely, and it was sued for violation of copyright[214]. The prosecutors and police pointed out that, according to the latest interpretation of Intellectual Property Office, Ministry of Economic Affairs at the end of July 2005, the use of Kuro platform for the exchange of MP3 music should be consented or authorized, or else one would have violations of "reproduction right " and "the right of public transmission"; "download" itself is an "reproduction" behavior, and one provides MP3 stored in his computer to other users through the Kuro for download, which is also the "public transmission" regulated by existing copyright law.

Kuro company representative and executive officers Shou-teng Chen, Guo-hua Chen, and Guo-hsiung Chen, knowing that its Kuro software and web services were available to members illegal download others works, but for the recruitment of members and earning fees, it

---

of the game based on legislative reference abroad for record industry, network music service provider and the general Internet users. http://cpro.com.tw / channel / news / content /? news_id = 8739 (search date: Nov. 15, 2005).

[214] Lawsuit that record industry against P2P file-sharing, Kuro refused to accept and continued to appeal in a press conference on September 9, and the company's web site would continue operating, but membership rights would not be affected; Kuro CEO Guo-hua Chen pointed out that, in the future they would actively promote to modify compulsory compensation system in system copyright law, the. See Wang, PH, "Kuro wanted to appeal, continue to operate", Litery Times, Sep. 10, 2005, http://www.epochtimes.com.tw/bt/5/9/10/n1047775.htm (search date: Nov. 22, 2005).

continuously advertised to induce substantial members, and therefore the result of its member's (Chia-hui Chen) infringing was significantly predictable on subjective, but it wasn't in breach of the member's intent, so in this case, the above three and the member were partners in crime, which should share responsibility for their behavior[215]. They were punishable by criminal responsibility and sentenced to a civil compensation.

Kruo case can be addressed to the guilty verdict, the "defendant-litigant structure" or "truth structure" shall have a critical impact. The structure that the prosecutor indicted made the collegiate bench judges consider defendant's "criminal intent" from the specific facts, and they can directly quoted the determine principles on the Taiwan traditional criminal laws, which is sufficient for IFPI to agree with the results[216].

Kuro (P2P software provider) had a vexatious suit when Taiwan record companies were sued; in mainland China, it was also sued infringement by Shanghai Busheng Music Culture Media, Beijing Second Intermediate People's Court has accepted it; according to (Xinhuanet) report, that was Chinese first P2P disputes. Shanghai Busheng called on Beijing Kuro to bear the civil liability of "cease the infringing act", "eliminate ill effects ", "public apology" and "compensation for economic losses"[217].

---

[215] Intellectual Property Office, Ministry of Economic Affairs, unauthorized P2P, platforms and users should take the responsibility, Sep. 9, 2005, http://www2.kuas.edu.tw/edu/copyright/docs.php?lang=big5&doc=5 (search date: Dec. 22, 2005).

[216] Wei, CH, P2P download user's legal risks, about the first-instance sentence of IFPI vs. Kuro, OFFICE Magazine, Issue 99, p.166, Oct. 1, 2005.

[217] Chen, H.L., "Kuro infringement case, P2P disputes of first case in China", ET News, http://tw.news.yahoo.com/ 051024/195/2g57y.html (search date: Nov. 16, 2005).

3. The Comparison of Cases

In addition to providing general music data indexing, Kuro and ezPeer websites also provided members with "hot new song this week", "download chart", and other express indexes; it was obvious that they were aware of the content transmitted by members, but they still encourage them with express index for music exchange. If Kuro and ezPeer didn't provide those, members couldn't do such transmission and exchange, and therefore against the copyright holder's right of public transmission, and they should hold criminal and civil liabilities. Incidentally, because of Kuro and ezPeer website knowing that the majority of MP3 music files without copyright authorization, still open to provide online file-swapping services, and accordingly charged to the members for profit, which had a high commercial benefits, and was bound to a very great impact on the record market, so it didn't belong to the situation of fair use[218].

According to two sentences of above-mentioned IFPI toward individual ezPeer or Kuro copyright infringement lawsuit, judges of the two collegiate benches all viewed that if user download unauthorized music or video through the network software, such as copyrighted material, unless it was in "fair use", otherwise it was against the law. However, why the final outcomes of two judgments were contrary?

---

[218] LI, G.Y., Chou, W.C., Chen, C.L., Analysis on legal issues of P2P – a case of Napster in United States, supplemented by ezPeer and Kuro cases in Taiwan, http://66.102.7.104/searc h?q=cache:_o2xArXAux0J:163.25.107.30/ecpp922/b8943030/%E9%9B%BB%E5%AD% 90%E5%95%86%E5%8B%99%E6%9C%9F%E6%9C%AB%E5%A0%B1%E5%91%8A. doc+%E6%9D%8E%E5%86%A0%E5%84%80%E3%80%81%E5%91%A8%E7%B6 %AD%E7%9C%9F%E3%80%81%E9%99%B3%E8%8A%9D%E7%8E%B2&hl=zh-TW&lr=lang_zh-TW (search date: 2005年12月10日).

There was a very different point in the case of Kuro, it's "defendant-litigant structure" was different from that in ezPeer case. In Kuro case the P2P industry operators and users have been included in the defendant; ezPeer case was only P2P industry operator. The court held that ezPee industry itself was not involved in any criminal acts like "reproduction" or "public transmission", that is, the perpetrator was the members rather than ezPeer. ezPeer developed software, set up the network platform and provided members with transmission download files, the court said that although it did not filter unauthorized music files, such omission was not in violation of copyright law, not the unauthorized "reproduction" or "public transmission".

However, in Kuro's judgment, the court found that industry operator and members had the criminal intents and constituted an accomplice[219]; according to Explanatory Letter Chi-Chu-Tze-Di#0921600565-0, Intellectual Property Office at the end of July 2003, exchange copyrighted works with P2P platform on the Internet should be in line with fair use required as copyright law, as well as get the author or copyright holder's consent or authorization, Otherwise, it was at risk of both violations of "reproduction right" and "the right of public transmission". In which, "download" is the "reproduction" behavior, and providing MP3 stored in the computer to other for download through P2P website is the "public transmission" according to copyright law[220].

---

[219] Wu, C.Y., "Discussion on problems in network download music copyright based on the decision of Kuro copyright infringement case (1)", Nov. 3, 2005, http://cpro.com.tw/channel/news/content/index.php?news_id=8763 (search date: Nov. 22, 2005).

[220] Tsai, L., "Taiwan's first infringement lawsuit on network P2P file exchange - Kuro case",

Although the focus of judges' consideration and actual operational behavior of ezPeer and Kuro were different, it can be identified that the judgments in two cases were based on fair use of P2P software; if it exceeded the scope of fair use, it would constitute infringement.

Table 2-1   Comparison of KURO and ezPeer Cases

Case	KURO Case	ezPeer Case
Truth	Accused as setting up the file exchange website for MP3 download without legally authorized, forming a unlimited and free data files environment.	ezPeer published software to provide members with a data files environment for download popular songs, films and others
Punishment	Taipei District Court ruled Kuro case, provided that it had copyright infringement, the defendants in this case most were sentenced to three years.	Shihlin District Court ruling, there was no legal requirement for the P2P industry operator, which must be responsible for the action that consumers send contents in the network, provided that P2P file-sharing software had no reproduction or public transmission, so not guilty.

4. Taiwan Copyright Law New Amendments

The study period of this paper coincided with the amendments and the addition of Copyright Law by Legislative Yuan on Jan 12, 2010; its contents are as follows: Article 87, Paragraph 1, Item 7: "without property rights holder's consent or authorization, the intention is public transmission or reproduction through the network, against property

Feb. 4, 2004, http://www.ipnavigator.com.tw/news/news_view.asp?NewsID=200402020925 49 (search date: Nov. 22, 2005).

rights, or do above for profits." Article 87, Paragraph 2: "if the doer of preceding 7 items takes ads or other positive measures to abet, induce, incite, or convince the public infringe through computer programs or other technologies, he/she has the criminal intention."

Article 93, paragraph 4: "one person in violation of article 87, paragraph 1, item 7 should be penalized two years imprisonment, criminal detention, or a fine of $ 500000 NTD." Article 97, paragraph 1: "one unit infringes Article 91, 92 and Article 93, paragraph 4 through open transmission, convicted by the courts, it should cease its acts; If not stop, and the case is serious, seriously impacting on holder's property rights and interests, the competent authority should make it correct within a month, otherwise issue an order to suspend or close." Based on foregoing provisions, the legal discussion of Taiwan' s copyright infringement has expressly provided, but how the effective is, time will tell.

VII. Conclusions

In June 2005, the Supreme Court of the United States made a decision to Metro-Goldwyn-Mayer Studios, Inc. V. Grokster, Ltd. [221], the Court held that Grokster should bear the secondary liability, even if the court considered Grokster's software didn't pose any infringing use[222], and it clarified and corrected a number of legal opinions from

---

[221] 125 S. Ct. 2764 (2005).

[222] Id. At 2780; see also Sony Crop. Of America v. Universal City Studios, Inc., 464 U.S. 417, 442 (1984).

the lower courts before based on this case; since the case of A & M Records, Inc. v. Napster, Inc. [223], the Ninth Circuit Court of Appeals assumed that Napster should bear the secondary liability, and then took the case of In re Aimster[224] as the example, the Seventh Circuit of Appeals' opinion was significantly different; the above-mentioned three companies, Napseer, Grokster and Aimster' software systems in fact allowed the direct copyright infringing[225].

In addition to court opinions on network copyright infringement or P2P related issues, Congress also hoped that legislation could complement and level the deficiencies in existing laws and practice[226], such as the Induce Act[227], Senator Hatch said the copyright groups' (such as the record, audio-visual industries) opinion on the Ninth Circuit Court of Appeals' judgment in the above-mentioned case of Grokster[228]; P2P software providers were opposed to passing this bill; when the inventor and the network users immersed in supporting opinions, however, the Federal Supreme Court's decision in 2005 was in favor of the copyright holder[229].

According to evolution from the above cases, we can see that the courts take different views, the dispute resorts to the legislation, but legislation is not comprehensive, and then once again returns to

---

[223] 239 F.3d 1004, 1024 (9th Cir. 2001).

[224] 334 F. 3d 643, 650 (7th Cir. 2003).

[225] Grokster, 380 F. 3d at 1158; Aimster, 334 F.3d. at 645; Napster 239 F.3d at 1013.

[226] 150 Cong. Rec. S7189 (daily ed. June 22, 2004) (statement of Sen. Hatch).

[227] See Sen. Orrin Hatch's proposal, S. 2560, 108th Cong (2004).

[228] 150 Cong. Rec. S7192 (daily ed. June 22, 2004) (statement of Sen. Hatch), the decision supported Grokster in 2004.

[229] See Metro-Goldwyn-Mayer Studios, Inc. v. Grokster, Ltd., 125 S. Ct. 2764, 2780 (2005).

the court and legislation; even such evolution still can not solve the controversy of copyright law. In Grokster case, the Supreme Court of the United States made Grokste removed the tort liability, even if it was proved true that some P2P software deliberately hurt others in essence, its secondary liability was also evaded[230]; and the Induce Act was to strengthen the provisions in Article 501 of copyright law, overturning District Court's opinions in previous cases, and maintaining partial opinions of the Ninth Circuit Court of Appeals.

The implementation and passing of a new bill always has positive and negative two opinions; the one opposed to the Induce Act, such as the software industry operators, which firmly believe that the secondary liability would discourage the efforts of R & D, it is bound to impede the technology update; network users, of course, support such technology, which makes download music and movies quickly and cheaper; In addition, the copyright holder, including the artists, creators and business groups strongly hope to prevent violations from happening[231], this situation is all around the world alike. In view of the American common law's spirit, the copyright law of 1976 did not specifically regulate the secondary liability, such as the case of Gershwin Publishing Corp. v. Columbia Artists Management, Inc[232], the Court held that orchestra manager should have a shared responsibility for violations as the orchestra performed. The Court demonstrated that,

---

[230] Metro-Goldwyn-Mayer Studios, Inc. v. Grokster, Ltd., 259 F. Supp. 2d 1029, 1046 (C.D.Cal.2003), aff'd, 380 F. 3d 1154 (9th Cir. 2004), vacated, 125 S.Ct. 2764 (2005).

[231] Aranda Ben, Inducing a Remedy or Courting a Solution? A Comparative Institutional Analysis of the P2P Dilemma. 50 St. Louis U. L.J. 863 (2006).

[232] 443 F. 2d at 1162-63.

when the doer: 1) know that violations occurred; 2) guides , assists or participates in violations, the one in line with these two elements must bear the responsibility of contributory infringer[233]. The court should determine the manager had the ability and right to know Orchestra events, and profit from it directly[234].

In this paper, it is recommended to reduce the price or increase the capacity of CD and DVD. Record films can attach posters, gifts, signatures, etc., so as to attract fans to buy, rather than download; that is, to make the CD or DVD packaging has a greater incentive and competitiveness. Public consumers generally think that CD or DVD price is too high, particularly in the groups of students, their income and job are not fixed, most of them consider records, and tapes expenditures affect its quality of life[235]. Take music industry as an example, cultivating artists (e.g. performer, artist) to meet the requirements of music producers and so on, are the reasons for record high prices; in fact, the interesting sidelights, behind-the-scenes or recalling fragment, production process, introduction paragraphs, NG screen and so on accompanied by CD or DVD, are all the practice based on the market, making consumers more have choices, not to do illegal download; in addition, improve software technology, so users are difficult to copy or excerpt CD; coupled with a need to log in and register with account numbers to solve problems; however, if

---

[233] Id. at 1162.

[234] Id.

[235] Taiwan's current CD and DVD price level do lie a burden to students, young students think that lower price is really attractive, because a real favorite songs or programs issued by the original publication company has a better quality

the numbers are shared, they will be opened, but at least can achieve a warning, or recommended that such registration numbers can exist in world's common ways, so as to reach the cross-boundary functions[236]..

In recent years, the most successful and well-known example is iTunes, issued by Apple Computer in April 2003, so that consumers could download songs with the price of 0.99 U.S. dollars[237], and the introduction of Apple Computer ipod made MP3 download and listening more convenient; iTunes sales a year was about one million songs, to March 2005, accounting for about one percent of the United States market[238]; if such promotion and performance for music market could reach an agreement on its use in international copyright law, so as to reconcile the disputes between copyright holder and users[239], it is a feasible measure. Taiwan's largest online music website (Kuro)

---

[236] Michael Landau, Digital Music Downloads and Copyright Infringement, 758 Pat. 405, 435 (2003).

[237] Overview Apple-iTunes, Apple.com, http://www.apple.com/itunes/overview/ (last visited, Nov. 11, 2005).

[238] Shahid Khan & Peri Shamsai, Digital Music's Comeback: How Can Record Companies and Music Publishers Seize the Opportunities? Bearing Point Inst. For Exec. Insight (Mar. 2005), http://www.bearingpoint.com/portal/binary/com.epicentric.contentmanagement. servlet/ published/pdfs/protected/C2967a-BEI_Music_WP.pdf.

[239] The largest weak of P2P industry operator's compensation system lies in deliberately neglect the essential difference of network software and hardware; the compensation system is applicable in the CD writer, CD or others to re-produce, rather than download; because WIPO passed WIPO Copyright Treaty (WCT) and WIPO Performances and Phonograms Treaty (WPPT) in 1996, giving the copyright holders new rights in network environment, including the rights of public transmission in WCT and WPPT, as well as reproduction right, distribution right, and rental rights. But P2P industry operator's proposal diverged from the international development trend, it is worthy of deep reflection whether this system can be used in Taiwan or not.

and the record company reached a settlement agreement; in September 2005, the court decided Kuro losing the suit, the two sides started reconciliation talks; for the recent record companies facing significant decline in CD sales, they finally succeeded after years to combat illegal music platform. In July 2006, the music platform industry operator also belong to P2P, the global digital and record companies reached a settlement agreement, Kuro expressed it would transfer into a legal music platform at the end of 2006[240].

Rather than spending time and money charging individual users or software designers, the copyright holders change the patterns of business management, such as the development of copyright protection software (such as anti-piracy device) and re-educate people to respect intellectual property rights; From the other side, in fact, developed electronic technology also opened up and extended the showing type of copyright holder's works, more diverse market models are developed, enabling music authors collect more profit. Instead, legal proceedings are in fact the lowest-order mode of relief, which undermine relations between the two sides and damage the unsuccessful party's reputation possibly, perhaps the above-mentioned approaches could solve P2P-related issues and disputes, and we would like to see copyright holders an users communicate more, system company is more willing to set up a communication platform to create win-win situation.

---

[240] He, Y.W., Online music curse: compensation-Kuro's largest pain, Business Times/Sec. A4, Sep. 5, 2006.

References

Chinese

1. Books

Wu, S.K., "Network Living and the Law", Jan. 2005, San Min Books.

"Case study on"attached resolution of the new amended Copyright Law, May 2004, Intellectual Property Office, Lee & Li Attorneys at Law.

Chao, J.M., Tsai, K.C., Chou, H.F., Hsieh, M.Y., Chang, K.N., "Introduction to Intellectual Property Rights", Feb. 2004, Angle Publishing.

Liu, C.B., "Case Analysis on Law and Management of Intellectual Property(1)", Oct. 2003, Hua Tai Publishing.

Lai, W.C., Chen, C.L., Lai, Y.L., Liu, C.C., "IS Law-Web", July, 2002, IS Law Office.

2. Articles

Yu, D.C., "Criminal responsibility of illegal use of the Internet", master's thesis, Department of Law, Tung Hai University, 2000.

Lin, C.M., "Uncovered P2P thieves through analysis of network traffic", Information and Computer, Issue 306, Jan. 2006.

Chen, C.C., "Copyright issues of temporary storage in RAM (I) - talking about from MAI v. Peak case - And the discussion of the impact on network environment", Intellectual Property, Jan. 2000.

Tzeng, S.C., Hsu, Y.H., "Related questions analysis on online music-take P2P technology of MP3 music download as the core", 2006 the second seminar of information management and project management practices, Institute of Information, Kai Nan

University hosted, May 5, 2006.

Yeh, Y.B., "P2P concepts and their practical significance of society", Information Society Journal of the Institute of Sociology, Nan Hua University, Issue 7, July 2004.

Wei, C.H., "P2P download user's legal risks, about the first-instance sentence of IFPI vs. Kuro", OFFICE Magazine, Issue 99, Oct. 1, 2005.

3. Electronic articles

"IFPI vs Kuro", Angle Law Network, http://www.angle.com.tw/focus/focus117.htm (Search date: Nov. 23, 2005).

Edited by Li, J.H., The unlimited prospect of P2P file-sharing, http://www.epochtimes.com/b5/6/3/30/n1271944.htm, (Search date: April 14, 2006).

Wang, P.H., "Kuro want to appeal, continue to operate", Liberty Times, Sep. 10, 2005, http://www.epochtimes.com.tw/bt/5/9/10/n1047775.htm (Search date: Nov. 22, 2005).

He, Y.W., Online music services are network killer application, but the industry operator generally has not yet been profitable, http://www.digitalcontent.org.tw/e/files/94/0511/940511-2.htm, (Search date: Dec. 23, 2005).

Wu, C.Y., Liao, W.J., "Discussion on problems in network download music copyright based on the decision of Kuro copyright infringement case (2)", Nov. 10, 2005, http://cpro.com.tw/channel/news/content/?news_id=8739 (Search date: Nov. 15, 2005).

Wu, C.Y., "Discussion on problems in network download music copyright based on the decision of Kuro copyright infringement case (1)", Nov. 3, 2005, http://cpro.com.tw/channel/news/content/index.php?news_id=8763 (Search date: Nov. 22, 2005).

Li, G.Y., Chou, W.C., Chen, C.L., Analysis on legal issues of P2P - a case of Napster in United States, http://66.102.7.104/search?q=ca che:_o2xArXAux0J:163.25.107.30/ecpp922/b8943030/%E9%9B %BB%E5%AD%90%E5%95%86%E5%8B%99%E6%9C%9F%E 6%9C%AB%E5%A0%B1%E5%91%8A.doc+%E6%9D%8E%E5 %86%A0%E5%84%80%E3%80%81%E5%91%A8%E7%B6%AD %E7%9C%9F%E3%80%81%E9%99%B3%E8%8A%9D%E7%8E %B2&hl=zh-TW&lr=lang_zh-TW (Search date: Dec. 10, 2005).

Shen, Y.C., Brief discussion on copyright and privacy rights issues in information society, Nan Hua University, Issue 39, May 15, 2004, http://mail.nhu.edu.tw/~society/e-j/39/39-04.htm (Search date: Jan. 3, 2006).

The US and Dutch court stroke two serious blows at RIAA, http:// taiwan.cent.com/news/ce/0,2000062982,20086544,00.htm(Search date: Apr. 11, 2006).

National Tsing Hua University Life Information, Copyright of music downloaded by users through network exchange software, March 2005, http://www.nthu.edu.tw/Hot-New/property/property.htm (Search date: Dec. 23, 2005).

Chen, C.S., Chung, L.F., Evaluation in copyright law on transmission and reproduction of P2P resource-sharing architecture, p.11, http:// www.ntpu.edu.tw/law/paper/07/2003/79271202c.pdf (Search date: Jan. 4, 2006).

Chen, H.L., "Kuro infringement case, the first Chinese P2P disputes", ET News, http://tw.news.yahoo.com/051024/195/2g57y.html (Search date: Nov. 16, 2005).

Chang, C.H., "Kuro case analysis", Nov. 4, 2005, http://www. copyrightnote.org/crnote/bbs.php?board=6&act=read&id=58(Sear

ch date: Nov. 25, 2005).

Tsai, L., "Taiwan's first infringement lawsuit on network P2P file exchange - Kuro case", Feb. 4, 2004, http://www.ipnavigator.com. tw/news/news_view.asp?NewsID=20040202092549 (Search date: Nov. 22, 2005).

Hsiao, B.G., The impact of Peer-to-Peer software on the network copyright in post-Napster time. http://www.apipa.org.tw/Area/ Article-ViewAdA.asp?intAreaType=2&intAdAArticleID=149, (Search date: Nov. 23, 2005).

Chian, R.C., When the P2P case of copyright la, http://taiwan.cnet. com/enterprise/column/0,2000062893,20101695,00.htm (Search date: Jan. 13, 2006).

Chuan Ping Law Network, Apr. 2001, www.cyberlawyer.com.tw (Search date: Nov. 15, 2005).

Intellectual Property Office, Ministry of Economic Affairs, Unauthorized P2P, platforms and users should take the responsibility, Sep. 9, 2005, http://www2.kuas.edu.tw/edu/ copyright/docs.php?lang=big5&doc=5 (Search date: Dec. 22, 2005).

4. Newspapers

He, Y.W., Online music curse compensation flight Nets the most pain, Business Times, Sec. A4, Sep. 5, 2006.

He, H.Y., P2P transmission, United Daily News Sec. A7, Jan. 3, 2006.

English

1. Articles

Alice Kao, RIAA v. Verizon: Applying the Subpoena Provision of the DMCA, 19 Berkeley Tech. L.J.405(2004).

Anna E. Engelman & Dale A. Scott, Arrgh! Hollywood Targets Internet Piracy, 11 Rich.J.L.&Tech. 3 (2004).

Aranda Ben, Inducing a Remedy or Courting a Solution? A Comparative Institutional Analysis of the P2P Dilemma, 50 St. Louis U. L.J. 863 (2006).

David Gorski, The Future of the Digital Millennium Copyright Act(DMCA)Subpoena Power on the Internet in Light of the Verizon Cases, 24 Rev. Litig. 166(2005).

Elizabeth Miles, Note, In Re Aimster & MGM, Inc. v. Grokster, Ltd.: Peer-to-Peer and the Sony Doctrine, 19 Berkeley Tech.L.J. 21 (2004).

Elliot M. Zimmerman, P2P File Sharing: Direct and Indirect Copyright Infringement, Fla. B.J., at 40 (May 2004).

Gigi B. Sohn, Radical Act Would Induce Big Chill, Legal Times, at 19 (Oct. 11, 2004).

Itza Wilson, Online Music Distribution Compromise: Protecting the Artist's Copyright While Not Stifling Digital Development, 2001 Syracuse L. & Tech. J. 3(2001).

Jesse M. Feder, Is Betamax Obsolete?: Sony Corp. of America v. Universal City Studios, Inc. in the Age of Napster, 37 Creighton L. Rev. 859, (2004).

Jordana Boag, The Battle of Piracy versus Privacy: How the Recording Industry Association of America (RIAA) is Using the Digital

Millennium Copyright Act (DMCA) as its Weapon Against Internet Users' Privacy Rights, 41 Cal.W.L. Rev. 241(2004).

Llewellyn Joseph Gibbons, Entrepreneurial Copyright Fair Use: Let the Independent Contractor Stand in the Shoes of the Fair User, 57 Ark. L. Rev. 539-547 (2004).

Matthew Green, Note, Napster Opens Pandora's Box : Examining How File-Sharing Services Threaten the Enforcement of Copyright on the Internet, 63 Ohio St. L.J. 799 (2002).

Matthew Rimmer, Hail to the Thief:.A Tribute to Kazaa, 2. U. Ottawa L. & Tech. J. 173, (2005).

Michael Landau, Digital Music Downloads and Copyright Infringement, 758 Pat. 405 (2003).

Michael Suppappola, Note, The End of the World as We Know It? The State of Decentralized Peer-to-Peer Technologies in the Wake of Metro-Goldwyn-Mayer Studios v. Grokster, 4Conn. Pub. Int. L.J. 133 (2004).

Peter Katz, Copyright Infringement: The Perils of Indirect Liability, 16 J. Proprietary Rts.1 (2004).

Rebekah O'Hara, You Say You Want a Revolution : Music & Technology-Evolution or Destruction? 39 Gonz. L. Rev. 247 (2004).

Sarah Lai Stirland, Talks Collapse in Effort to Reach Deal on File-Sharing Bill, CongressDailyAm (Oct. 7, 2004).

Seth. A. Miller, P2P File Distribution: An Analysis of Design, Liability, Litigation, And Potential Solutions, 25 Rev. Liting. 183 (winter, 2006).

Steve Seidenberg, Senate Bill Puts Power in Hands of Copyright Owners, Corp. Legal Times, at 16 (Sept. 2004).

Steven a. Heath, Contracts, Copyright, and Confusion Revisiting the Enforceability of 'shrinkwrap' licenses, 5 Chi.--Kent J. Intell. Prop 12 (2005).

Tim Wu, When Code Isn't Law, 89 Va. L. Rev. 679 (2003).

Tom Graves, Picking Up the Pieces of Grokster: A New Approach to File Sharing, 27 Hastings Comm. & Ent. L.J. 165 (2004).

Wendy M. Pollack, Note, Tuning In: The Future of Copyright Protection for Online Music in the Digital Millennium, 68 Fordham L. Rev. 2445(2000).

2. Electronic Articles

Alex Veiga, Unlikely Alliances From in File-Sharing Case, Associated Press, Feb. 27, 2005, http://www.post-gazette.com/pg/05058/463051.stm.

Andrew Kantor, File-Sharing Is a Lot More than Stolen Music, USA Today, Mar. 29, 2005, http://www.usatoday.com/tech/columnist/andrewkantor/2005-03-16-kantor_x.htm.

Explanatory Memorandum from Copyright Office, http://www.copyright.gov/docs/S2560.pdf (last visited, Apr. 24, 2006).

Grant Gross, P-to-P Case May Have Far-Reaching Impact, PC World, Mar. 25, 2005, http://www.pcworld.com/resource/printable/article/0,aid,120189,00.asp.

Katie Dean, Techies Talk Tough in D.C., Wired, Jan. 20, 2005, http://www.wired.com/news/politics/0,1283,66329,00.html.

Lorraine Woellert, Hobbling Grokster-and Innovation, Too, Bus. Week, Mar. 24, 2005, http://www.businessweek.com/print/technology/content/mar2005/tc20050324_0001.htm.

Mark Cuban, Grokster and America's Future, CNT News, Feb. 2, 2005, http://news.com.com/2102-1028_3-5559340.html.

Martyn Williams, Mark Cuban to Finance Grokster's Fight, PC World, Mar. 28, 2005, http://www.pcworld.co/resource/printable/article/0,aid,120198,00.asp.

Musicians Break Ranks in Grokster Case, Wash. Times, Mar. 1, 2005, http://washingtontimes.com/upi-breaking/20050301-1222226-6223r.htm.

Overview Apple-iTunes, Apple.com, http://www.apple.com/itunes/overview/ (last visited, Nov. 11, 2005).

Penny Nace, Ernie Allen & Chuck Canterbury, P2P Pressure: A Copyright Case Has Implications for Tracking Down Child-Porn Brokers, Nat.Rev. Online, Feb. 17, 2005, http://www.nationalreview.com/script/printpage.p?ref=/comment/nance200502170751.asp.

Redefining the Debate Over Protecting Intellectual Property, Ecoustics. Com, (Mar. 19, 2005), http://news.ecoustics.com/bbs/messages/10381/127979.html.

Reuters, Metallica Raps Napster, Mar. 29, 2001, http://www.cbsnews.com/stories/2001/03/29/archive/technology/main282384.shtml.

Shahid Khan & Peri Shamsai, Digital Music's Comeback: How Can Record Companies and Music Publishers Seize the Opportunities? Bearing Point Inst. For Exec. Insight (Mar. 2005), http://www.bearingpoint.com/portal/binary/com.epicentric.contentmanagement. servlet/published/pdfs/protected/C2967a-BEI_Music_WP.pdf.

3. Cases

A&M Records, Inc. v. Napster, Inc., 114F. Supp. 2d 896 (N.D Cal. 2000) [hereinafter Napster I].

A&M Records, Inc. v. Napster, Inc., 239 F.3d 1004 (9th Cir. 2001) [hereinafter Napster II].

Casella v. Morris, 820 F. 2d 362 (11th Cir. 1987).

Fonovisa, Inc. v. Cherry Auction, Inc., 76 F. 3d 259 (9th Cir. 1996).

Ga. Television Co. v. TV News Clips, Inc., 718 F. Supp. 939 (N.D. Ga.1989).

Gershwin Pub. Corp. v. Columbia Artists Mgmt., Inc., 443 F.2d 1159 (2d Cir. 1971).

In re Aimster Copyright Litig., 334 F. 3d 643 (7th Cir. 2003).

In Re Verizon Internet Servs., Inc., 257 F. Supp. 2d 244 (D.D.C. 2003).

Matthew Bender& Co. v. West Publ'g Co., 158 F. 3d 693 (2d Cir. 1998). Metro-Goldwyn-Mayer Studios, Inc. v. Grokster, Ltd., 259F. Supp.2d 1029 (C.D Cal. 2003).

Metro-Goldwyn-Mayer Studios, Inc. v. Grokster Ltd., 380 F. 3d 1154 (9th Cir. 2004).

Metro-Goldwyn-Mayer Studios, Inc. v. Grokster, Ltd., 125 S. Ct. 2764 (2005).

Oak Indus., Inc. v. Zenith Elec. Corp., 697 F. Supp. 988 (N.D Ill. 1988).

Recording Indus. Assn. of Am. v. Charter Commun. Inc., 393 F.3d 771(8th Cir. 2005).

Religious Technology Center v. Netcome On-Line Communications Services, Inc. 907 F.Supp.1361 (N.D. 1995).

Sony Corp. of Am. v. Universal City Studios, Inc., 464 U.S. 417 (1984).

Universal City Studios, Inc. v. Reimerdes, 111 F. Supp. 2d 294 (S.D.N.Y. 2000).

第三章 網路著作權管理新思維*

曾勝珍

* 本文所有圖表由嶺東科大財務金融研究所廖敏淳、張秀如、李佳亭三位同學協助整理，作者特此表達最誠摯的謝意。

■摘要 SUMMARY

　　科技技術日新月異如網站、點對點技術的廣泛運用，使著作權
人也嘗試以科技保護措施規範防止網路濫用藉以避免侵害行為，並

發展防盜拷技術運用，即科技保護措施及權利管理電子資訊系統，藉此防範使用人未取得授權蓄意侵害著作權，破壞TPMs系統進而分配著作的行為，然而著作權人維護其權益的措施，是否與公平交易政策有相違背的情形，或是二者可相以為用；我國於2009年4月21日通過修正「著作權法」，主要針對網路服務提供者，因使用者利用其所提供之服務侵害他人著作權或製版權，得主張不負責任之範圍及要件，後於2010年1月12日立法院三讀通過，「著作權法部分條文修正草案」及「著作權仲介團體條例修正草案」，將「著作權仲介團體」修正為「著作權集體管理團體」使我國著作權授權制度將有重大變革；此外，2009年11月17日亦公布網路服務提供者民事免責事由實施辦法。本文以我國新修正之著作權法為主，兼論美國及加拿大法制、實務經驗，輔敘述中國大陸現況，藉以說明網路著作權的種種規制，希冀本文對網路著作權管理之分析，能為我國在相關案件之處理，提供適用法律之依據，以供參考。

關鍵詞

- 智慧財產權
- 著作權
- 公平交易
- 網際網路
- 不公平競爭

壹、前　言

　　智慧財產權是一項重要的法律權利，它賦予權利人一定的專屬權與發展優勢。在經濟全球化的國際背景下，智慧財產權更是成為衡量一個企業組織甚至一個國家，財富和競爭能力的重要指標。國內近年科技產業蓬勃發展，除面臨國外大廠專利訴訟，鉅額權利金索取外，反傾銷控訴案件等屢有所見，且持續產生爭議。企業廠商熟悉專利訴訟、授權實務及法律攻擊防禦，成為產品研發與市場行銷的重要關鍵因素。也只有依靠智慧財產權制度與規範市場經濟，鼓勵和保護正當的競爭，並反對不當的競爭行為，才能有效地建立公平、合理的市場秩序。

　　網路興盛使得資訊的傳播在彈指之間無遠弗屆，重製及散播的速度遠遠超越著作權人或影音製作公司所能掌控的範圍，科技技術日新月異如網站、點對點技術（Peer to Peer，簡稱P2P）的廣泛運用，使著作權人也嘗試以反規避（Anti-Circumvention）規範防止網路濫用藉以避免侵害行為，並發展防盜拷技術運用，即科技保護措施（Technological Protection Measures，簡稱TPMs）及權利管理電子資訊（Digital Rights Management，簡稱DRM）系統，當使用人未取得授權蓄意侵害著作權，破壞TPMs系統進而分配著作，如運用於非私人目的的使用時之錄音時，是否有牴觸公平交易政策的可能。

　　本文以我國甫修正之著作權法為主，兼論美國立法過程及加拿大暨中國大陸現況，參酌網路使用的多面相及其法律規範的探討，再佐以實務案例對網路著作權管理，包含與消費行為有關的實務見解與理論依據，說明網路著作權的種種規制是否與公平競爭政策相符，或對公平交易造成的影響，並為目前適用及運用情形做出總結。最後鋪陳我國未來發展可建議的約制或對策，以維護健全發展的網路使用空間。

貳、網路著作權法發展現觀

　　美國詞曲創作人、作者、出版商協會（the American Society of Composers, Authors and Publishers，簡稱「ASCAP」）西元（下同）2006年收益為美金7億8,550萬元，傳播音樂機構（Broadcast Music Incorporated，簡稱BMI）2007年收益為美金8億5,000萬元，[1] 目前普遍運用網際網路及相關科技資訊為工具，資訊流通增加產業實力，亦使業者間之競爭更加激烈，因此為維持競爭優勢，以免相關資訊為他人知悉，成為自己競爭的對手，目前著作權法及各國的規範是否完善合理，將有以下說明。

一、我國法規定

　　網路科技發展使複製與傳輸技術更加便捷，亦使侵權行為產生侵害數量龐大且易於分散的特性，著作權人難以對網路無數的侵害使用者透過法律程序訴追，網路服務提供者亦面臨被告侵權之訴訟風險，我國經過多次修正著作權法部分條文，[2]參考國際間各國作法於網路環境中賦予網路服務提供者（Internet Service Providers，簡稱ISPs）

---

[1]　Howard P. Knopf, *CANADIAN COPYRIGHT COLLECTIVES AND THE COPYRIGHT BOARD: A SNAPSHOT IN 2008*, INTELL. PROP. J. 119 (2008).

[2]　如2008年2月14日舉行之「著作權法部分條文修正草案」公聽會，由台灣網際網路協會代表、著作權審議及調解委員會委員、智慧局著作權組、新世紀資通、數位聯合電信股份有限公司、IFPI、MPA、BSA、IPAPA、TBPA等5個團體代表、資策會科技法律中心及其他相關團體參與。「著作權法部分條文修正草案」公聽會紀錄可見於經濟部智慧財產局網站。http://www.tipo.gov.tw/ch/ AllInOne_Show. aspx?path=2770&guid=94b82b63-47e2-4def-8a9e-b1411e1ce4ac& lang=zh-tw&pat（最後瀏覽日2009/01/20）。

「避風港」，使著作權人得通知網路服務提供者移除網路流通之侵權資料，而網路服務提供者若遵循法律所定之程序，亦得就使用者侵害著作權及製版權之行為，主張不負損害賠償責任。[3]

二、我國法規

　　立法院再於2010年1月12日三讀通過之「著作權法部分條文修正草案」及「著作權仲介團體條例修正草案」，則使我國著作權授權制度產生重大變革。[4]立法理由說明由於旅館、醫療院所、餐廳、咖啡店、百貨公司、賣場、便利商店、客運車、遊覽車……等營業場所播放電視、廣播供客人觀賞，是社會上常見的利用行為，但因事先無法得知及控制播放之內容，且不易取得完全之授權，因此面臨刑事訴追之風險；此外，廣告中所用到的音樂係由廣告製作公司所選擇，電台、電視台無法決定，以致於廣告在電視台播出時，電視台與個別權利人洽商授權時常面臨刑事訴追之風險。[5]針對上述問題，此次修法係立法部門、廣大利用人、各家仲介團體及行政機關長期的努力所達成，希望未來在新法之下，利用人本「使用者付費」之精神，仲團本

---

[3] 96年3月28日總統公布智慧財產法院組織法，並於97年7月1日施行，為保障智慧財產權，妥適處理智慧財產案件，促進國家科技與經濟發展，故凡有關智慧財產之案件，無論係民事、刑事或行政訴訟，將由智慧財產法院集中管轄，增進智財訴訟之效率，目前世界網路使用者的數目迅速累積，比較網路人口及其使用態樣，常有感觸若未實體操作或親身經歷，不但無法瞭解網路活動及使用特性，更無從體認電腦技術多樣化，連帶使相關法規或紛爭複雜化。

[4] 「二次公播」、「廣告音樂」及著作權仲介團體授權制度之重大變革，經立法院三讀通過。智慧財產權電子報 44期，2010年2月5日。http://www.tipo.gov.tw/ch/EPaper_HistoryEPaper.aspx?path=2860&Department=1&Class=1（最後瀏覽日2010/02/06）。

[5] 此段說明詳見智慧財產局網站，亦可參考同前註之電子報內容。

「促進市場和諧」之原則，創造權利人與利用人雙贏。此外，2009年11月17日亦公布「網路服務提供者民事免責事由實施辦法」，網路業者的自律與互相競爭的關係，加上政府及立法機關提供的限制或規範，希冀促進著作權人與網路服務提供者合作，有效地行使法律所保障之權利，以減少網路侵權，進而促進網路資訊流通之自由及使用者接觸合法資訊之權利。[6]

　　我國於2009年4月21日通過修正「著作權法」，[7]主要針對網路服務提供者，因使用者利用其所提供之服務侵害他人著作權或製版權，得主張不負責任之範圍及要件，由於網際網路無遠弗屆，網路侵權亦

---

[6] 本次修正愛針對網路服務提供者因使用者不法利用其所提供之服務，侵害著作財產權或製版權所應負之責任及得主張不負責任之範圍，明文立法予以釐清，愛擬具著作權法部分條文修正草案，共計新增7條，其要點如下：一、明定得適用責任限制之四種類型網路服務提供者。（增訂第90條之4）二、釐清網路服務提供者就使用者利用其所提供之服務侵害著作權或製版權行為，課予防止損害繼續之義務。（增訂第90條之5）三、明定四種類型網路服務提供者進入避風港之要件。（增訂第90條之6）四、明定網路服務提供者執行移除、回復等措施時，應遵守之事項。（增訂第90條之7）五、明定網路服務提供者依規定移除侵害著作財產權或製版權之資訊，對使用者不負賠償責任。（增訂第90條之8）六、明定濫發通知或回復通知致他人受損害者，應就其所生之損害負賠償責任。（增訂第90條之9）七、授權以法規命令訂定網路服務提供者責任限制之實施辦法。（增訂第90條之10）。此為2008年5月7日資料，其後7月7日意見交流會議紀錄、8月27日「著作權法部分條文修正草案」（報行政院版）資料見經濟部智慧財產局，著作權法之修正。http://www. tipo.gov.tw/ch/AllInOne_Show.aspx?path=2770&guid=94b82b63-47e2-4def-8a9e-b 1411e1ce4ac&lang=zh-tw&pat（最後瀏覽日2009/1/20）。
[7] 立法院第7屆第3會期第9次會議通過之公報初稿資料，以下說明意見參見著作權法部分條文修正草案總說明，資料見經濟部智慧財產局，其他修法草案及討論可參考http://www.tipo.gov.tw/ch/AllInOne_Show.aspx?path=2770&guid= 94b82b63-47e2-4def-8a9e-b1411e1ce4ac&lang=zh-tw&pat（最後瀏覽日2009/5/25）。著作權法於中華民國98年5月13日總統令增訂著作權法第6章之1章名及第90條之4至第90條之12條文；並修正第3條條文，全文可見http://www.tipo.gov. tw/ch/AllInOne_Show.aspx?path=1362&guid=8f9352ad-820f-4040-bae1-0417ddc7a7fc &lang=zh-tw（最後瀏覽日2009/5/28）。

成為無國界、全球化之現象，早在著作權法本次修正通過前，世界
各國即已針對網路侵權制訂相關法規，[8]以健全網路著作權之保護環
境，並強化數位產業發展，修正要點如下：

1.增訂網路服務提供者之定義。（修正條文第3條第1項第19款）
明確定義網路服務提供者，包括連線服務提供者、快速存取服
務提供者、資訊儲存服務提供者、搜尋服務提供者所提供的服
務內涵。

2.網路服務提供者之民事免責事由，即避風港條款。參考國際間
各國作法，宜於網路環境中賦予網路服務提供者「責任避風
港」，使著作權人或製版權人得通知網路服務提供者移除網路
流通之侵權資料，而網路服務提供者若遵循法律所定之程序，
得就使用者涉有侵害著作權及製版權之行為，主張不負損害賠
償責任。為鼓勵網路服務提供者積極建構防止網路侵權之機
制，以有效遏止侵權，爰增訂專章加以規範。網路服務提供者
得適用新增章名第6章之1民事免責事由之共通要件。（修正條
文第90條之4）

3.因使用者利用其所提供之服務侵害他人著作財產權或製版權，
得主張不負責任之範圍及要件，明文立法予以釐清。各類網路
服務提供者對其使用者侵害他人著作權或製版權之行為，如業

---

[8]　如：(1)美國於1998年訂定之「數位千禧年著作權法」（Digital Millennium Copyright
Act of 1998, DMCA）」第512條規定。(2)歐盟於2000年通過之「電子商務指令
（Directive of Electronic Commerce）第12條至第14條規定。(3)日本於2001年通過之
「特定電信服務提供者損害賠償責任限制及發信者資訊提供相關法律」。(4)中國大陸
於2006年通過之「信息網路傳播權保護條例」。(5)韓國於2008年修正通過之「著作
權法第6章」。上述法規除歐盟之電子商務指令在立法體例上與美國法較為不同外，
其他國家多以美國數位千禧年著作權法第512條所架構之「通知／取下Notice & Take
Down」機制為本。經濟部智慧財產局，著作權法網路服務提供者ISP民事免責事由修
正條文Q&A。http://www.tipo.gov.tw/ch/ArtHtml_Show.aspx?ID=59ef8638-4393-4560-
82b3-9729 cba61dff&path=3334（最後瀏覽日2009/6/5）。

者確實遵守本法所定程序，即可不負賠償責任。（修正條文第
90條之5至第90條之8）

(1)鼓勵連線服務業者配合著作權人或製版權人之要求而加以
轉送，並非課予連線服務業者義務，縱連線服務業者未配
合轉送，如有其他已具體履行著作權保護措施之情事者，
仍得依第90條之4之規定，適用本條責任限制規定。（修正
條文第90條之5）

(2)快速存取服務提供者接獲著作權人或製版權人之通知後，
並不負侵權與否之判斷責任，只要通知文件內容形式上齊
備，應立即移除或使他人無法進入該涉嫌侵權內容。（修
正條文第90條之6）

(3)指網路服務提供者之獲益與使用者之侵權行為間不具有相
當因果關係。又「財產上利益」指金錢或得以金錢計算之
利益，廣告收益及會員入會費均屬之。（修正條文第90條
之7）

(4)搜尋服務提供者對其使用者利用其所提供之服務，不法侵
害他人著作權或製版權之行為，不負賠償責任應具備之要
件。（修正條文第90條之8）

4.提供資訊儲存服務之網路服務提供者執行回復措施時，應遵守
之事項。（修正條文第90條之9）。考量降低資訊儲存服務提
供者通知之成本及其掌握之使用者聯絡資訊未必真實等情事，
特規定以其與使用者約定之方式，或依使用者留存之聯絡資訊
通知即可。另顧及資訊儲存服務提供者因其提供服務之性質，
而未留存使用者連絡資訊之事實，例如架設論壇供使用者發表
意見，多未留存連絡資訊，爰於但書規定予以排除。

5.網路服務提供者依規定移除涉嫌侵害著作權或製版權之資訊，
對使用者不負賠償責任。（修正條文第90條之10）由於網路服
務提供者不負侵權與否之判斷責任，只要通知文件內容形式上

齊備，應立即移除或使他人無法進入該涉嫌侵權內容，除可不
負著作權侵害賠償責任外，縱令事後證明該被移除之內容並不
構成侵權，網路服務提供者亦無須對使用者負民事賠償責任。

6.不實通知或回復通知致他人受損害者，應就所生之損害負賠償
　責任。（修正條文第90條之11）為避免本章規定之「通知／回
　復通知」機制遭濫用，對網路服務提供者造成營運上之困擾，
　明定濫發通知或回復通知之法律責任，提醒著作權人及使用者
　審慎為之。

7.授權主管機關以法規命令訂定前揭相關增訂條文之各項執行細
　節。（修正條文第90條之12）。

8.新修正著作權法第90條之6至第90條之8所規定之「通知／取
　下」（Notice/Take Down）機制如何運作，權利人之行為有無
　可能構成權利濫用，甚或影響公平競爭交易原則，依據智慧財
　產局說明的程序如下(1)權利人之「通知」：權利人一旦發現
　網路上有侵害其著作權之內容時，只需依新修正著作權法之規
　定通知ISP，即可經由ISP之配合取下而迅速排除侵權行為，並
　避免損害範圍之擴大。[9]同時，ISP為配合收取權利人之通知，
　亦需指定窗口。(2)ISP之「取下」ISP對於使用者利用其服務
　從事著作權侵權之行為，只要(a)依權利人通知，立即取下該涉
　嫌侵權之內容；或(b)ISP因其他管道知悉該等侵害情事，善意
　取下該涉嫌侵權之內容者，該ISP對權利人及使用者均不負賠
　償責任。

---

[9]　權利人通知之格式，智慧局將會在相關實施辦法中予以明文。

三、著作權仲介團體條例之修法內容

我國「著作權仲介團體條例」自1997年11月5日公布施行，由於本制度在我國係第1次施行，而有加以檢討修正之必要。另著作權仲介團體及利用人雙方均對本條例提出修正之建議，如使用報酬率之審議制度、著作財產權目錄及使用清單製作之義務、會員退會後之權利義務關係等問題，2008年完成之修正草案版本[10]將「著作權仲介團體」修正為「著作權集體管理團體」（以下簡稱「集管團體」），並修法增訂著作權法第37條第6項第2款、第3款及第4款，就未加入集管團體，權利人個別行使權利之情形，將營業場所公開播送之二次利用著作行為，以及著作經個別權利人授權重製於廣告後，後續公開播送或同步公開傳輸行為，免除利用人刑事責任。

本草案立法通過後，前述利用人將不必再擔心遭受個別權利人刑事訴追，但仍有依法支付使用報酬之義務，不支付者，則仍須負擔民事侵權法律責任。至於關於集管團體管理之著作部分不受本次修法之影響。本次修正最重大之突破在於增設「共同使用報酬率」及「單一窗口」之制度。由於我國目前已經成立之仲介團體共有7家，且同種著作類別之仲介團體不只1家，利用人於實務上常發生需同時與5、6家團體洽取授權之不便，也造成團體個別向利用人收費之困難，為使授權更為簡便，爰增訂多家團體就專責機關指定之利用型態有訂定「共同使用報酬率」之義務，並應由其中一個團體向利用人收取。

可能會被指定的利用型態包括：旅館、美容業等公開場所二次利用行為、KTV、卡拉OK及伴唱機之利用等大量利用著作之利用型態。由於共同使用報酬率之訂定有其複雜性，於修正條文中規定兩

---

[10] 著作權仲介團體條例之修正，更新日期：2009/11/19。http://www.tipo.gov.tw/ch/AllInOne_Show.aspx?path=2770&guid=b023b882-4024-4862-8e05-145faf60225f&lang=zh-tw&pat（最後瀏覽日2010/2/5）。

年之過渡期間，我國經濟部智慧財產局積極協助各仲團實施此一新制度，並為使收費標準及共同使用報酬率之內部分配更為客觀合理，並研擬著作權集體管理團體條例相關之辦法，以使未來集管團體之申請及使用報酬率審議之新制得順利施行；規劃相關教育宣導工作，讓各界充分瞭解本次修法內容。

四、美　國

　　美國著作權法法源起於憲法的規定，進而成為聯邦法規，保障創作者及藝術家對其作品的專屬權，並給於智慧財產權上的保護，[11]從而促進科技與文明的更新，提昇全民福祉與利益，[12]至於所有權人本身的利益則為輔；美國法典第17章第106條[13]明定著作人所有權的權利保障，侵害著作權的侵害人則有直接與間接兩種侵害責任。[14]

　　著作權法維護的公共利益當然包括技術面進步而獲致的整體社會利益，國會立定新法及法院制定判決，皆須留意技術創新與法規保障之間的平衡。若營運新事業體的目的乃為侵害他人的著作權，當然不被允許，此乃法院在適用著作權法解決P2P相關案件時，發展而來的間接侵害責任，亦即適用法律規範（特別在法官造法的情形時）反而導致結果不公平時，須重新審視對該規範的適用合理與否。

　　美國法規範反而更形嚴格，採納公約精神並針對TPMs技術，提供全面禁止規避規定，美國是首度將1996年世界智慧財產權組織（World Intellectual Property Organization，簡稱WIPO）條約規範

---

[11] U.S. Const. art. I, § 8.

[12] Id.

[13] 17 U.S.C. § 106.

[14] *Kalem Co. v. Harper Bros.*, 222 U.S. 55, 63 (1911).

置入法令的國家，[15]1998年美國制定電子千禧著作權法（the Digital Millennium Copyright Act，簡稱DMCA），[16]內容有關反規避條文之定義及罰則，如規避DRM系統以取得著作物，[17]追蹤裝置以獲得使用途徑進行規避[18]及追蹤破解，DRM在複製及分配文件限制，[19]DMCA規範使著作權人增加對著作保障之權利。[20]

五、美國法規

　　將網際網路視為檔案自由交換的境地，與認為侵害其財產權的所有人間，在未來仍存在相當多的爭議，因此聯邦與州立法的增訂或修改，是解決紛爭的方向之一，目前已有DMCA, 家用影視錄音法（Audio Home Recording Act），[21]著作權引誘侵害法（The Inducing Infringement of Copyright Act of 2004，簡稱 Induce Act），[22]家庭娛樂著作權法（The Family Entertainment and Copyright Act of 2004）[23]等既存法規，電子業者在忙於研發新產品及程式，並著力維持市場的競爭力及提高國際消費市場的同時，也不應忽略在提案及立法上的努力，唯有完善的法規及制度才能更有益於公平市場的競爭，並使消費

---

[15] 如制定電子千禧著作權法。

[16] Pub. L. No. 105-304,112 Stat. 2860 (1998).

[17] § 1201(a)(1)(A).

[18] § 1201(2).

[19] § 1201(b)(2)(B).

[20] DMCA內容有對於侵害行為刑罰規定，增加著作權人求償管道及可能性。

[21] 17 U.S.C. §§ 1001-1010.

[22] S. 2560, 108th Cong. (2004).

[23] 18 U.S.C.S. § 2379B. Digital Media Consumers' Rights Act of 2005, H. R.1201, 109th Cong. (2005). 共和黨議員Rep. Rick Boucher 提案2005年電子影音消費者法－Digital Media Consumers, Rights Act of 2005, H.R. 1201, 109th Cong. (2005).

者擁有更多權限與餘裕度做選擇，因此電子業者應增加與聯邦政府的互動，使公部門更瞭解私人企業的需求。

　　美國國會通過DMCA後積極鼓勵其他國家在與美國簽署貿易雙邊條約時，亦能遵守DMCA之法規內容。[24]P2P隱私預防法（P2P Privacy Prevention Bill）[25]並非規範違法下載侵害著作權的首宗立法。1998年網路服務提供者（Internet Service Providers，簡稱ISPs）擔憂其使用者直接侵害著作權，DMCA此法亦建立ISP業者合法的避風港，[26]極少法規試圖解決P2P技術侵害著作權的部分；至2002年眾議員Howard Berman支持P2P隱私預防法，規範著作權人避免在不傷害使用人的情形下，可使用任何科技有效防堵及避免任何未經授權的使用。

　　2003年1月，另一法案「電子媒介消費者保護法」（the Digital Media Consumer's Rights Act[27]），內容有關保障合法CD使買賣盜版CD違法，有論者以為考量憲法上的人民權益，既不能忽略消費者行使其財產上的權利（如使用網路功能），也不希望減損科技人士研發成長的機會，[28]然而此二法案皆未獲通過。

　　2004年9月，加州通過州法第1506號提案，此法科處散播P2P及發展著作權內容的部分刑罰，[29]包括系統業者若未盡合理努力以保障其使用者散佈未擁有著作權資訊之內容，將被罰美金2,500元及一年

[24] Matthew Rimmer, *HAIL TO THE THIEF: A TRIBUTE TO KAZAA*, 2. U. OTTAWA L. & TECH. J. 173 (2005).

[25] H.R. 5211 pmbl., 107th Cong. (2002).

[26] Elliot M. Zimmerman, *P2P FILE SHARING: DIRECT AND INDIRECT COPYRIGHT INFRINGEMENT*, FLA. B.J.40, 41 (MAY 2004).

[27] H.R. 107, 108th Cong. (2003).

[28] Rebekah O'Hara, *YOU SAY YOU WANT A REVOLUTION: MUSIC & TECHNOLOGY—EVOLUTION OR DESTRUCTION?*, 39 GONZ. L. REV. 247, 288 (2004).

[29] Cal. Penal Code § 653a.

的徒刑，欲使用P2P軟體的人必須先在州內註冊，否則亦有刑事處罰。[30]州立法（如加州部分）仍無法妥當解決整體著作權侵害問題，而隨著電子技術的更新及進步神速，法規內容的用語及規範亦不能過於廣泛或特定，仍需所有使用人間的共識，而非一味限制使用人及科處刑責，影音業者若朝向接納多元化的新科技，選擇更多面向的思考，以解決此類紛爭的產生。

六、美國實務

　　1984年Sony[31]一案為科技的革新創造良好的避風港，甚或是以科技政策為主的一項重大指標，[32]也為電腦科技業者在發展如P2P技術時，突破著作權法對間接侵害責任行為人的種種要件要求，Napster[33]案則涉及使用第一代點對點傳輸網路架構，中央目錄伺服器系統，[34]每位使用者或該系統顧客，連接到網路形成一個連結點（Node），中央目錄伺服器維持在每個點上有可供瀏覽的完整內容明細，而每個點有其獨特專用的網址，[35]為維持功能及控制，使用者每次進入皆須註冊以獲得最新的文件目錄索引，中央伺服器可接收及傳送所有的搜尋資料及指令，當供需相對應時，提出要求的顧客會收到與其要求呼

---

[30] *Id.*

[31] *Sony Corp. of Am. v. Universal City Studios, Inc.*, 464 U.S. 417, 431 (1984).

[32] Elizabeth Miles, *NOTE, IN RE AIMSTER & MGM, INC. V. GROKSTER, LTD.: PEER-TO-PEER AND THE SONY DOCTRINE*, 19 BERKELEY TECH. L.J. 21, 25 (2004).

[33] *A&M Records, Inc. v. Napster, Inc.*, 239 F.3d 1004-1029 (9th Cir. 2001).

[34] *See* Jesse M. Feder, *IS BETAMAX OBSOLETE?: SONY CORP. OF AMERICA V. UNIVERSAL CITY STUDIOS, INC. IN THE AGE OF NAPSTER*, 37 CREIGHTON L. REV. 859, 864-65 (2004).

[35] *Id.* at 864.

應的另台電腦網址，藉以滿足所需。[36]

　　美國聯邦最高法院在2005年6月27日針對Merto-Goldwyn-Mayer Studios, Inc. v. Grokster, Ltd.[37]判決認為當經銷或裝置某種設備，目的乃為侵害他人著作權時，即使採取相當手段以避免侵害，仍應對第三人因其侵權行為的結果負責。[38]針對網際網路之興起，著作權法規範的行為客體、態樣，變化多端，視聽及影音業者控告P2P業者，希望聯邦最高法院的判決不僅能產生禁制令的效果，亦能促使如Stream Case及Sharman Networks等視聽業者成立侵權責任，提供予大眾判定侵權責任的標準。

1. 音樂網站

　　2007年3月13日，Viacom提出對YouTube及Google侵害著作權的訴訟，[39]要求賠償金額高達10億美元，Viacom指稱即使YouTube網站的構成，來自使用者分享他們同意的原始作品，卻形成數種不同的侵害類型，如直接侵害、間接侵害、替代侵害及引誘侵害責任。此案件造成YouTube網站增加影音辨識技術（Audio Fingerprinting Technology），以排除侵害他人著作權之可能；2007年10月YouTube又再增加影像辨識技術（Video Fingerprinting Technology），著作權人可要求YouTube網站封鎖侵害其權益的影片或影音，或與YouTube合作自影片上載取得收益。[40]

---

[36] 此系統運作優點在於中央目錄包含完整目錄，並且搜尋迅速、有效，Id. at 865.因為憑藉中央伺服器的功能，因此亦可避免使用人使用彼此間分享檔案，Id. 也因此功能上不足促使新科技的發展與非中央集中管理的P2P文件分享方式。See Tim Wu, *When Code Isn't Law*, 89 VA. L. REV. *679, 726-36 (2003)*.

[37] *Metro-Goldwyn-Mayer Studios, Inc. v. Grokster, Ltd.*, 125 S. Ct. 2764, 2775 (2005).

[38] Seth. A. Miller, *P2P File Distribution: An Analysis of Design, Liability, Litigation, And Potential Solutions*, 25 REV. LITIG. 183 (2006).

[39] *Viacom Intl, Inc. v. YouTube, Inc.*, No. 07-02103 (S.D.N.Y. complaint filed Mar. 13, 2007).

[40] YouTube Video Identification Beta. http://youtube.com/t/video_id_about（最後瀏覽日

　　2006年11月17日環球音樂（Universal Music Group Recordings，簡稱UMG）控告我的空間（MySpace）金額亦近10億，UMG主張MySpace為蓄意參與者，未經取得授權卻上載UMG所有之影片及音樂，MySpace構成直接、幫助、替代及引誘著作權侵害，此案最終仍在審理中。[41]UMG（原告）控告世界最大的連絡網站，指稱MySpace網站涉嫌造成或引誘他人侵害原告之著作權，並質疑該網站的律師事務所不適格；經加州地方法院法官A. Howard Matz, J.拒絕此項控訴，[42]認為代表被告的律師事務所不適任與本案涉及著作權侵害的爭點無關。

　　在Viacom一案中，原告主張YouTube怠於架設標準化的技術支援，避免著作權人在YouTube網站發現侵害其權益的錄影作品，若使用人可利用YouTube網站功能，和其他人分享，而未監督其網站是否怠於提供標準化的技術支援，同理可證，若UGC的三大網站皆無此類技術支援，則此技術如何「標準化」；此外YouTube網站未盡監督該站作品之責，YouTube雖未得到直接收益（direct financial

2008/5/31）。在YouTube網站的說明中，有關錄影帶辨識內容，有下述3種目的：(1)辨別性（identification），和Google公司合作，使全世界的著作權人能使用該辨識系統，確認是否有他人未經取得其授權，咨意利用著作侵害著作權人的權益。(2)選擇性（choice）著作權人可選擇封鎖、展示其作品或與YouTube網站合作，增加商機獲得利潤，數以百萬計的人們及公司對原始著作的需求皆不同，有希望完全掌控的，也有私自放上網路供人瀏覽的，甚或也有家庭完全排斥私人生活被公開，或一些希望增加知名度的人，也許盼望更多大眾參與其創作過程，或觀賞其成果；因此，最好的結果乃與YouTube合作，可以從著作權人的選擇中，由YouTube網站協助達成。(3)使用者經驗（User Experience），為使創作人能有安全且迅速的服務管道，YouTube針對使用人就其使用者經驗，維護其權益與分擔責任，例如使樂團或歌唱者的樂迷能有機會與他們所喜歡的媒體結晶有良好互動。

[41]　*UMG Recordings Inc. v. MySpace Inc.*, No. 06-07361 (C.D. Cal. Complaint filed Nov. 17, 2006).

[42]　*UMG Recordings Inc. v. MySpace Inc.*, United States District Corut (C.D. California. Dec. 10, 2007).

benefit），然而若未放置大量侵權資料，即未經著作權人同意之作品，無法形成YouTube網站吸引人之處，YouTube網站亦自網站廣告獲得直接收益。[43]

　　即使有直接收益，網路服務提供者仍可主張512(c)的免責條款保護，Napster案承審法院認為Napster公司有能力監督使用者並能移除構成侵害之作品；[44]YouTube及MySpace的情形則又不同，UGC不易被辨識，即使目前有辨識技術支援，但不足以改善現況，因此認為被告不必擔負完全的監督責任；有廣告收益的商業網站監督網站內容誠為合理，惟如何監督及移除不當內容，仰賴網站本身的社會責任感及道德心。

2. P2P檔案分享與散佈權

　　2008年有數起與P2P檔案分享與散佈權有關的案件，如*Atlantic Recording Corp. v. Brennan*[45]案中，唱片公司控告個別使用人於網路分享音樂檔案，康乃迪克州地區法院認為原告指稱被告散佈原告所有著作之指控不成立，因為「散佈」必須符合事實上的散佈行為；[46]另外，*Elektra Entm't Group, Inc. v. Barker*[47]案，原告指控被告於Kazaa（運用P2P技術分享檔案的一個軟體）與人分享611個音樂檔案，紐約州南區地區法院駁回原告申請，認為被告行為不構成侵害，[48]原告採行「使大眾廣為散佈理論」（Making Available），著作權法雖未明文定義散佈（Distribution），但有定義「發表」（Publication）指：為公共表演或展示之目的而將複製品分配給一般大眾，美國著作

---

[43] *Id.*

[44] *A&M Records, Inc. v. Napster, Inc.*, 239 F.3d 1004-1013 (9th Cir. 2001).

[45] *Atlantic Recording Corp. v. Brennan*, 534 F. Supp. 2d 278 (D. Conn. 2008).

[46] *Perfect 10, Inc. v. Amazon.com, Inc.*, 508 F.3d 1146, 1162 (9th Cir. 2007).

[47] *Elektra Entm't Group, Inc. v. Barker*, 551 F. Supp. 2d 234 (S.D.N.Y. 2008).

[48] *Elektra*, 551 F. Supp. 2d at 238-39

權法第106條第3 款定義趨近於散佈，[49]僅對他人提出要約不構成「散佈」，[50]因原告無法舉證被告符合供他人廣為散佈的要件，法院判決原告敗訴。

麻薩諸薩州地區法院於*London-Sire Records, Inc. v. Doe 1*[51]案則有不同判決結果，法院最終做出結論，原告已充分證明被告不僅實際從事散佈的步驟，也有實際散佈的事實，符合第106條第3 款的規定。*Atlantic Recording Corp. v. Howell*[52]案，亞利桑那州地區法院拒絕原告之控訴，認為原告未能證明被告有違法散佈的事實，原告指控被告使用Kazaa軟體上傳未取得授權的音樂檔案，供不特定之大眾下載分享，法院判決在只能證明被告有意圖散佈，並無破壞原告對其著作的專屬散佈權，[53]但未牽涉到著作本身被移轉的情形，因著作權法未針對意圖犯有罰責，亞利桑那州地區法院認為若要處以刑責，應訴諸立法政策付諸執行。[54]

本案採取和*London-Sire Records, Inc. v. Doe 1*一案類似見解，「發表」與「散佈」並非同義詞，「發表」有散佈或向他人要約即將散佈的意義，「散佈」則包括買賣或其他所有權的移轉，本案原告怠於證明被告有散佈影音著作的實際行為，[55]法院亦認為原告未釐清直接侵害與間接侵害責任，若被告僅提供檔案分享的途徑給公眾中的不特定人分享，被告則不能被歸責為直接侵害人，只能認為是危害原告再製權（reproduction right）的間接侵害人；其次，原告亦無說明KaZaA文件分享系統的構造，使被告擁有直接破壞原告專屬散佈權

---

[49] *Id*. at 240.

[50] *Id*. at 243.

[51] *London-Sire Records, Inc. v. Doe 1*, 542 F. Supp. 2d 153 (D. Mass. 2008).

[52] *Atlantic Recording Corp. v. Howell*, 554 F. Supp. 2d 976 (D. Ariz. 2008).

[53] *Atlantic Recording*, 554 F. Supp. 2d. at 983.

[54] *Id*. at 984.

[55] *Id*. at 984-85.

的能力，或只提供第三人侵害原告著作的管道（輔助侵害原告的再製權）；[56]最終，若能舉證被告之輔助侵害責任成立，原告須再證明第三人已取得該著作之複製品，即直接侵害已確定發生，而此案結果原告敗訴。

3. Sprint &Cogent Communications網路公司之戰

2008年10月30日美國緬因州政府（Maine）處理Sprint Nextel及Cogent Communications兩家網路公司間，因為網路樞紐連線中斷的問題而焦頭爛額，對於因而造成美國與加拿大間眾多大學失聯的情形，緬因州政府與其他鄉鎮失去連繫，數以百萬的Sprint寬頻無線用戶無法上網，美國FCC和加拿大主管機構——加拿大廣播電視及通訊委員會（the Canadian Radio-Television and Telecommunications Commission）無計可施，全球通訊與網路連線中斷了整整三天。[57]

上述現象說明現今網路管理仍建立在私人公司間的私契約關係上，有別於政府部門的管制，事實上從上述無論大學或公部門間的連繫，都有可能完全停止三天，可見政府對此類活動的管控或協助，還有許多可以改進的空間，更甚者可想而知一網路是否根本不在被規範的範圍，亦意味著存在許多潛藏的危險？前述事實發生後Sprint在Virginia州地方法院提出Cogent的控訴，因為Cogent違背了當時雙方簽訂保密契約的精神，將雙方如何在網路世界中運作的情形公告於世，而不甘示弱的被告也即提出反訴控告Sprint。

2002年Cogent及Sprint彼此協議以無償的方式交換彼此的網路系統且簽訂契約，然而線路需經往另一第三人的路徑而進行，Sprint提出Cogent對此疑惑的解答，若二者間要有直接途徑則Cogent需另

[56] Id. at 986.

[57] Scott Wooley, *The Day the Web Went Dead*, Forbes, Dec. 2, 2008. http://www.forbes.com/technology/2008/12/01/cogent-sprint-regulation-tech-enter-cz_sw_1202 cogent.html. (last visited:2/6/2010).

外付費，Cogent當然無法理解互益的雙方，為何只有自己需要付費？Sprint堅持要有90天的試運期，若雙方往來的量數及比例相當，Sprint才願意以無償的方式進行合作；經過試鍊Cogent與Sprint直到2006年9月19日才簽訂正式契約。

雙方的合作關係直到2007年6月已在美國六個城市及全球其餘地區建立高效頻的網路聯結，然而Sprint最終仍堅持對測試期的結果不滿，Cogent需支付90天試驗期共美金478,000元的費用，至此Cogent發現也許Sprint自始至終根本無心與其共構免費的網路互享，兩家公司因而陷入冷戰，Sprint每個月寄發給Cogent近100,000元的帳單，到2008年7月底累積成120萬美金，Sprint決定提出訴訟；Cogent認為既已盡力於測試成果，Sprint若不滿意雙方的聯結與配合狀況，最簡單的做法便是中斷聯結，Sprint果真如此執行，首先切斷完全依賴Sprint系統如：美國聯邦各級法院，再切斷完全依賴Cogent系統：如各大律師事務所。

Sprint的行為造成2008年10月30日到11月2日整整三天網路系統的全面停擺，私人企業的經營關係竟可導致如此嚴重的社會現象，令人不可思議，也從此事件後，激發美國官方及學界的探討，[58]網路樞紐提供者與伺服器業者間的糾紛，竟然可以造成如此大的波瀾，換言之，私人企業間的紛爭竟然可以造成社會大眾的紛擾，實在值得檢討。網路樞紐提供者可以完全不考慮使用者（消費者）的立場，與伺服器業者展開如此的爭端，如果停止供應服務的時間不是三天，而是更長的時間或是造成更大的損失，整體社會成本必定仍由政府部門承受，換言之亦是全民買單，因此思考其他模式的建立管理秩序更有意義。

---

[58] 有關本事件的敘述本文整理自Weiser, P.J. (2009). *The Future of Internet Regulation.* U.C. Davis L. Rev. 43, 529.與Scott Wooley, *The Day the Web Went Dead*, Forbes, Dec. 2, 2008).

七、加拿大

1995年以來TPMs受到極大討論並被廣為運用，而DRM系統超越TPMs，是近年來發展迅速，但仍處於早期階段之技術。TPMs是檢測未經授權之電子檔使用技術，[59]可管控網路路徑及保障依據不同使用目的之電子資料內容，如複製、傳送、顯示及表現，也許是一個最簡單的使用者密碼，或複雜且反複製技術，[60]DRM是混合TPMs形成較複雜之資訊系統，包含與受保護資訊間之特殊授權內容，[61]如電子資訊分配方式，使著作權人可透過遙控方式管理及操作顧客使用情形，此功能正是經由DRM而來，[62]運用此項技術充滿彈性並可適用於各式產品中。

八、草案C-60

DRM技術使著作權人不僅擴充法律權利，更重要是使其限制具有可行性，如記載資料於一天內被讀取內容與次數，及被授權情形，此系統並可限制個人使用及被授權前與其他DRM內容之交換情形，上述限制皆必須在DRM技術運用之下，如唱片工業下載情形也

---

[59] Ibid.

[60] Ibid.

[61] See D.J. Gervais, "*Electronic Rights Management and Digital Identifer Systems*" (1999), The Journal of Electronic Publishing, online: University of Michigan Press http://www.press.umich.edu/jep/04- 03/gervais.html.

[62] See C. Hoofnagle, *Digital Rights Management: Many Technical Controls on Digital Content Distribution Can Create a Surveillance Society*, (2004) 5 CoLUM. SCI. & TECH. L. REV. 3, CoLUM. SCI. & TECH. L. REV. 3, online: http://www.stlr.org/html/volume5/ hoofnagle.pdf.

屬於本處所涉及之資訊內容。[63]DRM系統一再被更新及發展，曾估計至2006年約有20% 全球化系統會使用DRM系統以保障電子化之內容，[64]而此類技術能經由政治與技術面做為考量而更新。

2005年6月20日加拿大文化局長（the Minister of Canadian Heritage）將草案C-60（內容為著作權法最新的修正版），送交議會（the House of Commons）審議，本草案內容主要有關著作權電子化議題，同年11月29日決議未獲通過，內容有關反規避規範及防止網路濫用、保障教育目的之使用……等，關於網際網路使用人在文件搜尋及引用上之權利，目前仍停滯於政府高層，雖持高度關切但未獲執行階段；[65]後於2008年草案C-61延續前述大致內容，再度被送交議會[66]仍未通過。加拿大希冀修正著作權法主要來自網路點對點傳輸技術的盛行，下載電子文件檔之快速興盛，導致使用者日益增多的應用現狀，因應個人使用上配合除外規定及保障網路隱私的需求外，增添更多不確定性於實際使用，前述草案C-60配合WIPO下之各式公約規定，其中又以WIPO著作權條約（Copyright Treaty）及WIPO表演及錄音條約（Performances and Phonograms Treaty）最為重要。[67]

C-60草案主要內容為下述四項重點，對於TPMs及RMI 技術使

---

[63] F. von Lohmann, *Don't Sue the Customer*, IP Law and Business (December, 2004), online: IP Law and Business http://www.ipww.com/texts/1204/music1204.html; D. McCullagh, P2P's little secret, CNET News.Com (8 July 2003), online: CNET http://news.com. com/2100-1029_3- 1023735.html.

[64] Eweek Staff, Analysts Predict Swellong of DRM Use, eWeek.com (31 March, 2004), eWeek. com http://www.eweek.com/article2/0,1759,1572171,00.asp. (last visited: 4/16/2008).

[65] Bruce M. Green, Intellectual Property Law (Copyright), Annual Review of Law & Practice, 327-328, The Continuing Legal Education Society of British Columbia (2006).

[66] Bill C-61: An Act to amend the Copyright Act, Law and Government Division, Parliament of Canada, 12 August 2008. http://www2.parl.gc.ca/Sites/LOP/LEGISINFO/ index.asp?Language=E&query=5466&Session=15&List=ls (last visited:2/23/2010).

[67] *Id*. at 329.

得著作權電子化速度日新月異，並落實WIPO條約主要議題在此草案中，包括對(1)表演者固定及現場表演內容給予著作人格權（Moral Rights），(2)使錄音表演之著作權達50年，(3)對攝影工作者之著作權歸屬及其作品分類在此法案中有所改變，(4)規範網路服務提供者責任歸屬亦有不同，和影音媒介業相同，網路服務提供者提供資訊服務及網站，而使用者間的文件分享，即使透過ISPs的軟體系統或硬體設備，亦不能全部歸責於ISPs業者。ISPs業者能做即是當收到權利人，指稱其著作遭受不當分布或複製時所應有之回應，法院可要求網站關閉或停止此類行為，ISPs並應保存相關資訊至少6個月。

新法案包括圖書館及教育機構，處理著作權相關內容物時，對於電子化文件及資訊使用方面，包含教育及研究目的之範圍，遠距教學及電子傳送資料、圖書館之間互動及資訊傳遞。[68]提供錄影作品為公眾使用，特別容易造成使用人侵害著作權，為避免侵害行為，發展防盜拷技術運用，即科技保護措施（Technological Protection Measures，簡稱TPMs），使用人未取得授權亦有可能蓄意侵害著作權，破壞TPMs系統進而分配著作，如運用於非私人目的使用時之錄音；其他如權利管理訊息（Rights Management Information，簡稱RMI），管控著作權侵害之技術本身即已侵害著作權，前述使用人亦可能以侵害著作權之前提下，移除或變更RMI系統，無權散布他人之著作物。

九、實　務

1995年Society of Composers, Authors and Music Publishers of Canada v. Canadian Assn. of Internet Providers[69]一案，為加拿大著

---

[68] *Id.*

[69] Supreme Court of Canada, 2 S.C.R. 427, 2004 SCC 45 (2004).

作權法中，針對網路服務提供者至今最醒目之案例，本案事實有關SOCAN提出的Tariff 22提案，規定任何人於加拿大境內使用電子音樂檔案，即透過網際網路使用者間下載或分享檔案之行為人，必須支付SOCAN授權金才能取得授權，原先提案內容乃包括任何與音樂檔案傳達的行為人，皆須繳交授權金，其後將提供網路服務給ISPs的終端伺服器業者免責，而是針對使用的個人收費。本案為SOCAN代表音樂著作權人對著作權委員會提出Tariff 22提案，希冀規範網路使用人在下載音樂著作（廣泛引用P2P技術，為MP3音樂或影片下載免費使用增加管道）。

　　本提案主要訴求對加拿大國內使用網路下載音樂作品者，收取授權金，著作權委員會考量下述重點：(1)只要從主伺服器（儲存文件檔）到終端使用者，即構成對公眾之傳輸，符合著作權法第3條(1)項(f)內容。(2)ISPs之買賣條件在於，若僅提供他人做為溝通及傳送使用，在形成內容主要供應者時（Content Providers），亦即不僅只是傳輸功能，還包括提供大量題材（著作物）供他人下載，或以電子郵件互相傳送，則違背ISPs免責條件。(3)依據著作權委員會解釋，當被他人以侵害著作權為目的之使用ISP，並不構成ISP授權侵害行為，除非ISP知情且允許使用人之侵害（CA s.3）。(4)只有發生於加拿大國內網路通訊，受加拿大著作權法管轄，同時也只有放置於加國境內伺服器上之資訊內容必須繳交授權金（Royalty）給委員會。

　　基於上述裡由，SOCAN不服，繼而上訴至上訴法院，希望司法單位能更正對著作權委員會的若干見解，聯邦上訴法院也認為委員會，不能因為主伺服器在加拿大國內之情形才能收取授權金，著作權法s.2.4 (1)之情形，關於對大眾必須之無線通訊範圍，並非由ISPs提供快速存提（Caches），即必須是大眾需要通訊，如(a)款中提到公寓大廈、飯店客房住宿……等，必需透過主伺服器再到個別終端使用人，即是公眾必須使用之通訊，若為個人需求，如下載影片或音樂，不透過付費使用，而利用無線通訊上之便利行事，的確違背合理使用及使用者付費間之平等原則，[70]本案其後由ISP業者上訴，將聯邦上訴法院判決結果，繼續上訴至加拿大聯邦最高法院，形成本案之爭點探討。

著作權法保護公眾利益，鼓勵創作及發明分享，並獎勵創作人，[71]網際網路能廣為散布人類思想文化及創作之結晶，此種便利性應被鼓勵，而非淪為剽竊或利用他人著作成果之工具，電子商務成為現代人購物、消費的重要市場，因此規範網路法律責任勢在必行，[72]著作權人有權對其著作從事各種使用，[73]1988年修正版增加「對大眾以無線通訊方式傳播及授權如此行為，[74]著作權委員會音樂檔案傳遞即是無線通訊形式，因此被上訴人（SOCAN）認為上訴人（被告）參與音樂作品傳遞，應負擔Tariff 22提案中之補償費[75]」。著作權委員會在Tariff 22中對「發生於加拿大」定義為一下載音樂或影片檔，必須傳遞自加拿大國內伺服器，除非內容提供者蓄意和位於加拿大境內接收者連絡；[76]最高法院判決理由書，對此定義深感不解，因網路連繫往往發生於跨國行為，對委員會非創始於加拿大國內伺服器，則

---

[70] 加拿大在近年來的案件，以本案（SOCAN案）最為受人矚目，除此之外，有關MP3音樂檔案下載，使用P2P技術之案件並不多。

[71] 相關判決中，皆曾出現此類見解，如 *The' berge v. Galerie d'Art du Petit Champlain inc.*,(2002)2 S.C.R. 336, 2002 SCC 34, at para.30., *CCH Canadian Ltd. v. Law Society of Upper Canada*, (2004) 1 S.C.R. 339, 2004 SCC 13, at para. 10.

[72] 在SOCAN案中，法官Binnie J.彙整其他法官意見書後，在判決理由書中對此點亦提出強烈訴求，see 2 S.C.R. 427, 2004 SCC 45 (2004).

[73] S.27 (1).

[74] S.3 (1) (f).

[75] 美國1998年制定通過電子千禧著作權法規範，the Digital Millennium Copyright Act, 17 U.S.C. § 512 (1998)；澳洲於2000年制定著作權法增訂版本（電子篇），Copyright Amendment (Digital Agenda) Act 2000, No.110 of 2000，加拿大法院亦嘗試，使其國內法規能配合1886年伯恩公約（the Berne Convention for the Protection of Literary and Artistic Works of 1886，1980年於柏林更新，其後並有連番補充更新版本）。

[76] *See* Tariff 22, at P. 459-460.

不能算發生於加國境內解釋，不予接受。

　　以MP3音樂下載為例，終端使用者擁有其先前未曾付費使用之音樂作品，涉及管轄法院及法律主體間問題，在之前法院判決，如Libman v. The Queen[77]涉及股票買賣規避，美國買方與多倫多賣方以電話連繫，並匯款至加拿大，判決書中法官認為只要二者之間有真正且實質的連繫，無論是透過無線通訊由別州到加拿大，或加拿大到其他國家，重點不在於當事人與相對人所在的位置與區域，而是整個交易買賣過程，甚至還有涉及第三國之可能；因此，另一案Canada (Human Right Commission) v. Canadian Liberty Net[78]及Kitakufe v. Oloya[79]曾有相同見解。[80]對運用著作權法及國際間網路交易或聯繫之行為，找出合理客觀之標準，衡量網路行為時，內容提供者（Content Provider）、主伺服器（Host Server）、中間人（Intermdiaries）及使用者（End User）所在位置，及交易性質和種類，皆是考量因素。

　　本案最終經過對著作權法條文，如s.2.4 (1)(b)解釋，並對ISP業者引用快速存提（Caches）使使用人可免費下載音樂或影片作法，是否符合條文規範，亦參考歐盟電子商務導引規範會員國ISP業者免責規定（art.13 (1)），因此著作權委員會認為使用者透過中間媒介，應用快速存提作法亦落實在s.2.4 (1)之免責規定中；此外，SOCAN指控

---

[77] 2 S.C.R. 178 (1985).

[78] 1 S.C.R. 626, at para 52 (1998).

[79] O.J. No.2537 (QL) (Gen.Div.) (1998).

[80] 關於真正且實質連繫（real and substantial connection）由近年來法院判決中，歸納出一種避免過度解釋，對擴大區域性，即跨國買賣或交易，能做適度限縮，並符合公平原則之應用，如Holt Cargo Systems Inc. v. ABC Containerline N.V. (Trustees of), (2001) 3 S.C.R. 907, 2001 SCC 90, at para. 71; Spar Aerospace Ltd. v. American Mobile Satellite Corp., (2002) 4 S.C.R. 205, 2002 SCC 78; Beals v. Saldanha, (2003) 3. C.R. 416, 2003 SCC 72.

若主伺服器（ISP業者）雖未侵害著作權，也需負擔授權內容提供者（因為中間媒介、仲介人一定明白內容），即重大引誘使用人從事侵害著作權之責任，快速存提中間媒介必須在知悉侵害發生時，移除或消滅該侵害內容。

十、後續發展

上述C-60法案雖未獲通過，但希冀草案通過之重要爭點在其他國家，尤其美國早已如火如荼從事許多法令更新及制定新法的措施，我國順應國際潮流陸續更新法規；[81]加拿大立法速度與作法配合國際趨勢，望之保守實則有其堅持，可能是其國土幅員廣大、國情單純及政治穩定，才能有如此「獨立」的作法，[82]不問DMCA內容是否反映國際公約及美國著作權法立法真諦，事實則為其罰則加強部分造成使用人恐懼，[83]因此，加拿大著作權法並未照單全收，加拿大以DMCA做為參考標的與對照，法案C-60可發現加入反規避條文，1997年加拿大簽署加入WCT及WPPT條約，[84]2005年6月C-60法案加入補充規定。[85]

---

[81] 我國部分，可參閱立法院歷年立法理由及修正重點，本文不另敘述。

[82] 作者在蒐集資料的過程，深切感受此點，特別是智慧財產權領域，加拿大未如其他國家急切配合國際公約或規章的腳步。不過，這也許是作者才疏學淺一己之見。

[83] 曾勝珍，著作權侵害罰則之探討─以美國電子千禧著作權法為主，法令月刊，第58卷第3期，頁106-126，2007。

[84] Government of Canada - Canadian Heritage, News Release, *Canada Commits to Sign International Copyright Treaties*, 18 December (1997). online: http://www. canadianheritage. gc.ca/newsroom/news_e.cfm?Action=Display&code=7NR135E

[85] Industry Canada, News Release, *Government of Canada Introduces Bill to Amend the Copyrigh Act*, 20 June (2005). http://www.ic.g.ca/cmb/welcomeic.nsf/261ce500 dfcd7259852564820068dc6d/85256a5d006b9720852570pwnDocument. (last visited: 4/16/2008).

　　有關保障TPMs技術及反規避條文規範於第34.02(1)內容中，即任何著作物之所有人，對附著於錄音形式表演或形諸於表演當中之錄音部分，依據加拿大著作權法，當任何人未取得著作權人之授權而利用該著作時，應給予著作權人精神及實質上補償，雖然上述條文以禁止侵害著作權為原則，然而在判斷及推論侵害人之責任時，不須證明當事人實際侵害行為，相異於美國DMCA內容，而以當事人之犯意為準，因此解釋當事人之犯意更形重要，條文文意簡易卻同時造成解釋上困難，如DMCA規定在(1)禁止規避，(2)禁止提供任何產品或服務以規避控制路徑DRM技術，(3)禁止利用上述規避手段而取得著作。

　　C-60第34.02(1)中並未如DMCA般，特別明文禁止對DRM技術管制條文（即禁止規避情事之規定）。在第2條條文中定義DRM，指保障著作權人作品專有權，如寫作、表演或錄音工業……等方面之著作權，然而此種定義付諸實際，卻與設計DRM系統有多元性之目的不同，因為DRM系統乃為保障對著作物之使用與路徑方式，非如前述純為保障著作人專有權，因此歸納C-60與DMCA最大差別乃在對故意要件之定義，C-60第34.02(1)規定仍以科技方式規避他人之著作者之犯意為主。

參、網路著作權管理

　　目前眾多網站採用套裝包裹（Package Media），並透過由使用者同意發行的方式（Publication of User-Generated Content，簡稱

UGC或稱Consumer-Generated Media），[86]有別於以前電腦公司販售軟、硬體或週邊商品，即藉由影音頻道、同學錄或相片集，達到使用人本身也是作品提供者，多樣式使用狀態和以往如部落格或聊天室、個人網站所提供的功能又有不同。

在大型電腦公司發展新軟體給使用者的開發過程中，長期耗時費力的研發過程是支出成本的大宗，而除了回收並能長期獲利的模組，架構在使用者的數目能迅速累積及提昇，目前網路人口及使用態樣的比較，世界網路E-mail使用人數已達1億3,190萬，[87]2007年2月YouTube瀏覽頁數為1億7,600萬人，[88]Facebook使用者人數目前邁向6,000萬，預測2008年後Facebook 使用者人數將突破1億2,500萬人大關，[89]如同眾多定型化契約的型態，在我們使用網路的經驗中，會發現「一按即成」（Shrink-Wrap or Click-Wrap）的設置十分普遍且便利，[90]如微軟公司的使用者註冊契約（End User License Agreement，簡稱EULA）形成軟體免費使用或分享的先驅。

2003年Myspace設立，2年後該網站價值已超過美金5億8,000萬

---

[86] See Robert P. Latham, Carl C. Butzer, Jeremy T. Brown, *Legal Implications of User-Generated Content: Youtube, Myspace, Facebook*, 20 No.5 INTELL. PROP. & T ECH. L.J. 1, May (2008).

[87] 全球新趨勢 教授虛擬世界開課。http://www.peopo.org/portal.php?op=viewPost&articleId=13367（最後瀏覽日2008/5/20）。

[88] 根據哈佛國際回顧（Harvard International Review）2007年12月30日根據統計市場調查顯示，電子商務時報。http://www.ectimes.org.tw/shownews.aspx?id= 10291（最後瀏覽日2008/5/20）。

[89] 預測2008年的Facebook。http://mmdays.com/2007/12/31/facebook-2008（最後瀏覽日2008/5/20）。

[90] 參考原文自Molly Shaffer Van Houweling, *The New Servitudes*, 90 Geo. L.J. 889 (2008). 指的是在普通法（Common Law）的規範下，往昔對地主與承租人間的制約規範，不論經手幾次或轉手數人，原所有人對土地所加的限制會一直隨「物」存在，在目前智慧財產權及電子商務普通應用及保障的情況下，由使用人直接觸碰「接受鍵」（I agree），即可進入該系統或使用軟體中，使架設軟體的速度十分快捷。

元，而2004年針對大專學生成立的Facebook，亦為大眾廣泛使用分享資訊、相片、錄影短片，2006年Google以美金16億5,000萬元的價格買下YouTube。[91]網路經營者及使用者在UGC的架構下大量運用其便利性，YouTube上傳及下載影片的速度，數量驚人，Facebook點閱及公布訊息的人數也遠超想像，[92]使用如此便利故無可避免觸及智慧財產權保障相關問題。美國著作權法規範重製、預備重製、散佈或公開播放他人文學、音樂、戲劇、動畫及其他影音作品，[93]亦包含以電子媒體的方式侵害著作權法第106至122條規定中，[94]保障著作權人的專屬權利。[95]

　　回歸網路使用的主要精神，最起始的源由來自於「分享」，利用網路架設平台——分享新資訊與見聞，按觸鍵盤是最快也最廣為人使用的方式，可快速傳遞前手所定的規則由後手承接，網路著作權管理首重對消費行為的保障，若無法使消費者與業者在互益公平的平台進行交易而公平交易法立法目的，在於維護交易秩序與消費者利益，確保公平競爭，促進經濟之安定與繁榮，與產業界及消費者均屬息息相關。我國司法院司法官釋字第548號解釋中，將禁止權利濫用的原

---

[91] 每天約有65,000部錄影作品被上傳至YouTube，約一億支影片每日被欣賞，資料來源引用 See Robert P. Latham, Carl C. Butzer, Jeremy T. Brown, *Legal Implications of User-Generated Content: Youtube, Myspace, Facebook*, 20 NO.5 Intell. Prop. & Tech. L.J. 1, May (2008).

[92] 只要周遭有青年學子或習慣上網者，皆會熟悉此類網站的運用，光在「Google搜尋」打YouTube或Facebook，便可進入一個恍若異地的精彩世界。

[93] 17 U.S.C. §501(a).

[94] 17 U.S.C. §106(1)-(6).

[95] 包括未經授權的使用，如未經著作權人同意或在第107至122條文中的除外及限制規定，並不單指直接侵害者才有侵害責任，對非直接侵害者，但對該等侵害事實有某些程度的參與或涉及，則科予第二順位侵權責任，並且不在1976年修改的著作權法內容中(1976 Copyright Act)，國會在立法過程中知悉此種侵害責任之存在。17 U.S.C. § 501(a) (2003). H.R. Rep. No. 1476, 94th Cong., 2d Sess. 61, 159-60 1976).

則導引至智慧財產權的領域，公平交易法第45條規定，「依照著作權法、商標法或專利法行使權利之正當行為，不適用本法之規定。」綜上所述，網路著作權現況與公平競爭政策重疊或競合的關係值得探究，其次再探討美國法在理論及實務上能提供借鏡之處。

一、我國不公平競爭

我國「公平交易法」乃促進公平交易的法律，亦即維持自由市場經濟的基本秩序而訂定企業活動規則，我國在1992年2月4日開始施行「公平交易法」，[96]中國大陸則在1993年9月2日開始實施並稱為「反不正當競爭法」，2007年8月30日通過反壟斷法。[97]內容維護自由競爭的反壟斷法，規範事業濫用獨占地位之行為、結合行為以及聯合行為，並確保公平競爭的反不當競爭法，維持轉售價格的禁止、妨礙公平競爭、仿冒、虛偽不實廣告、損害他人營業信譽、不當多層次傳銷及其他足以影響交易秩序之欺罔或顯失公平行為。

公平交易法第45條規定：「依照著作權法、商標法或專利法行使權利之正當行為，不適用本法之規定。」此一規定兼顧智慧財產權法制之壟斷特性與公平交易法之維護公平交易特性，祇有在行使智慧財產權法制所賦予之權利有「不正當行為」時，才得適用公平交易法。雖然智慧財產權法制與公平交易法有可能同時適用，亦即侵害智慧財產權行為可能亦違反公平交易法，但實際上，當著作權法、商標法或專利法得以適用時，公平會一向均不介入處分。[98]

我國公平交易法於2002年2月6日進行最近一次的修正，立法目

---

[96] 1991/2/4日經總統公布，1992/2/4施行。

[97] 第10屆全國人大常委會通過，同日公布，自2008/8/1起施行。

[98] 章忠信，「智慧財產權基本概念」，2000/2/18發表，2003/2/19最後更新。http://www.copyrightnote.org/crnote/bbs.php?board=1&act=read&id=37（最後瀏覽日2009/2/12）。

的「為維護交易秩序與消費者利益，確保公平競爭，促進經濟之安定與繁榮[99]」。公平交易法第19條第5款規定，[100]脅迫、利誘或其他不正當方法獲取營業祕密之侵害類型，侵害類型顯然規定不足；消費者在處理不同種類資訊時，若在結果涉入時產生負面效果，對消費者而言，負面資訊相較具有診斷性，在消費者不確知企業資訊時會過濾各種資訊，如此延長消費者判斷的時間，也容易使競爭商家有機可趁。

2005年2月5日公布行政罰法第15條私法人之董事或其他有代表權之人，因執行其職務或為私法人之利益為行為，致使私法人違反行政法上義務應受處罰者，該行為人如有故意或重大過失時，除法律或自治條例另有規定外，應並受同一規定罰鍰之處罰。法人之職員、受僱人或從業人員，因執行其職務或為私法人之利益為行為，致使私法人違反行政法上義務應受處罰者，私法人之董事或其他有代表權之人，如對該行政法上義務之違反，因故意或重大過失，未盡其防止義務時，除法律或自治條例另有規定外，應並受同一規定罰鍰之處罰。依前二項並受同一規定處罰之罰鍰，不得逾新臺幣100萬元。但其所得之利益逾新臺幣100萬元者，得於其所得利益之範圍內裁處之。

公平交易法第19條第5款「以脅迫、利誘或其他不正當方法，獲取他事業之產銷機密、交易相對人資料或其他有關技術秘密之行為。」即禁止妨礙公平競爭行為，應屬於公平交易法第24條，禁止不公平競爭行為之概括條款範圍內，「即事業不得為其他足以影響交易秩序之欺罔或顯失公平之行為」，不公平競爭行為，凡具有不公平競爭本質之行為，如無法依公平交易法其他條文規定加以規範者，則可檢視有無該法第24條規定之適用。

公平交易法第24條「不公平競爭之概括條款」，運用在網路交

---

[99] 見公平交易法第1條。

[100] 公平交易法第19條第5款，以脅迫、利誘或其他不正當方法，獲取他人事業之產銷機密、交易相對人資料或其他有關技術秘密之行為。

易行為及電子商務，有發展出新類型，例如「榨取他人努力成果」。依第24條處理原則規定，判斷是否違法原則上應考量：(1)遭攀附或高度抄襲之標的，應係該事業已投入相當程度之努力，於市場上擁有一定之經濟效應，而已被系爭行為所榨取；(2)其攀附或抄襲之結果，應有使交易相對人誤以為兩者屬同一來源，原系列產品或關係之企業之效果等。惟倘其所採行手段可非難性甚高（如完全一致之抄襲）者，縱非屬前述二因素之情形，仍有違法之虞，應依個案實際情形，綜合判斷之。[101]

　　所謂不公平競爭，係指行為具有商業競爭倫理之非難性，商業競爭行為違反社會倫理，或侵害以價格、品質、服務等效能競爭本質為中心之不公平競爭，國人積極在先進科技領域、包括電腦資訊、醫藥生化方面賣力經營，或循技術授權、技術合作、企業購併，乃至現金購買等方面積極引進尖端技術，期以強化現有技術研發水準，提升企業獲利能力及經營格局。期待我國在保護智慧財產權的同時，能避免形成不公平競爭，使同業競爭者基於公平互利的立場展開交易模式，如此可望達成公平交易活絡市場，具體保障投資人與消費大眾的需求，刺激經濟景象加強良性循環的榮景。

　　因此著作權等智慧財之行使權利行為與一般有體物之所有權應該是一致的，只要屬正當行使權利之行為，即不違反公平法之規定，這也是著作權等智慧財適用公平法之當然結果。公平交易法第45條有關「依照著作權法、商標法或專利法行使權利之正當行為，不適用本法之規定」之解釋，應有平衡智慧財產權保護政策與競爭保護政策之立法意涵。[102]

---

[101] 陳櫻琴，「科技產業的第五元素－競爭法的建構與解讀」，頁88-89，台北，翰蘆圖書出版有限公司，2005。

[102] 智慧財產權於防止不公平競爭之功能方面與公平法有部分相同，著作權禁止盜用他人之智慧財產之行為，亦帶有保護競爭秩序之法律意涵，但另一方面智慧財產權亦會限

二、美加及中國大陸競爭法

1967年7月14日簽定於斯德哥爾摩之「建立世界智慧財產權組織公約（Convention Establishing the World Intellectual Property Organizations）規定[103]智慧財產權包括：(1)文學，藝術與科學之創作，(2)表演藝術，圖像與廣播之演出，(3)各個人類努力領域之發明，(4)科學上之發現，(5)工業設計，(6)商標，服務標章，與商業名稱和設計，(7)防止不公平競爭之保護，(8)以及所有其他在工業，科學，文學或藝術領域之智力活動成果之權利。

1993年12月15日「關稅貿易總協定」（General Agreement on Tariffs and Trade，簡稱GATT協定）達成最終協議，烏拉圭回合談判「與貿易相關之智慧財產權協定」（Agreements on Trade Related Aspect of Intellectual Property Rights, Including Trade in Counterfeit Goods，簡稱Agreements on TRIPS），[104]規範(1)著作權及相關權

制一部分之自由競爭，智慧財產權法政策與自由競爭政策期間應有適當之調和，例外不適用說認為，著作權等智慧財之保護與公平法之競爭政策並非相容，但基於該等智慧財於文化及產業政策上等公益性考量，故規定該等智慧財行使法律所賦予之權利行為時，可例外不適用公平法之規範，因此該等智慧財產行使權利之正當行為，雖形式上侵害公平法上所保護之法益而應受公平法之規範，但因認為該等行使權利之行為，屬於公平法上正當行為，故例外不適用公平法之規定，適用說認為，著作權法主要之法目的，在於鼓勵、促進創作，並保障其效果之實施與交易，並於立法技術上將原本屬於無體物之智慧財產權利，擬制為有體物之所有權加以保護，基於對無體智慧財之保護只要與私有財產採同一保護標準即可，與法律政策上對智慧財產之保護亦無須制定高於私有財產權之保護標準，因此上述之適用說或例外不適用說，均失之偏頗，此處理論引自汪渡村，「公平交易法」，五南圖書出版有限公司，2007，頁299。

[103] 「建立世界智慧財產權組織公約」第2條第8款，本公約中英文版本請見經濟部智慧財產局網站。http://www.tipo.gov.tw/ch/AllInOne_Show.aspx?guid=c1df1827-6e28-46c8-b71a-f08b5880c35b&lang=zh-tw&path=393（最後瀏覽日2009/5/28）。

[104] 謝銘洋，「智慧財產權法之基礎理論」，頁10，台北，翰蘆圖書出版有限公司，1995。

利，(2)商標，(3)產地標示，(4)工業設計，(5)專利，(6)積體電路之電路佈局，(7)未公開資訊之保護，(8)對授權契約中違反競爭行為之管理。由國際公約規範的範疇觀察防止不公平競爭之保護，與對授權契約中違反競爭行為之管理皆被列入。

　　TRIPS第40條規範針對授權契約所可能發生的限制競爭實務，TRIPS承認會員國處理違反公平競爭的授權行為，和授權行為或其條件構成權利濫用或違反公平競爭之情事時，鼓勵以政府間的諮商予以解決，至於權利濫用的救濟則應配合TRIPS的相關條款。[105] 最早於1883年簽訂「保護產業（工業）財產權巴黎公約」（Paris Convention for the Protection of industrial Property，簡稱巴黎公約）時，「防止不正當競爭」即被列入「產業（工業）財產權」（Industrial Property Rights）之範疇。

　　競爭秩序之維護被納入智慧財產權之範圍有其重要意義，因為精神創作人欲實現其創作成果之經濟價值，通常須藉由交易行為，如將其創作成果商品化後在市場上銷售，或者直接將其創作成果之實施權讓與他人行使，而正當之交易秩序則能保障並有助於精神創作人實現其權利之經濟價值[106]。著作權法為保障著作人著作權益，調和社會公共利益，促進國家文化發展，依照著作權法、商標法或專利法行使權利之正當行為，不適用公平交易法規定之解釋，除依據各該智慧財產權法規定判斷其所具有之權利，亦須依公平交易法相關規定，審視權利之行使是否正當，權利人有無權利濫用形成不公平競爭行為之情

---

[105] 馮震宇，「智慧財產權發展趨勢與重要問題研究」，頁13，台北，元照出版有限公司，2003。

[106] 謝銘洋，「智慧財產權法之基礎理論」，頁13，台北，翰蘆圖書出版有限公司，1995。CHARLES R. MCMANIS, INTELLECTUAL PROPERTY AND UNFAIR COMPETITION, 29-30, WEST PUBLISHING CO. (2004).

事，方屬妥適。[107]

　　我國如雅虎公司自行關閉無名小站部分部落格功能，造成付費會員權益受損乙事，公平會將主動瞭解[108]雅虎公司是否有利用因結合而取得之市場地位，以不正當方法阻礙競爭者網頁連結、電子郵件之接收與傳送、或其他服務之提供等情事。考量產業政策及總體社會經濟利益，保護智慧財產權與公平競爭秩序實為一體兩面的利基，調和二者以先尊重著作權人行使於著作權法所賦予之權利，在考量其行使權利之行為是否正當，不以權利濫用之法理作為先入為主的概念，而是以客觀角度衡量該權利行使之行為在保護智慧財產權之效益與限制競爭所造成的不利益，比較利弊得失而做出判斷；[109]以下說明網路著作權法與公平交易法相關案例，及實務上運作所造成的法益衝突或相輔相成的情形。

---

[107] 「公平會審理事業發侵害著作權、商標權或專利權警告函案件處理原則」所稱「正當行為」之意義乙案，公平會2000年8月3日第457次委員會議審議，此則函釋所附「行政院公平會審理事業發侵害著作權、商標權或專利權警告函案件處理原則」，經本會2005年2月24日修正名稱為「行政院公平交易委員會對於事業發侵害著作權、商標權或專利權警告函案件之處理原則」。http:// www.ftc.gov.tw/internet/main/doc/docDetail. aspx?uid=126&docid=10553（最後瀏覽日2009/5/28）。

[108] 公平會5月28日表示，有關媒體報導無名小站於26日關閉部分部落格功能，對於付費會員不公平，造成渠等權益受損乙事，公平會將主動對此事進行瞭解，如涉有違反該會96年間不禁止雅虎公司與無名小站結合所附加負擔：「申報人不得利用因結合而取得之市場地位，以不正當方法阻礙競爭者網頁連結、電子郵件之接收與傳送、或其他服務之提供。」之情事，將依公平交易法規定予以查處。雅虎公司如未履行前揭該會對於結合所附加之負擔，可依公平交易法規定限期命其分設事業併處以新臺幣10萬元以上5千萬元以下罰鍰。http://www.ftc.gov.tw/ internet/main/doc/docDetail. aspx?uid=126&docid=10553（最後瀏覽日2009/5/28）。

[109] 汪渡村，「公平交易法」，頁299，台北，五南圖書出版有限公司，2007。

三、美　國

　　拜數位科技與網際網路之賜，創作品取得、再製、傳送的成本變得極低。數位時代核心的創作品，「資訊」而非「實體」，先天上便具有「公共財」無排他性與競爭性的特性。出於避免創作誘因不足的理由，著作權法的產權控制與程式碼的技術控制日趨嚴密。其結果是兩種極端主義的對抗僵局：一邊是越來越嚴苛的著作權管制主義，另一邊是越來越囂張的盜版無政府主義。對方各自成為自身強化武裝的理由，造成了相互增強的惡性循環。

　　美國於1890年通過「薛爾曼反托拉斯法」（The Sherman Anti-trust Act），[110]該法主要禁止以契約、協定或其他共謀之方式，限制洲際或國際貿易[111]或以獨占、企圖獨占或共謀獨占洲際或國際貿易；[112]1914年通過「克萊頓反托拉斯法」（The Clayton Act），[113]補充前法不足之處，禁止壟斷、兼併及不正當競爭，同年亦通過「聯邦貿易委員會法」（The Federal Trade Commission Act），阻止非在前二法案禁止之列，不利交易秩序及市場競爭之行為態樣。[114]與公

---

[110] The Sherman Anti-trust Act of July 1890, c. 647, 26 Stat. 209, 15 U. S. C. § 1 -7, as amended 1998 & Supp. IV 1992. See Robert P. Merges, Peter S. Menell & Mark A. Lemley, *Intellectual Property in the New Technological Age*, 1138 (2007), Aspen Publishers Co..

[111] 15 U. S. C. § 1 (1988). 亦可見陳家駿、羅怡德，「公平交易法與智慧財產權」，頁137，台北，五南圖書出版有限公司，1999。

[112] 15 U. S. C. § 2 (1988).

[113] Act of Oct. 15, 1914, c. 323, 38 Stat. 730, as amended, 15 U.S.C. § 12 -27 (1988). 該法確定對防止不正當競爭方法的管轄，對有可能造成削弱競爭或造成壟斷的商業活動，限制已售物的轉售價格，或獨家銷售、搭售協定（tying agreement），陳家駿、羅怡德，「公平交易法與智慧財產權」，頁138，台北，五南圖書出版有限公司，1999。另可參考曲三強，「知識產權法原理」，頁620，北京市，中國檢察出版社，2004。

[114] Act of Sept. 26, 1914, c. 311, 38 Stat. 717, as amended, 15 U.S.C. § 41 -58 (1988). 陳家駿、羅怡德，同前註113，頁139。曲三強，同前註113，頁620。

平交易有關的重要法規最後為「羅賓森反托拉斯法」（The Robinson Patman Act），[115]擴大「克來頓反托拉斯法」中有關價格歧視條款的適用範圍。[116]

如申請專利，一般而言大型藥廠（如Merck及Pfizer）投注大筆金錢與人力進行研發，一種新藥物的產生與發明耗時曠日，然而專利時效過後，藥廠唯有加強公司的內部組織與管理，才能降低成本與其他仿效者競爭，獨佔型的缺點在於為維持其獨佔性，隨時要有訴訟的準備，避免他人冒用或仿效，同時有可能違反公平競爭（造成壟斷）而犧牲市場的獨佔性。[117]著作權之行使在公平交易法上可能引起之問題，大抵以著作權授權實務為多，如區域限制、整批授權、價格限制、用途限制、搭售限制過程中著作權人欲以其專屬權限作不當之控制所衍生之問題，及著作權之權利濫用等問題等最令人矚目。[118]

---

[115] 15 U.S.C. § 13 (1988). *See* CHARLES R. MCMANIS, INTELLECTUAL PROPERTY AND UNFAIR COMPETITION, 443-445, WEST PUBLISHING CO. (2004).

[116] 大型連鎖店可由廠商取得較低的進貨價格，小型商店因而無法與之競爭，為保障小型商店之生存，禁止廠商對於購買相同品質貨物之買主，在價格上有所歧視。15 U.S.C. § 13(a) (1988).

[117] Robert R. Trumble, Bradley S. Butterfield, Kevin J. Mason and Joseph B. *Payne, Human Resources and Intellectual Property in a Global Outsourcing Environment,* 15 WINTR INT' L HR J. 2-3 (2006).

[118] 著作權僅保護「觀念之表達」（the expression of an idea），而不保護「觀念」本身（idea）；任何人均有權表達同一個觀念，惟不可使用他人已採用之表達方式。著作權法並不保護著作物所有意表達之觀念，故任何人均可採用不同表達方式，表達其他著作人已於著作物中表達過之觀念，因此不同的著作物之間，便產生出高度的替代性，使任何著作權人相對而言均不容易在相關產品市場中，取得可以控制市場之力量。陳家駿、羅怡德，「公平交易法與智慧財產權」，頁328，台北，五南圖書出版有限公司，1999。

1. Data General Corp. v. Grumman Systems Support Corp.[119]案

原告Data General Corp.為一家設計、製造電腦並對其買家提供服務的公司，原告拒絕對被告及其他從事維修工作之第三者，提供維護其新產品之軟體工具—ADEX，只有與原告有授權關係的經銷商對ADEX有獨家使用權，被告Grumman Systems Support Corp.使用曾受僱於原告之離職工程師自行複製的備份，原告控告被告侵害其著作權及違反僱傭契約中保密義務，不當洩漏營業秘密；被告反訴原告不願提供ADEX的授權，形成獨占並造成對市場的壟斷。[120]

一審的地方區域法院駁回被告之請求，判決理由認為原告向社會大眾公開授權，並未獨占市場亦未造成壟斷，被告隨即上訴；美國聯邦第一巡迴法院以為，著作權人原本即有權利可決定其著作被他人使用的範圍及內涵，不會因為單方面的拒絕（unilateral refusal）著作權之授權而形成壟斷，[121]最終維持原判原告勝訴。[122]

2. Independent service organization (ISO) v. Xerox Corporation[123]案

美國聯邦第10巡迴法院以為，影印機製造商拒絕銷售或授

---

[119] *Data General Corp. v. Grumman Systems Support Corp.*, 36 F.3d 1147(1st Cir. 1994).

[120] *See* 15 U.S.C. § 2. *Moore v. Jas. H. Matthews & Co.*, 473 F .2d 328, 332 (9th Cir. 1973).

[121] *See* 15 U.S.C. § 106. 著作權人對其著作原本即有專屬權，可以出賣、出租、出借或排除他人之使用。*Fox Film Corp. v. Doyal*, 286 U.S. 123, 127 (1932)., *Stewart v. Abend*, 495 U.S. 207, 229 (1990). See also supra note 89, Robert P. Merges, Peter S. Menell & Mark A. Lemley, 1143

[122] 聯邦第一巡迴法院只有對賠償金額部分重新考量，其餘維持原判。*Id.*

[123] Independent service organization (ISO) v. Xerox Corporation, 203 F.3d 1322, 2000-1 Trade Cases P 72,795, 2000 COPR.L. Dec. P 28,026, 53 U.S.P.Q.2d 1852 (2000).本案自 CSU, L.L.C. v. Xerox Corp., 23 F.Supp.2d 1242 (D.Kan.1999) 而來，原告原在坎薩斯州地院提出請求，主張Xerox不願出售其擁有專利之零件給獨立的維修商，一審判決原告敗訴，上訴法院維持一審見解，原告繼續上訴。

權其擁有著作權之原料及軟體,並未違反反托拉斯法(Sherman Act),[124]本案有關Xerox公司製造、販售、授權高品質的影印機,並與經銷商簽訂維修契約,地院判決Xerox公司若為維護其專利及著作權,可以理解其拒絕提供維修零件的做法,並未違反公平競爭的原則,[125]原告所提起的理由並未構成影響法院判決的事實爭點,[126]上訴巡迴法院則找尋巡迴法院及聯邦判決中的相關論點,認為被告之拒絕銷售乃為維護其專利物件的權利,而無論以著作權或專利權的角度,不能因此就認為被告違反托拉斯法的規範,[127]智慧財產權的維護絕非為了牴觸公平交易的原理原則,[128]商業利益的考量不僅在新技術的研發創造,更避免造成權利人的壟斷,[129]本案為其後案件形成重要影響。

四、加拿大

科技中立並非忽視著作權人之利益,科技中立冀求維護科技更新,謀求更多數人福祉,國際社會(即使加拿大仍未積極加入國際組

---

[124] Sherman Ac), § 1 et seq., as amended, 15 U.S.C.A. § 1 et seq.; 17 U.S.C.A. § 106(3).

[125] *See* Petrolite Corp. v. Baker Hughes Inc., 96 F.3d 1423, 1425, 40 USPQ2d 1201, 1203 (Fed. Cir.1996) (citing Meyers v. Asics Corp., 974 F.2d 1304, 1306, 24 USPQ2d 1036, 1037 (Fed. Cir.1992)).

[126] *See* Transmatic, Inc. v. Gulton Indus., Inc., 53 F.3d 1270, 1274, 35 USPQ2d 1035, 1038 (Fed. Cir.1995).

[127] *See* Nobelpharma AB v. Implant Innovations, Inc., 141 F.3d 1059, 1068, 46 USPQ2d 1097, 1104 (Fed.Cir.1998). Pro-Mold & Tool Co. v. Great Lakes Plastics, Inc., 75 F.3d 1568, 1574-75, 37 USPQ2d 1626, 1631 (Fed.Cir.1996). Midwest Indus., Inc. v. Karavan Trailers, Inc., 175 F.3d 1356, 1360, 50 USPQ2d 1672, 1676 (Fed.Cir.1999).

[128] *See* Intergraph Corp. v. Intel Corp., 195 F.3d 1346, 1362, 52 USPQ2d 1641, 1652 (Fed. Cir.1999).

[129] *See* Abbott Lab. v. Brennan, 952 F.2d 1346, 1354, 21 USPQ2d 1192, 1199 (Fed.Cir.1991).

織或成為會員國之類）在保障著作權及取得和諧間，其實已有相當共識，WIPO之後明確規範國際著作權保障型態及主旨，1996年WIPO增加對TPMs保護規定，加拿大法如何看待此項規定，而對法律保護部份更新也受到相當期待，著作權人受到WCT（the WIPO Copyright Treaty）及WPPT（the WIPO Performances and Phonograms Treaty）的保障，如WCT第11條內容中有關締約雙方將提供足夠法律保障與賠償，遵循WIPO著作權條約中規範反規避條文，WPPT第18條也有類似規範。

　　TPMs及DRM 系統使著作權人更有優勢，當面臨與個別使用者簽訂契約時，DRM提供予著作權人絕大的利基，通常這類契約甚至賦予著作權人優於著作權法的保障，而更傾向於提供公平交易及平等競爭的法令、政策保護，若著作權人可對行使規避TPMs及DRM系統的個人，運用反規避條款提出訴訟，則使反規避與反裝置條款（Anti-Device Provisions）形同著作權的新規範，實際上美國及我國正是此種做法，加拿大如前文所提卻遲遲未通過新法案，也因而面臨生存於國際社會的重大考驗，[130]2009年美國貿易代表署新近公布的「2009特別301報告」，該份報告首度將加拿大列入「優先觀察名

---

[130] 美國貿易代表署於5月7日公布「2009特別301報告」，該份報告首度將加拿大列入「優先觀察名單」，台灣因為保護智慧財產權績效良好，沒有被列入「優先觀察名單」以及「觀察名單」，南韓情況亦然，中國則因網際網路盜版以及假冒活動的執法不足，連續第五年被列入「優先觀察名單」，並繼續列入「306條款監管」，此為美國將實施貿易報復的最後通牒。美國貿易代表署針對全球77個國家和地區的智慧財產權保護情形提出檢討，今年被列入「優先觀察名單」的12個國家，分別是阿根廷、委內瑞拉、智利、中國、俄羅斯、印度、印尼、泰國、巴基斯坦、阿爾及利亞、以色列以及加拿大。該署表示，中國和俄羅斯在保護智財權上略有進步，不過成績不佳，報告特別引用中國《百度》網站作為網路盜版的代表，表示中國50%～75%的非法音樂下載和百度有關，阿里巴巴和淘寶網等中國電子商務網站則提供客戶侵權產品。編譯陳柏誠、記者曾慧雯／綜合報導，「301觀察名單 我獲除名」，自由時報電子報。http://www. libertytimes.com.tw/2009/new/may/2/today-e4.htm（最後瀏覽日2009/6/4）。

單」，美國的電影、視訊遊戲和唱片在加拿大受到歡迎，但美國認為加拿大沒有及時更新著作權相關法規，跟不上技術發展，導致對著作權的保護不足。[131]以下就加拿大「競爭法」（Competition Act）內涵及實務案例說明與網路著作權的關係。

1. 加拿大「競爭法」

「競爭法」規範妨礙競爭秩序的不當行為，[132]高科技產業發達使電腦化應用及資源分配、資訊分享的管道多元化，對競爭法的需求更加迫切，以統轄解決經濟及商業層面的糾紛，使消費者在貨品的選購範圍及價格的穩定度更有保障，[133]本法立法目的為鼓勵加拿大境內的商業競爭行為，以促進其經濟發展，並能獲得加拿大立足國際社會與各國偕同參與更多經濟活動，確保中、小型企業於提供消費者貨物及維持價格穩定度上有其均等機會，主管機關為「競爭局」（the Competition Bureau），亦出版「智慧財產執行指南」（Intellectual Property Enforcement Guidelines），對競爭法與智慧財產相關爭議有模擬問題與詳盡解答，與有關此法的糾紛則由「競爭法庭」（the Competition Tribunal）管轄。[134]

維護著作權人，特別是對抗免費檔案下載及分享，形成全球化趨勢。[135]加拿大採取腳步及態度仍然有待觀望，加拿大競爭法第32條

---

[131] 連邦國際專利商標事務所。http://www.tsailee.com/_ch/_ipn/default01.asp?PKID=1306（最後瀏覽日2009/6/4）。

[132] R.S.C. 1985, c. C-34, as amended.其後有法案C-23提出並於2002/6/21執行。George S. Takach, *Computer Law*, 427-428, Irwin Law Inc. (2003).

[133] Sec.1.1 R.S.C. 1985.

[134] The Competition Tribunal Act, R.S.C. 1985, c. 19 (2d Supp).

[135] 音樂產業發起新一波訴訟案與起訴，以對抗整個歐洲檔案分享，其效力之一是遏止線上海盜行為以及鼓勵使用合法音樂服務。大約有2,000個案子在10個國家當中進行，這些數字並沒有包含美國，RIAA囊括大約18,000件官司。如葡萄牙其所販售之實體CD在過去四年內銷售量下滑40%，主要是因為嚴重檔案分享使用所致，尤其是大學

第1項對任何有關專利、商標、著作權或積體電路佈局法有關的智慧財產權法，給予其權利及利益完整的保障，惟應遵守不得：[136](1)不當限制運輸、製造、供應、儲存或交易任何物品、貨物構成買賣的相關事項；(2)不當對限制或侵害與交易有關的物品、貨物；(3)不當避免、限制、減少物品、貨物之製造、生產或無端不合理的提高價格；(4)不當避免、減少物品、貨物之製造、生產、買賣、運輸、供應之競爭行為。第32條第2項則針對前項行為規定，聯邦政府得於必要時頒發命令，如宣布該項智慧財產權無效，[137]此外，並需配合第3項遵守國際公約的各項規範。[138]

「智慧財產執行指南」中「競爭局」明確指出，對32條的解釋

生。IFPI法律訴訟並非只針對非法下載音樂個人，也包括「上傳者」，將具有版權之音樂放入檔案分享網路當中。IFPI表示，數位音樂的銷售量在2005年上揚，但不足以補償實體媒體格式，例如：CD持續下滑銷售量約為3%。音樂產業在歐洲發起更大規模的法律訴訟。http://www. nytimes.com/reuters/technology/tech-media-music-lawsuits.html（最後瀏覽日2006/ 4/15）。倫敦2005年4月12日報導，反制網路音樂檔案的最大一波法律行動在針對963個位在歐洲及亞洲11個國家中的個人所發起之新案件。由IFPI代表1450家以上唱片公司整合之新一波訴訟，所影響對象不僅止於Kazza網路（KaZaA, KazaaLite, iMesh），也包括eDonkey、eMule與各個Gnutella服務〔Bearshare、Limewire〕、OpenNap、WinMX及Winny、DirectConnect和BitTorrent等新檔案交換服務業者。IFPI更提出最新證據顯示反制行動已產生效果。德國在2004年音樂檔案下載數量銳減，從前一年6億2百萬減少35%而至3億8,200萬個檔案。2005年3月德國IFPI委託GFK機構針對10,000人所做調查結果。Kazaa曾是最大與最流行之檔案交換服務業者，自從採取包括訴訟和警告反制行動後，其用戶數量減少約45%（從4,200萬至2,300萬經常用戶）。2004年西班牙及瑞典音樂產業皆遭受盜版重創，銷售量分別下跌12.5%及18%，他們以即時通訊方式警告那些正在檔案分享服務網路上非法散布音樂的人。迄今已對美國以外12個國家之利用檔案分享服務的個人發出1,200萬則警告通知。音樂檔案交換者面臨迄今最大規模法律行動，許多人已經付出違法代價。http:// wwwifpi.org.tw/news/音樂交換法律行動新聞稿（最後瀏覽日2005/4/15）。

[136] R.S.C. 1985, c. C-34. s.32(1).

[137] Ibid., s.32(2).

[138] Ibid., s.32(3).

必須限縮且嚴格，執行要件除必須符合「競爭法」的規定外，尚需證明競爭利益受危害乃直接來自權益的被否決，[139]當事人行使其某項智慧財產權－如著作權、商標權、專利權、積體電路電路佈局權，因而排除他人之使用，然而此種排除不能侵害其他第三人的創作意願，[140]但依據32條提出的侵害請求伴隨高度的舉證責任，乃為維持創作人之創作動機，且智慧財產權法規所強調的專用權與競爭法排除壟斷、不公平競爭的精神，在其間尋求和諧，[141]無論是著作權、商標權、專利權、積體電路電路佈局權，或其他智財法規，加拿大議會從來無意使其成為反競爭法的一部分。

其他與智財法有關為1986年增訂第79條第5項，有關「獨占防止」（Abuse of Dominant Position）[142]的規定，智財法規若無其他因素不足以構成違反公平競爭，加拿大競爭局在權衡公平競爭政策及智慧財產權案例適用法規，尤其是限縮著作權法對著作權人的保障或是擴張以增加保護，二者之間的考量使競爭局未來立法或增修條文時有另一番省思空間。

---

[139] *See* Canada, Competition Bureau, Intellectual Property Enforcement Guidelines (Ottawa: Industry Canada, 2000), Competition Bureau <http://strategis.ic.gc.ca/pics/ ct/ipege.pdf> [IPEGs] at 9. *See* also Alex Cameron, Robert Tomkowicz, "*Competition Policy and Canada's New Breed of "Copyright" Law*," MCGILL L.J., 297 (2007).

[140] 也因此截至2007年9月為止，並無依據加拿大競爭法第32條所判定的實際案例。Ibid.

[141] See Canada, Competition Bureau, supra note, at 1.

[142] 關於Abuse of Dominant Position的解釋，本文亦參閱Groklaw, EU Ct. of 1st Instance: Microsoft Abused its Dominant Position – Updated (September 17, 2007). http://www.groklaw.net/articlebasic.php?story=20070917053717322 (last visited June7, 2009). Sanoussi Bilal & Marcelo Olarreaga, Regionalism, Competition Policy and Abuse of Dominant Position, European Institute of Public Administration (May, 1998). http://unpan1. un.org/intradoc/groups/public/documents/NISPAcee/UNPAN007414.pdf (last visited on date: 2009/7/7).

2. 案　例

1997年Canada v. Tele-Direct[143]及Canada v. Warner Music Canada[144]為加拿大有名案例，此二案例皆未因競爭法對之產生影響，當著作權人拒絕他人使用其權利，乃依據智財法行使專屬權，如著作權人單純行使其授權契約，並無其他「搭售」（Tied Selling）亦為非反競爭之行為，則與競爭法並未產生競合或衝突，[145]特別是網路著作權人深恐其作品被侵害，當然仰賴「權利管理電子資訊（DRM）系統」及「反規避條款」，如加重著作權法規對侵害行為的處罰，然而如此亦限縮發明者及創作者的創意空間，加拿大聯邦最高法院法官Justice Binnie 曾在判決書中強烈支持此項論點，[146]因而要在權利管理電子資訊系統、契約、反規避法規中找到平衡點，則需要「競爭局」審慎評估公平競爭政策與著作權間的和諧關係。

聯邦上訴法院於BMG Canada Inc. v. John Doe[147]案之判決結果引起舉世注目，加拿大錄音唱片工業協會（the Canadian Recording

---

[143] Canada (Director of Investigation and Research) v. Tele-Direct (Publications) (1997), 73 C.P.R. (3d) 1.

[144] Canada (Director of Investigation and Research) v. Warner Music Canada (1997), 78 C.P.R. (3d) 321.

[145] Canada (Director of Investigation & Research) v. Xerox Canada Inc. (1990), 33 C.P.R. (3d) 83, C.L.D. 1146. 1990年此案對其後判決影響深遠，被告販售多年影印機並提供零件、機器維修，原先由美國總公司先做的決定，再由加拿大公司採用—為對抗個別獨立的零售業供應商也為Xerox機器提供的服務（independent service organizations，簡稱ISOs），Xerox不願提供零件以鞏固本身的二手維修市場，本案主要與競爭法第75條有關（R.S.C., 1985, c. C-34, s.75.），最終判決認為Xerox違反競爭法規定，不能無端拒絕供應（refusal to supply）維修零件給其他零售業供應商，如此形成獨占。

[146] The'berge v. Galerie d'Art du Petit Champlain, 2002 SCC 34, [2002] 2 S.C.R. 336 at para. 32, 210 D.L.R. (4th) 385 [The'berge]. *CCH Canadian Ltd. v. Law Society of Upper Canada*, (2004) 1 S.C.R. 339, 2004 SCC 13, at para. 41-42.

[147] 2005 FCA 193, May, 19 (2005).此案自先前2004年時於32 C.P.R (4th) 64 (F.C.)上訴而來。

Industry Association，簡稱CRIA）引用聯邦法院規則第233條及第238條內容，希望法院對網路服務提供者下達命令，要求其公布特定侵害網路著作權使用者名單，然而原告之上訴亦告失敗，因為要求內容侵害規則第81條，亦以該項指控純為傳聞（Hearsay）而非正確證據來源，法院也不接受依據規則第238條檢驗方式，更正確的說法應指原告是否為實質惡意指控，遠比表面控訴的理由更為重要。

　　本案仍自著作權侵害觀點進行，以1985年著作權法規觀之（s.80(1) of the Copyright Act, R. S. 1985, c. C-42），下載為個人目的所使用之歌曲，並不至於構成著作權之侵害，無適用s.80(2)的可能，音樂製品乃為買賣、租賃、分配給大眾而使用之目的，若使用者未使用「音響錄音媒介」（Audio Recording Medium），則私人複製使用之抗辯則不存在，法院亦認為讓使用人經由網路，複製及下載他人音樂作品構成對著作權之侵害，使用人應知情此侵害行為構成間接侵害責任（Copyright Act, s. 27(2)）。

　　其他如Albian Sands Energy Inc. v. Positive Attitude Safety System Inc.[148]案有關著作權侵害及契約授權，聯邦上訴法院則認為原告著作權有效；Columbia Pictures Industries, Inc. v. Gaudreault[149]案，有關著作權侵害及違反無線通訊法（the Radio communications Act），被告涉嫌對違反刑責部分提出上訴，希冀避免因審判而造成不當花費及利益；[150]再如Eurosport Event Management Ltd. v. 650621 B.C. Ltd.[151]及1395047 Ontario Inc. v. New Atlantico Cafe and Restaurante Inc.[152]等案中，原告亦主張相同論點，即著作權侵害及違

---

[148] 2005 FCA 332.

[149] 2005 FC 338.

[150] 本案之前有前例Columbia Pictures Industries, Inc. v. Frankl, 2004 FC 1454.

[151] 2005 FC 1359.

[152] 2005 FC 1358.

反無線傳播通訊法，皆被聯邦法院駁回，原告必須證明確實擁有被告侵害之權利，然而本案未能確認原告所有權及媒體出現之原告名稱，並不代表原告合法權益，亦不符合著作權法（s.34.1(2)）相關規定。[153]

現今國際社會對著作權規範，多半依隨國際組織及公約，然而加拿大迄今仍未積極遵守，仍從其本身規範法令對國內案件進行審理，是否加入國際公約或更新法規內容，至今仍無明確決定，維護國際間經濟利益，創造著作權人更願意投注創作環境，已是各國之間共識，網路音樂、影片下載之便利性及普及性，呼應加強對網路著作權保障之重要性；加拿大著作權法規並未詳盡規劃，[154]和其他智慧財產權法規未必能完全配合，同時建議研究加拿大法規，應先著眼[155]其國家體制面，比較不會出現疑惑，如為何修法速度如此緩慢？發現加拿大智慧財產權法專業領域發展，仍未如其他商法、民事、刑事法規蓬勃發展，因此，著作權法仍有相當大發展空間，也許這也是政府部門考量，寧可慢慢觀望以確保品質。[156]

---

[153] 2005年7月9日在溫哥華另一個案子Raincoast Book Distribution Ltd. v. Loblaw Companies Ltd. (9 July, 2005), Vancouver SO53789 (B.C.S.C.). 法院發出禁制令，限制被告John及Jane Does 或其他代表被告之自然人，在取得J.K. Rowling （J.K.羅琳，英國有名的作者）所作哈利波特（Harry Potter）系列著作，在該書2005年7月16日正式出版前，不能複製或公開任何與該本著作（Harry Potter and the Half-Blood Prince）有關之內容或資訊題材，而此禁制令乃來自於在正式出版日前，已銷售15本書而起，因而要求購買或影印人須返還或交回，避免影響正式銷售日的銷售數量。

[154] See David Vaver, Copyright Law, 292, Irwin Law Inc. (2000).

[155] 加拿大十分重視環保，而先民多來自歐洲，因此表面祥和平靜，實則有其自行認定步驟與系統，以往多以為北美地區－美國、加拿大為兄弟之邦，然而兩國關係友好，卻未必承襲相同體系傳統，加國著作權法一直未見更新，乃因其本國自身考量，加上加國訴訟案件，系爭金額並不大，若考量訴訟成本、律師費用，不見得會願意興訟，此乃本文作者個人見解，僅供參考。

[156] 若從此處考量，加國智慧財產權學者或業者實在比我國動輒修法輕鬆許多。

五、中國大陸現狀

　　1993年9月2日中國大陸開始實施反不正當競爭法，[157]其他有關經濟壟斷及限制競爭行為，則自97年8月1日施行維護自由競爭的反壟斷法，[158]反壟斷法第55條規定，經營者依照有關知識產權的法律、行政法規規定行使知識產權的行為，不適用本法；但是，經營者濫用知識產權，排除、限制競爭的行為，適用本法。以下說明反不正當競爭法前，先一窺目前中國大陸知識產權案件及分類件數。

　　最高人民法院於2008年12月10公布[159]日召開的全國法院「司法護權、激勵創新」加強知識產權司法保護行動月總結新聞發佈會，地方各級法院集中宣判了962件知識產權案件，其中包括專利案件179件、商標案件243件、著作權案件444件、反不正當競爭案件38件、知識產權合同案件21件，其他案件37件。[160]從上述數據得知中國大陸知識產權案件以著作權案件為大宗。

---

[157] 經第8屆人大常委會第3次會議通過，自1993年12月1日起施行。

[158] 2007年8月30日第10屆全國人大常委會通過，同日公布，自2008年8月1日起施行。反壟斷法不反對知識產權的權利人依照知識產權的法律獲得和行使知識產權，在保護知識產權的同時，還須防止和制止濫用知識產權排除、限制競爭的行為，以維護競爭和保護消費者利益。李有軍 劉曉林，「反壟斷法 今起實施 不會影響企業做大做強」，新華網人民日報海外版，發表日期：2008/8/1。
http://big5.xinhuanet.com/gate/big5/news.xinhuanet.com/fortune/2008-08/01/content_8885737.htm（最後瀏覽日2009/6/20）。

[159] 最高人民法院於2008年12月10日召開全國法院"司法護權、激勵創新"加強知識產權司法保護行動月總結新聞發佈會。

[160] 行動月期間，地方各級法院公開開庭審理知識產權案件1,352件，邀請人大代表857人、政協委員598人以及其他社會公眾7,321人旁聽了庭審，舉辦有關座談會110餘次，參加座談會的人數達2,300餘人。「公開開庭，接受群眾監督；召開代表性人士座談會，徵求對加強知識產權審判工作的意見，這些都是人民法院提高知識產權審判水準的重要途徑。」最高人民法院知識產權庭副庭長孔祥俊在新聞發佈會上說，人民法院知識產權審判工作的健康發展和審判水準的不斷提高，不僅需要社會各界的關心、支援和幫助，也需要社會各界給予監督、提出批評和建議，需要真切認識和理解人民群眾對知識產權保護的新要求和新期待並最大限度地予以滿足。楊維漢，全國法

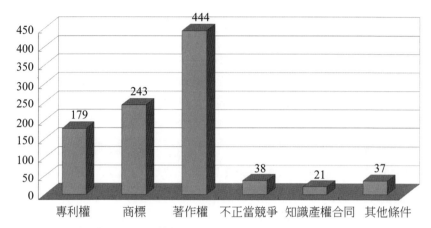

資料來源：PPAC中國專利保護協會，袁定波、張亮（編譯），http://www.ppac. org. cn/lcontent.asp?c=15&id=3680，最後瀏覽日：2009/2/8。

圖3-1　2008年中國大陸知識產權案件曲線圖

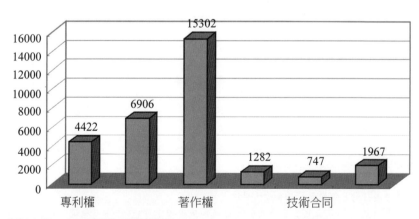

資料來源：中國保護知識產權網，http://www.ipr.gov.cn/xwdt/gnxw/bw/615488. shtml，最後瀏覽日：2010/3/11。

圖3-2　2009年中國大陸知識產權案件曲線圖

院集中宣判近千件知識產權案件。http://www.ppac.org.cn/lcontent.asp?c=15&id=3680 （最後瀏覽日2009/2/12）。

　　抄襲、仿冒和篡改他人的網路作品，擴充自己的經營內容與同業
對手進行競爭，網路登入和傳輸信息量的多寡，網路統纜各類資訊的
多少、網路發布的資訊的品種、質量等，都是一個網站與同類網站爭
取網民的重要原因。有的網路服務商雖然取得上述效應而躍躍一試，
但又不願支付合理的費用，在未經作品權利人同意之下，便擅自將他
人在網下或網上的作品上載或移轉到其網上，予以登載和傳輸；還有
的將所開設的公告欄作為其招攬網民的途徑，任人上載作品，即使明
知所刊登的作品是抄襲之作，也不加以干涉，任其泛濫。[161]

　　禁止不正當競爭行為，是反不正當競爭法的基本內容。各國認
定的不正當競爭行為範圍寬窄不一，對不正當競爭主體在立法形式上
處理也各有特色。中國大陸「反不正當競爭法」從中國經濟的實際需
要出發，注重規制實行經濟生活中亟需加以約束的不正當競爭行為，
將目前不十分突出的典型的經濟壟斷和限制競爭行為留待獨立的反壟
斷法制理。[162]最高人民法院21日通過中國法院網公布2008年中國知識
產權司法保護10大案件和2008年中國知識產權司法保護50件典型案
件，[163]2008年中國知識產權司法保護50件典型案件中包括45件知識產

---

[161] 楊鈞，「論網路經營活動與制止不正當競爭侵害」，兩岸智慧財產權保護與運用，頁
　　309，台北，元照出版有限公司，2002年。

[162] 費安玲、郭禾、張今，「知識產權法學原理」，頁275，北京市，中國政法大學出版
　　社，1999。

[163] 此為最高人民法院開展2009年「知識產權宣傳周」活動期間的內容安排之一。50件典
　　型案件中包括45件知識產權民事案件，5件知識產權行政案件。知識產權民事案件中
　　有專利侵權案件10件、著作權侵權案件15件、商標侵權案件8件、植物新品種侵權案
　　件2件、不正當競爭案件8件、知識產權合同案件2件。知識產權行政案件包括，4件專
　　利商標授權確權案件，1件一般知識產權行政案件。最高法院公布2008年中國知識產
　　權司法保護10大案件和50件典型案件，發表日期：2009年4月22日，中華人民共和國
　　國家知識產權局。
　　http://big5.sipo.gov.cn/www/sipo2008/yw/2009/200904/t20090422_455625.html（最後瀏
　　覽日2009/6/21）。

權民事案件，不正當競爭案件8件。

反不正當競爭法保障現有知識財產權法保護不及的創作結果和識別性標誌，制止超出專項立法保護範圍的不正當競爭行為，制裁前述侵權行為以維護市場經濟秩序，是違反不正當競爭法的任務之一。在市場經濟活動各個環節中，不正當競爭行為無處不在，不正當價格行為，巨額獎項銷售行為，欺騙性廣告宣傳行為等等，表現形式日益複雜多樣，為了適應市場經濟的需要，反不正當競爭法的調整範圍擴大到知識產權以外的領域，中國大陸反不正當競爭法有規範市場、維護公平競爭的主要目的。[164]

2009年第1季中國大陸全國工商機關競爭執法機構大力推進創新工作，並以反不正當競爭作為執法重點。反限制競爭執法工作取得新進展。今年第一季度共查處限制競爭案件76件，比上年同期減少26件，下降25.49%。中國各地工商機關競爭執法機構認真落實「反壟斷法」和反壟斷執法職能，對重點行業市場競爭狀況進行調查研究，大力開展反壟斷執法培訓活動，加強反壟斷宣傳教育；繼續依據「反不正當競爭法」的規定，查處公用企業和依法具有獨占地位的經營者限制競爭行為，以及地方政府及其所屬部門濫用行政權力排除，限制競爭行為等違法案件。[165]

---

[164] 正如世界知識組織編寫的知識財產權教材中所指出，通過限制不誠實經營行為，反不正當競爭法不能提供保護的情況下提供保護。費安玲、郭禾、張今，「知識產權法學原理」，頁280，北京市，中國政法大學出版社，1999。

[165] 國家工商總局今年第一季度共查處反不正當競爭案件4,944件，比上年同期增加302件，增長6.51%。實現監管領域由低端向高端延伸，堅持把反不正當競爭執法放在突出位置，深入調查研究，採取有力措施，實現重點突破；圍繞群眾反映強烈的熱點，難點問題，加大反不正當競爭案件查處力度；繼續深入開展打擊"傍名牌"執法行動，對假冒，仿冒等違法行為進行集中整治，加強指導和考核，進一步明確職責，提升反不正當競爭執法辦案水平。童紀，「全國工商機關今年第一季度競爭執法工作取得新成績」，發表日期：2009/5/13。http://www.cicn.com.cn/ docroot/200905/13/kw05/13010104.htm（最後瀏覽日2009/6/1）。

肆、我國著作權保護現況暨結論

　　以下圖表乃針對2008年我國智慧財產權法院，(1)民事類案件數及百分比，(2)行政類案件數及百分比，(3)民事賠償金額；觀察目前我國實務發展現況得知，雖然著作權案件數及賠償金額遠低於專利權案件數及賠償金額，公平交易法案件賠償金額則僅次於專利權案件，然而為防免未來網路及電腦使用造成更多糾紛，圖表的數據鋪陳後本文將提出對我國的立法建議。

一、比較圖表

智慧財產權法院民事類案件				
	裁定	判決	著作權	專利權	商標
相關案件數	68	25	10	76	7
百分比	73.12%	26.88%	10.75%	81.72%	7.53%

資料來源：PPAC中國專利保護協會，袁定波、張亮（編譯），http://www. ppac.org. cn/lcontent.asp?c=15&id=3680，最後瀏覽日：2009/2/8。

圖3-3　2008年我國智慧財產權法院民事類案件比例圖

　　根據圖3-3再細分民事類案件中著作權及公平交易法案件曲線圖。

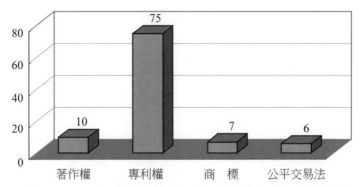

圖3-4　2008年我國智慧財產權法院民事類案件曲線圖

智慧財產權法院民事類案件					
	裁定	判決	著作權	專利權	商標	公平交易法
案件數	156	268	84	263	70	7
百分比	36.79%	63.21%	19.81%	62.03%	16.51%	1.65%

資料來源：法源法律網，各式業務統計，http://www.lawbank.com.tw/index.php，最後瀏覽日：2010/3/1。

圖3-5　2009年我國智慧財產權法院民事類案件比例圖

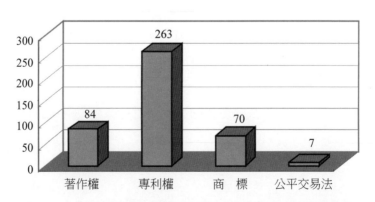

圖3-6　2009年我國智慧財產權法院民事類案件曲線圖

　　亦針對2008年我國智慧財產權法院行政類案件之分配比例做一說明，可以發現專利案件仍為最多，其次為商標案件，著作權及公平交易法案件仍以民事案件提起，因為未如專利和商標須做申請及登記等法定程序，因而會產生需要公部門做出評定等情事，或是權利人對註冊程序不滿產生爭議。

智慧財產權法院行政類案件							
	裁　定	判　決	商標異議	商標註冊	商標評定	發明專利	新型專利
相關案件數	106	52	33	16	17	28	64
百　分　比	67.09%	32.91%	20.89%	10.13%	10.76%	17.72%	40.51%

資料來源：法源法律網，各式業務統計，http://www.lawbank.com.tw/index.php，最後瀏覽日：2009/2/8。

圖3-7　2008年我國智慧財產權法院行政類案件比例圖

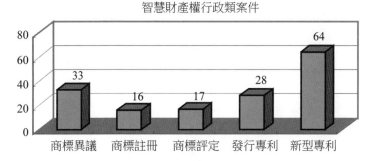

圖3-8　2008年我國智慧財產權法院行政類案件曲線圖

智慧財產權法院行政類案件							
	裁　定	判　決	商標 異議	商標 註冊	商標 評定	發明 專利	新型 專利
案件數	175	359	138	120	65	68	143
百分比	32.77%	67.23%	25.84%	22.47%	12.17%	12.73%	26.78%

資料來源：法源法律網，各式業務統計，http://www.lawbank.com.tw/index.php，最後瀏覽日：2010/3/11。

圖3-9　2009年我國智慧財產權法院行政類案件比例圖

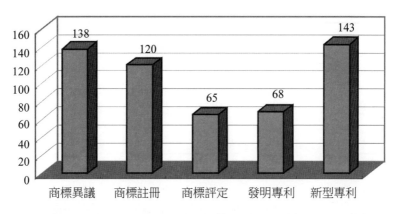

圖3-10　2009年我國智慧財產權法院行政類案件曲線圖

以下為民事賠償金額。

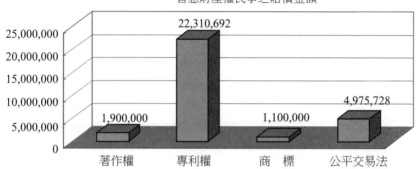

智慧財產權民事之賠償金額

資料來源：法源法律網，各式業務統計，http://www.lawbank.com.tw/index.php，最後瀏覽日：2009/2/8。

圖3-11　2008年我國智慧財產權民事賠償金額曲線圖

二、結　論

　　立法院[166]通過著作權法部分條文修正案增訂所謂「三振條款」，網路使用者只要三次被認定侵權就會被停權，目前實務上往往使用者會更換帳號，就可以躲過被停權。但經濟部智慧財產局指出，修法是為謀求權利人、ISP、使用者三贏的局面，相信目前網路著作權的侵權問題會有顯著改善。現行著作權法第3條第1項並沒有明確規範網路服務提供者的定義，修正案通過之後，才增訂了網路服務提供者，

---

[166] 也就是只要網路使用者如果遭3次認定侵權，網路服務提供者就可以將使用者停權。修正案中也增訂「避風港條款」，網路業者只要對使用者侵權行為盡到告知義務，就可以避免連帶法律責任。網路侵權 3 次可終止服務！立院三讀通過（2009月4月22日），法源法律網。http://www.lawbank.com.tw/fnews/news. php?keyword=&sdate=&edate=&type_id=1&total=18212&nid=69331.00&seq=317（最後瀏覽日2009/6/19）。

包含連線服務提供、快速存取服務提供、資訊儲存服務提供者以及搜
尋服務提供。

　　於網路環境中賦予網路服務提供者「責任避風港」，一方面使
著作權人或製版權人得以依法要求網路服務提供者移除網路流通之侵
權資料，而另一方面網路服務提供者亦可依法針對使用者涉有侵害著
作權及製版權之行為，[167]主張不負損害賠償責任。著作權法的更新因
應網路環境並觸及公平競爭政策等議題，在前述Yahoo奇摩再併購無
名小站一例，是否二者一旦結合將形成市場壟斷，造成市場不公平競
爭，或是網路主導權已從網路經營者回到網友手中，二者的合併提供
給網友更好的服務與選擇，[168]公平會最終仍核准此合併案。[169]

---

[167] 參照著作權法部分條文修正草案總說明可知，被稱為「ISP法案」主要因為網路侵權
氾濫，為劃清責任界線，規範業者只要遵守「通知／取下」（Notice & Take Down）
的原則，就可以免除民事賠償責任。

[168] Yahoo！奇摩網站到達率達98%，佔台灣整體網路廣告市場達五成以上，是全台灣最
大的入口網站。目前台灣最知名的社群網站為無名小站，有近3,000,000名的會員。
2006年網路拍賣市集要向商家及賣家收取商品交易手續費，就引來賣家串連抗議，
也曾經向公平會提出申訴。但公平會最後判決並未違反公平法。何英煒，「雅虎
奇摩併購無名小站網路業聯手反制」，工商時報，2007年1月23日。http://blog.yam.
com/jlth0325/article/16860505（最後瀏覽日2009/6/1）。競爭對手網絡數碼（Webs-TV.
com）執行長陳銘堯表示堅決反對Yahoo奇摩再併購無名小站，因為這將助長「大者
恆大」的不公平局面，若公平會同意此結合案，等於同意其擁有台灣十大網站80%瀏
覽網頁數的絕對市場地位。不僅讓台灣網路使用者幾乎被Yahoo！奇摩所主宰，無名
小站使用國家學術資源創站卻賣給近乎市場獨占業者的行為也形成不當示範。他依
據創市際2006年11月統計指出，無名小站每月總瀏覽網頁數高達1947177130頁，佔
台灣前十大網站總瀏覽頁數的17%；Yahoo奇摩則佔63%，約7009980300頁。結合後
兩家公司每月總瀏覽網頁數將接近90億頁，占台灣前10大網站總瀏覽頁數的80%。
姚詠馨，「Yahoo併無名是否壟斷公平會：依法行事」，2007年1月23日。http://www.
wretch.cc/blog/leekming/10369326（最後瀏覽日 2009/6/1）。

[169] 公平會認為，瀏覽網頁數與業者提供網頁數量與內容高度相關，代表網站聚集潛在消
費者數目多寡，這是廣告代理商或廣告主對該網站的評價重點。但實際的價值，仍
須透過交易來實現。無名小站雖然匯集眾多網友，但廣告收入仍有限，因此市占率不
高。以當前網站經營模式，網站經營者多透過提供各項免費服務、資訊，吸引使用者

2009年Yahoo 4月27日公布終止部分9項服務，[170]無名小站未先徵求會員同意或舉行內部會員公開意見調查與投票，主要影響付費會員。但後因輿論力量無名小站於6月3日恢復網誌備份的功能。在在說明網路使用者與當今政策的息息相關，本文探討的公平競爭與網路著作權有別於以往傳統法學的更迭速度，由使用者（廣大網民）的使用習慣與偏好可以影響立法，因為網路不受地域及時間的限制，各國之間互通聲息頻率快速，從著作權人嘗試以科技保護措施規範防止網路濫用藉以避免侵害行為，並發展防盜拷技術運用，藉此防範使用人未取得授權蓄意侵害著作權，破壞TPMs系統進而分配著作的行為，與網路公司單方採取停止服務的舉動，再經由消費者反撲又恢復服務的例子觀察，確實是實務引領政策與立法。

三、網站、使用人、系統服務提供者之間能架設互相溝通的平台

網站、使用人、系統服務提供者摒棄私益為整體創作環境考量，才會打造使用人、著作權人雙贏的局面，亦即使彼此間脫離敵對立場，同心使整體文化提昇，技術共享，嘉惠社會大眾的利益面出

前往網站駐足瀏覽，聚集大量的潛在消費者，吸引廣告代理商或廣告主青睞來獲取廣告收益。時報資訊，「Yahoo！奇摩與無名小站結合准了」，2007年3月30日。http://tw.stock.yahoo.com/news_content/url/ d/a/070330/3/cyls.html（最後瀏覽日2009/6/1）。

[170] 無名小站欲停止的服務有：(1)PK擂台服務，(2)哈啦討論區，(3)網誌備份XML下載，(4)網誌投票功能，(5)Mypage，(6)中華電信MMS上傳照片網誌服務，(7)NOKIA上傳電信服務，(8)發表網誌文章時可以塞入整張電子地圖（即地圖出現功能），(9)網誌邊欄「我的訂閱」功能。無名小站宣佈5/26起將停止部份網路服務及網誌功能，其中包括網誌備份、RSS「我的訂閱」等，網友應注意5月底前先完成內容備份、移轉。蘇文彬，「無名小站5月底將停止網誌備份等多項功能」，2009年5月11日。http://www.ithome.com.tw/itadm/ article.php?c=54939（最後瀏覽日2009/6/27）。

發，才是最佳對策。網路跨國界、跨地域使用的特色，使用人享受免費或低廉的服務時，亦應維護安全與合理的使用秩序與空間。智慧財產權法的領域保障人類智慧結晶及研發成果，以促進社會整體經濟並提升文化（如著作權法）、產業競爭力（如專利法）、產品標示度（如商標法）、競爭秩序（如營業秘密法），從維護創作發明人的小我出發，進而建立人類群體的大我利益。

四、簽訂多方契約

　　要使參與整體運作的每一方都能得到滿意的結果，並不容易，首先必須符合公平性及穩定度兼具、並為各方謀求最大利益，包括終端使用人的福祉、程式設計者及寬頻服務提供業者之間的折衝，但重點在於若有一方或各方乃以追求自身投資的最佳獲益為出發點，枉顧他人的投資心血，那類似Sprint Nextel及Cogent Communications的案例仍會發生，亦使如此的策略性行為與計畫毀於一旦。[171]以下建議乃基於我國現狀及美加經驗而提出的綜合看法，建立新的合作模式也許可以使合作的平台更加圓滿。

　　使各方－終端使用人、程式設計者及寬頻服務提供業者基於互助合作的精神，制定多方契約。沒有任何一家公司或企業能獨立擁有規範網路活動的核心準則，在莫衷一是的自由貿易體系裡，尤其是網路活動的跨地域、跨產業、無時間限制（特別是網路商店，不像實體店面有一定的營業時間）的特性，誠如網際網路工程特別工作小組（the Internet Engineering Task Force, IETF）[172]是一個開放的組織，規範如個人電腦及網路工作者在管理工具（TCP/IP protocol）的準

---

[171] Weiser, P.J, *The Future of Internet Regulation.* U.C. DAVIS L. REV. 43, 538 (2009).

[172] Internet Engineering Task Force, Wikipedia, the free encyclopedia. http://en. wikipedia.org/wiki/Internet_Engineering_Task_Force (last visited: 2/15/2010).

則，幕後雖受到美國安全局的贊助，但仍是一個被普羅大眾所能接受的私人組織，也是目前在國際社會中被普遍認同的標準，存在於當今高度商業化下的網路環境，寬頻服務提供業者在產品升級與提昇管理的層面上，兼顧傳統的網路生態與其他業者的合作誠屬不易，對終端使用人、程式設計者而言，能對寬頻表現及其服務產生信任感是很重要的事，避免如上述案件而產生的不安定感。

　　寬頻服務的平台提供者盡力使其平台更有經濟價值，線上影音愈盛行使有線數據機的需求更加興盛，[173]網路直接促進了數據機的銷量。在衡量是否有造成公司斷線的危機再度發生的可能性時，程式設計人如BitTorrent，能不能信任寬頻平台服務提供者如Comcast，是一個很大的疑問，姑且不問平台服務提供者是否能避免程式設計人與其的競爭，程式設計人更應憂慮當程式被成功的運用後，平台服務提供者會切斷與程式設計人的關係，如減少支付給程式設計人的酬金、設計費、月租金或其它對價，相對地，程式設計人也會降低設計的誘因，放慢更新程式的速度或以折騰人的策略迴避平台服務提供者，平台服務提供者將遭遇程式提供不穩定的資料傳送（Quality of Service, QoS）[174]結果，如此惡性循環下，減損整體表現的品質與商業競爭力，實在不是眾所樂見的結果。

---

[173] 此段敘述來自Comcast的總裁Brian Roberts在受訪時的回答。*See* Vishesh Kumar, *Comcast Reports Strong Results in Web Services*, Wall St. J., July 31, 2008, at B8.

[174] Quality of Service (QoS) 乃是提供穩定、可預測的資料傳送服務，來滿足使用程式的需求。QoS並不能產生新的頻寬，而是依據應用程式的需求以及網路管理的設定來有效的管理網路頻寬。一般的Traffic Shaping, Queuing, Policy Management 或是Caching的產品，或許能夠增加網路的效能，但卻不能保證重要網路應用的穩定運作及反應速度（Consistent response time）。QoS則能夠將既有的頻寬資源作最佳化的調整，相關機制的完整應用，對網路上的交通做到真正完全的控管。宜蘭縣教育局，「新世代骨幹網路」。http://nmc.ilc.edu.tw/ page3.htm#4（最後瀏覽日2010/2/18）。

五、維繫交易秩序與和諧競爭

　　依據學者（Weiser, 2009: 561-584）建議將提供三階段策略供網路著作權管理者參考，以解決寬頻提供者與網路樞紐連線[175]業者的爭端與疑義，首先FCC可以扮演成企業家準則的角色，制定各個公司或企業間遵奉的規定與標竿，同時將通用的用語與準則一致化；其次，FCC可以透過私人的團體管理方式運作，統籌成共同管理暨管制的集體合作模式；最後，不採用預先規範而採用事後繳納授權金的方式，並以私人管理的形式達成各個企業間的合作。如此，可以預見在未來會使網際網路的運用與活絡更上層樓，使用的彈性與限度也會更加寬廣。

　　本文雖提供智財案件的數據及曲線圖，然而實際案件絕不僅於此，因為著作權涉及公平競爭或反壟斷的案件，有可能因為怕影響著作權人（如發行公司）的聲譽，毀壞其市場佔有率因而私下和解，也有可能在當事人怠於提出訴訟的情形下不了了之，這一切現象不代表著作權間接侵害理論與公平競爭秩序間的例子不多，相反地，目前一般大眾使用點對點傳播使用網路的情形普遍，影音、影片上傳及下載成為日常生活的循環——即生活的一部分，更甚者造成使用氾濫；[176]網路廠商競爭激烈的情況下，使用者的滿意度會影響其繼續使用的意願，因此提供更貼心好用的服務才能留得住使用者，[177]亦即在著作權

---

[175] Vanberg, M.A. (2003). Internet Interconnection: Market Power in the Backbone Industry? ZEW (Centre for European Economic Research), Mannheim, March 2003. http://userpage.fu-berlin.de/~jmueller/its/conf/helsinki03/abstracts/Vanberg.pdf (last visited: 2/6/2010). Also see Backbone network, From Wikipedia, the free encyclopedia. http://en.wikipedia.org/wiki/Backbone_network (last visited: 2/6/2010).

[176] 在作者任教及演講的機會中，發現莘莘學子習慣下載影片或音樂，不全然為欣賞目的，更甚者乃收藏或供他人借閱等情形，且下載數量之龐大有時十分驚人。

[177] 台灣消費者沒理由再對權益損傷沉默，知名社群網站無名小站曾在今年5月底宣布終

人、網路業者及消費者間，維繫交易秩序與和諧競爭上亦有異曲同工
之妙，並兼論美國、加拿大、中國大陸和我國在法規、實務面上的種
種規範，希冀為未來二者間的配合或競合有所建議。

參考文獻

中文部分

1. 書　籍

曲三強，「知識產權法原理」，北京市，中國檢察出版社，2004。

汪渡村，「公平交易法」，台北市，五南圖書出版有限公司，
　　2007。

陳家駿、羅怡德，「公平交易法與智慧財產權」，台北市，五南圖書
　　出版有限公司，1999。

陳櫻琴，「科技產業的第五元素－競爭法的建構與解讀」，台北市，
　　瀚蘆圖書出版有限公司，2005。

費安玲、郭禾、張今，「知識產權法學原理」，北京市，中國政法大
　　學出版社，1999。

馮震宇，「智慧財產權發展趨勢與重要問題研究」，台北市，元照出
　　版有限公司，2003。

止備份網誌功能，引發網友出走潮，之後無名小站收回這項決定。儘管無名小站對外
表示會員數成長率依舊維持每個月3%～5%的水準，不過無名小站為了鞏固市場地
位，特別祭出了「大赦條款」，不再對超過180天未登入的使用者強制刪除帳號，中
國時報。台灣消費者沒理由再對權益損傷沉默，A21／時論廣場，2009年7月15日。
http://tol.chinatimes.com/CT_NS/CTContent.aspx? nsrc=B&ndate=20090715&nfno=N0129
.001&nsno=1&nkeyword=%b5L%a6W%a4p%af%b8&SearchArgs=Keyword%3d%b5L%a
6W%a4p%af%b8%26Attr%3d%26Src%3d7%26DateFrom%3d20090620%26DateTo%3d2
0090719%26ShowStyle%3d2%26PageNo%3d1%26ItemsPerPage%3d10&App=NS（最後
瀏覽日2009/7/20）。

楊鈞，「論網路經營活動與制止不正當競爭侵害」，兩岸智慧財產權保護與運用，台北市，元照出版有限公司，2002。

謝銘洋，「智慧財產權法之基礎理論」，台北市，翰蘆圖書出版有限公司，1995。

2. 期刊論文

曾勝珍，著作權侵害罰則之探討－以美國電子千禧著作權法為主，法令月刊，第58卷第3期，頁106-126，2007。

3. 其　他

李有軍　劉曉林，「反壟斷法今起實施不會影響企業做大做強」，新華網人民日報海外版，發表日期：2008/8/1。http://big5.xinhuanet.com/gate/big5/news.xinhuanet.com/fortune/2008-08/01/content_8885737.htm（最後瀏覽日2009/6/20）。

何英煒，「雅虎奇摩併購無名小站 網路業聯手反制」，工商時報，2007/1/23。http://blog.yam.com/jlth0325/article/16860505（最後瀏覽日2009/6/1）。

法源法律網，各式業務統計。http://www.lawbank.com.tw/ index.php（最後瀏覽日2009/2/8）。

宜蘭縣教育局，「新世代骨幹網路」。http://nmc.ilc.edu.tw/ page3.htm#4（最後瀏覽日2010/2/18）。

袁定波、張亮（編譯），PPAC中國專利保護協會。http://www.ppac.org.cn/lcontent.asp?c=15&id=3680（最後瀏覽日2009/2/8）。

姚詠馨，「Yahoo併無名是否壟斷公平會：依法行事」，2007/1/23。http://www.wretch.cc/blog/leekming/10369326（最後瀏覽日2009/6/1）。

連邦國際專利商標事務所。http://www.tsailee.com/_ch/_ipn/default01.asp?PKID=1306（最後瀏覽日2009/6/4）。

章忠信，「智慧財產權基本概念」，2000/2/18發表，2003/2/19最後更新。http://www.copyrightnote.org/crnote/bbs.php?board=

1&act=read&id=37（最後瀏覽日2009/2/12）。

陳柏誠、曾慧雯，「301觀察名單　我獲除名」，自由時報電子報。
http://www.libertytimes.com.tw/2009/new/may/2/today-e4.htm
（最後瀏覽日2009/6/4）。

童紀，「全國工商機關今年第一季度競爭執法工作取得新成績」，
發表日期：2009/5/13。http://www.cicn.com.cn/docroot/
200905/13/kw05/13010104.htm（最後瀏覽日2009/6/1）。

經濟部智慧財產局，「著作權法網路服務提供者ISP民事免責事由
修正條文Q&A」。http://www.tipo.gov.tw/ch/Art Html_Show.
aspx?ID=59ef8638-4393-4560-82b3-9729cba61dff& path=3334
（最後瀏覽日2009/6/5）。

蘇文彬，「無名小站5月底將停止網誌備份等多項功能」，
2009/5/11。http://www.ithome.com.tw/itadm/article.php?c=54939
（最後瀏覽日2009/6/2）

外文部分

1. 書　籍

BRUCE M. GREEN, INTELLECTUAL PROPERTY LAW
(COPYRIGHT), ANNUAL REVIEW OF LAW & PRACTICE,
327-328, THE CONTINUING LEGAL EDUCATION SOCIETY
OF BRITISH COLUMBIA (2006).

CHARLES R. MCMANIS, INTELLECTUAL PROPERTY AND
UNFAIR COMPETITION, 29-30, WEST PUBLISHING CO.
(2004).

DAVID VAVER, COPYRIGHT LAW, 292, IRWIN LAW INC. (2000).

2. 期刊論文

C. Hoofnagle, Digital Rights Management: *MANY TECHNICAL*

CONTROLS ON DIGITAL CONTENT DISTRIBUTION CAN CREATE A SURVEILLANCE SOCIETY, COLUM. SCI. & TECH. L. REV. 5, 3 (2004).

Elliot M. Zimmerman, *P2P FILE SHARING: DIRECT AND INDIRECT COPYRIGHT INFRINGEMENT*, FLA. B.J.40, 41 (MAY 2004).

Elizabeth Miles, *NOTE, IN RE AIMSTER & MGM, INC. V. GROKSTER*, LTD.: PEER-TO-PEER AND THE SONY DOCTRINE, 19 BERKELEY TECH. L.J. 21, 25 (2004).

F. von Lohmann, *DON'T SUE THE CUSTOMER*, IP LAW AND BUSINESS (2004).

Howard P. Knopf, *CANADIAN COPYRIGHT COLLECTIVES AND THE COPYRIGHT BOARD: A SNAPSHOT IN 2008*, INTELL. PROP. J. 119 (2008).

Jesse M. Feder, *IS BETAMAX OBSOLETE?: SONY CORP. OF AMERICA V. UNIVERSAL CITY STUDIOS, INC. IN THE AGE OF NAPSTER*, 37 CREIGHTON L. REV. 859, 864-65 (2004).

Matthew Rimmer, *HAIL TO THE THIEF: A TRIBUTE TO KAZAA*, 2. U. OTTAWA L. & TECH. J. 173 (2005).

Molly Shaffer Van Houweling, *THE NEW SERVITUDES*, 90 GEO.L.J. 889 (2008).

Obert R. Trumble, Bradley S. Butterfield, Kevin J. Mason and Joseph B. Payne, *HUMAN RESOURCES AND INTELLECTUAL PROPERTY IN A GLOBAL OUTSOURCING ENVIRONMENT*, 15-WINTER INT'L HR J. 2-3 (2006).

Rebekah O'Hara, *YOU SAY YOU WANT A REVOLUTION: MUSIC & TECHNOLOGY-EVOLUTION OR DESTRUCTION?*, 39 GONZ. L. REV. 247, 288 (2004).

Robert P. Latham, Carl C. Butzer, Jeremy T. Brown, *LEGAL*

IMPLICATIONS OF USER-GENERATED CONTENT: YOUTUBE, MYSPACE, FACEBOOK, 20 NO.5 INTELL. PROP. & TECH. L.J. 1, MAY (2008).

Seth. A. Miller, *P2P FILE DISTRIBUTION: AN ANALYSIS OF DESIGN, LIABILITY, LITIGATION, AND POTENTIAL SOLUTIONS*, 25 REV. LITIG. 183 (2006).

Tim Wu, *WHEN CODE ISN'T LAW*, 89 VA. L. REV. 679, 726-36 (2003).

3. 其　他

D. McCullagh, *P2P's little secret*, CNET News.Com (2003).

Eweek Staff, *Analysts Predict Swellong of DRM Use*, eWeek. com (2004).

第四章 美國經濟間諜法施行成效之探討

曾勝珍

■摘要 SUMMARY

　　電腦、網路興盛及使用的速度，使美國國家安全與營業秘密維護，結合科技成為一體兩面的關係，基此，美國於1996年制定公布經濟間諜法（the Economic Espionage Act of 1996, EEA），EEA是規範侵害營業祕密及從事商業間諜行為的聯邦法，特別針對由外國政府或機構在幕後支持，竊取美國研發科技或政府資訊的經濟間諜活動；EEA施行至今是否達成當時立法之施行成效，即維持在全球市場上的美國經濟競爭力，避免營業秘密被不當的剽竊或破壞，且有效防制外國經濟間諜行動，因而本文將先説明當時EEA之立法背景，其次，介紹美國規範經濟間諜及營業秘密之相關法規；再論述EEA施行後所面對之難題，如外國經濟間諜所造成的威脅，美國公司防止經濟間諜的步驟太慢，法律規範需要保障新的知識領域，因此EEA規範是否有不足之處；最後探討是否有制定美國聯邦營業秘密法之必要性，希冀本研究對營業秘密保護及經濟間諜等主題能提供若干新思維。

關鍵詞

■ 營業秘密 ■ 智慧財產權 ■ 保密契約
■ 經濟間諜 ■ 網際網路

壹、前　言

電腦、網路興盛及使用的速度，使美國國家安全與營業秘密維護，與科技結合為一體兩面的關係，基此，美國於1996年制定公布經濟間諜法（the Economic Espionage Act of 1996, EEA）[1]後，EEA是規範侵害營業秘密及從事商業間諜行為的聯邦法，特別針對由外國政府或機構在幕後支持，竊取美國研發科技或政府資訊的經濟間諜活動；美國聯邦調查局（FBI）顯示自2001年至2007年，以中國大陸在美國從事經濟間諜的數目為例，由150個增加到350個[2]，亦有數據顯示中國經濟間諜自2001年起以逐年10%的數據成長[3]。

時至2009年9月，美國官方亦公布北韓政府在7月4日起之美國連續假期期間，展開對美國政府及民間網路的一連串攻擊活動，包括駭客入侵網站[4]及眾多商業間諜藉助科技工具的力量，監看競爭廠商客

---

[1]　18 U.S.C. §1831-§1839.

[2]　Jonathan Eric Lewis, *The Economic Espionage Act and the Threat of Chinese Espionage in the United States*, 8 Chi.-Kent J. Intell. Prop. 192 (Spring, 2009).

[3]　Victor Epstein, *Chinese man in NJ accused of trade secret theft*, USA TODAY, http://www.usatoday.com/news/nation/states/newjersey/2009-04-10-725573065_x.htm (last visited: 2009/9/6).

[4]　*U.S. officials eye N. Korea in cyberattack*, USA TODAY, http://www.usatoday.com/ news/washington/2009-07-08-hacking-washington-nkorea_N.htm, (last visited: 2009/ 9/6).

戶名單、董事會成員密碼、蒐集競價資料及潛入系統更改資訊內容[5]
等等。

　　EEA施行至今是否達成當時立法之施行成效，維持在全球市場上
的美國經濟競爭力，避免營業秘密被不當的剽竊或破壞，且有效防制
外國之經濟間諜行動，本文將自EEA立法背景、美國規範經濟間諜及
營業秘密相關法規、EEA施行後所面對之難題，最後探討是否有制定
美國聯邦營業秘密法（Federal Trade Secrets Act, FTSA）之必要性；
希冀本研究對營業秘密保護及經濟間諜等主題能提供若干新思維。

貳、EEA立法背景

　　EEA立法前1934年贓物跨州運送法（Interstate Transportation of
Stolen Property Act of 1934）是唯一主要的聯邦法律，適用的對象主
要是有體物，對於無體財產權並無法律依據，而州法在適用上較無效
力，乃因為各州的檢警單位無足夠的資源執行保護，各州的判決對於
跨州或國際性的侵害也難以貫徹執行[6]，因為冷戰時期結束後，經濟

---

[5]　Byron Acohido, *Tech gadgets help corporate spying surge in tough times*, USA TODAY,
　　http://www.usatoday.com/tech/news/computersecurity/2009-07-28-corporate- espionage-
　　recession-tech_N.htm, (last visited: 2009/9/6).

[6]　美國聯邦調查局長在國會聽證會上歸納原因，強調：一、冷戰後，美國國內經濟發展
　　和國家安全重要性相等；二、許多國家為其經濟利益，不擇手段、積極介入偷取美國
　　的商業機密；三、既有的美國現行法規無法有效追訴經濟間諜，因此通過經濟間諜法
　　案使成為美國的聯邦法案，可有效防治美國國內跨州或國際間的經濟間諜。Louis J.
　　Freeh, *supra note* 2. 中文部份請參閱羅麗珠，「美國的經濟間諜法案」，經濟部科技
　　專案通報「技術尖兵」，第32期，頁12，民國86年8月；調查局長Louis J. Freeh 認為
　　冷戰過後，外國經濟間諜活動的次數及頻率並無改變，而是改變情報活動目標的客
　　體，包括俄羅斯情報單位亦以美國經濟資訊為其諜報工作的目標。CBS Evening News
　　(CBS television broadcast (1996/12/18); Michael T. Clark, *Economic Espionage: The Role*

間諜活動取代軍事行動，經濟勢力重新分配，外國政府參與競爭……等時空因素，無體財產權的特質極易被竊取，受雇人比起以往有更多的機會可接觸營業秘密相關資訊，此外，電腦駭客有眾多途徑可竊取機密，即使對距離相隔遙遠，其他類型的公司，因為網際網路的盛行，再如行動電話、傳真機的便利性，使得對營業秘密的蒐集更加快速[7]。科技文明的更新，竊取及洩漏營業秘密管道增多，聯邦政府考量國家安全與產業密不可分，因而成立專責單位，也使成立規範經濟間諜專屬法規之需求更形迫切。

一、經濟間諜活動盛行

以往間諜活動多半專注於刺探軍事秘密，但冷戰（Cold War）結束後逐漸改變型態，經濟上的優越性比軍事優勢更形重要，如*United States v. Hsu*[8]一案中，美國聯邦第七巡迴法院指出「冷戰時代」的結束，使得政府部門更積極刺探私人的商業行動，西元1996年之前，有關企業智慧財產權竊取造成每年高達24億美元的損失[9]。生物科技技術進步神速，成為21世紀最具發展潛力的科技產業[10]，專利權保護高科技產品成為此時代的趨勢，在未取得專利之前，如何保障相關配方、原料、製程及其成份不被洩漏，避免影響公司商機並能鞏固巨大投資成本，目前企業認為營業秘密的竊盜案件價值更高，因為冷戰時

---

of the United States Intelligence Community, 3 J. Int'l Legal Stud. 253, 254-255 (1997).

[7] Dareen S. Tucker, *The Federal Government's War on Economic Espionage*, 18 U.Pa. J. Int'l Econ L. 1113, http://web.lesix-nexis.com/universe/document?_m (last visited 2003/8/12).

[8] *United States v. Hsu*, 155 F. 3d 189 (3d Cir. 1998).

[9] *Id*. at 194.

[10] 由於生物科技研發出的藥品有許多使用於人體，因此在研發的過程中，必須經過長期嚴格的臨床試驗，可能要費上十餘年的時間以及龐大的研發人力，但只要在眾多的試驗中，有一項產品研發成功，則可能帶來高達數百億元的龐大利潤。

期結束，使以往投注於軍事、技術或機密上有關智慧財產權的資源，移轉到商業活動方面[11]。

　　高科技產業的盛行，使美國政府認為維護其國家科技產業及智慧財產權，是鞏固其強權之重要武器，比起殺戮戰場之血刃相見，經濟力量的侵犯、資源的掠奪，更是國家維持其國家主權強勢的象徵。冷戰時期結束後，美國不再以軍事活動或戰略勢力維持其領導地位，如何在經濟競爭上與其他國家一較長短，成當務之急，也因此產生對制裁經濟間諜的必要性，西元1991年美國總統布希曾宣告，美國人必須以情報單位遏阻，任何企圖不付出合理代價，竊取美國科技、資訊的人[12]，經濟間諜形成美國情報政策議題[13]中最熱門的話題[14]。美國不論在工業、政府部門或是社會體系上，資訊的流通性及獲得資訊的管道皆十分通暢，美國自忖智慧財產權居世界領導地位[15]。

　　聯邦調查局（Federal Bureau of Investigation，簡稱FBI）對173個國家的研究指出，至少有100個國家曾經投注經費在探求美國的相關科技[16]，其中57個國家，實際從事對美國相關的間諜行動[17]，局長Louis Freeh認為外國間諜活動及情報蒐集系統、安全措施十分活躍，

---

[11] Tucker, *supra note* 7, 1109, 1113-1114 (1997).

[12] Rob Norton, *The CIA's Mission Improbable*, Fortune, at 55 (Oct. 2, 1995).

[13] Jim Mann, *Woolsey Cites Dangers in Economic Espionage*, L.A. Times, A10 (quoting former Director of Central Intelligence R. James Woolsey) (Feb. 3, 1993).

[14] 美國總統柯林頓曾強烈反對削減中央情報局的預算，他認為冷戰時期的結束，不代表不再需要任何情報單位及情報蒐集行動，裁減情報單位的預算，亦即阻斷了中央情報局的工作，正如同當一個人健康時，取消了健康保險一樣不智。*President's Remarks at Central Intelligence Agency in Langley*, Virginia, 31 Weekly Comp. Pres. Doc. 1238 (Jul. 14, 1995).

[15] H.R. Rep. No. 104-788, at 4 (1996).

[16] Peter Schweizer, *The Growth of Economic Espionage: America Is Target Number One*, Foreigh Aff., Jan./Feb. at 11 (1996).

[17] Id.

如同在冷戰時期一樣，都以美國為首要目標，並非為了軍事活動的進行，而以經濟的滲透及利益的奪取為主[18]。再根據前中央情報局（the Central Intelligence Agency，簡稱CIA）局長Robert Gates指出有位於亞洲、歐洲、中東、拉丁美洲等各地，約有20個政府皆從事於獲取相關經濟利益、智財權上的活動[19]。

以美國而言，經濟間諜最容易發生且最頻繁的行業，屬於研究高科技的單位及公司，地區包括達拉斯（Dallas）、波士頓（Boston）、華盛頓特區（Washington, D.C.），吸引最多經濟間諜活動[20]，當然矽谷[21]亦被認為為最具挑戰性，且充滿誘因的地區；最受到外國經濟間諜喜愛的為IBM（International Business Machines）公司，IBM生產的產品供應許多政府部門，不論在硬體或軟體部份皆受到相當注目[22]，只要使用網際網路，任何資訊都非常容易被傳送到世界上任何角落[23]，網際網路是摧毀私密性及個人隱私，包括企業及公司之營業秘密最好的工具。

目前如電腦的程式設計密碼（computer source code）或是生化設計程式（biochemical formula）往往是整個公司最重要的資產，因

---

[18] Michael T. Clark, *supra note* 6, at 253.

[19] Ronald E. Yates, *Cold War: Part II, Foreign Intelligence Agencies Have New Targets - U.S. Companies*, Chi. Trib. , at C1, Aug. 1993. 根據西元1993年報告，最積極從事商業行為的國家，包括法國、日本、伊朗、德國、南韓、英國、蘇俄、中國、台灣、巴基斯坦、印度、埃及、古巴、東歐國家、敘利亞，CIA同時作出結論，因這些國家積極從事經濟間諜的活動而使美國的國家安全，特別是美國的國家經濟，遭受空前的威脅。

[20] John Berthelsen, *Friendly Spies*, Far E. Econ. Rev., at 28 (Feb. 1994).

[21] 矽谷集合了有關於電子科技、生物科技產業的地區，且其與遠東地區，包括在汽車、跨國性的工作配合上具有重要的聯繫。

[22] 根據IBM內部資料，在過去的10年間（西元1987年至1997年），IBM至少遭遇到非法的經濟間諜竊取高達25次，似乎可形容IBM隨時都處於攻擊之下。*Economic Espionage*, Seattle Times, at A3 (Nov. 6, 1991).

[23] Chris Carr, *The Economic Espionage Act: Bear Trap or MouseTrap*? 8 Tex. Intell. Prop. L.J. 164-165 (2000).

為現在電腦傳輸的技術，能迅速複製或傳送具有重大價值的營業秘密，受雇人極易使用公司的硬碟或軟體攜帶資料，或利用網際網路直接傳送至其他地區或其他人，因此，美國的企業容易喪失對其營業秘密的掌控[24]。受雇人比以往有更多的機會可以從所竊取的營業秘密得到利益，例如自行開業或者是變換工作。高階經理人皆有共識，商業上的電腦使用愈便利、連結愈容易，商業機密亦更容易被侵入，受雇人甚至在離職之前，只要利用一片磁碟，便可拷貝複製重要的營業秘密，高度科技文明的發達，使得營業秘密洩漏的管道更多，經濟間諜的形成與制裁更需加以重視。

二、外國政府謀求經濟勢力之新戰場

世界各國經濟競爭模式日漸複雜，智財權的維持形成美國經濟的重要關鍵，開發中國家持續採用傳統的工業模式，即傾向於往低收入的製造商或是在開發中國家設廠，利用薪資之差價賺取利潤，但目前美國的經濟不再仰賴於此，而是以日漸升級的科技產業，及發明者在技術革新上領先其他國家而佔優勢，因此美國的商業及發明者在智慧財產權及營業秘密的提昇上，有十分成功且卓越的貢獻。美國一向在領導全球的產品或技術更新上居龍頭地位，因此不論對於美國本土的人民或新移民，皆可在美國享有創造更新及技術提昇的自由。

此類更新或技術改革、技術方法的擴展往往耗資甚鉅，美國政府及公司耗費數以億計的研究成本，如果競爭者只是輕易利用竊取手段，而將營業秘密移轉，不用花費任何研發的成本，雖然競爭的價格降低，但也會使新發明的動機盪然無存，投資者無意願進行投資，因

---

[24] R. Mark Halligan, *The Economic Espionage Act of 1996: The Theft of Trade Secrets is Now a Federal Crime*, http://www.execpc.com/mhallign/crime.html (last visited 2000/8/28).

而無法增加工作機會的提供，如此對美國的經濟發展完全沒有幫助。特別是外國的政府或國際企業，往往希望竊取美國的營業秘密或無體財產權增加其競爭優勢[25]。對美國政府而言，經濟力量是國家安全致命的核心。

經濟間諜有別於傳統的工業間諜，經濟間諜往往涉及幕後有外國政府支持、配合或協助，針對美國聯邦政府、公司、機構或自然人，涉及不法竊取營業秘密的目的，包括經濟上、貿易上、財務上的政策資訊，由外國政府或機構，或與國內政府或公司所支持的機構；形成傳統的間諜活動，往往只牽涉對國際防禦資訊的掠奪，雖使用非法技巧或途徑蒐集資訊，但外國政府或機構並未介入。因此區分二者的關鍵乃在於經濟間諜定義上，牽涉到外國政府的支持，如南韓公司涉嫌竊取英代爾公司（Intel）的資訊，若南韓政府提供竊聽的器材，並且持有公司的股份，則此南韓公司的舉動可被視為經濟間諜。

美國工商業之所以成為外國經濟間諜所窺伺的目標，最主要乃因一、美國生產合格的商品提供給其他的政府，是國際上地位顯著的供應商；二、美國提供軍事或私人使用，特別是高科技產品，利潤誘人。再加上美國政府維持經濟安全的努力值得批判[26]。經濟間諜不只與美國的高科技資訊有關，對於一般工商業的企業資訊，如價格資料、顧客名單、產品發展、計畫、基礎研究、銷貨量評估及市場計畫亦感興趣，另外外國政府對於發展計畫、私有資訊報告、個人資料、企業投標金額、生產成本分析、軟體及策略計畫，亦想一窺究竟[27]。經濟間諜活動的盛行與利潤之誘因密不可分，竊取秘密之行為人可坐

---

[25] *Id.*

[26] Joint Hearing Before the Select Subcomm. On intelligence of the U.S. Senate and the Subcomm. On Terrorism, Tech., and Gov't Info. Of the Comm. On the Judiciary of the U.S. Senate, 104th cong., 2d Sess. 45 (1996). 此段論述乃出於FBI局長Louis Freeh於聽證會上所做的陳述。

[27] Ronald E. Yates, *supra note 19*, at C1. Also see Louis Freeh, *supra note.*

享暴利，不用花費任何研發及投資成本，嚴重打擊秘密所有人及產業經濟安全，對整體商業考量及國家安全造成雙重傷害。

防制經濟間諜的成本嚴重打擊美國企業，如賓州參議員Arlen Specter對參議院情報委員會的報告，指出經濟間諜對西元1996年之前10年間，造成高達600萬工作機會的喪失，並嚴重影響美國經濟[28]；再依據美國白宮科技委員會統計，美國企業因為外國經濟間諜的損失，每年高達100億美金。事實上，受害公司恐懼影響投資者的意願，不願呈報正確的計算內容及損失，這點亦是本文討論經濟間諜法立法過程中，考量商業利益的另一個關鍵，因此極難求証或精確計算。因為若將事實公開，有可能造成：(1)股價跌落，影響公司資產；(2)對公司而言，公司的信用以及商譽都會遭受打擊；(3)會使原本有意投資的股東或投資人因而卻步；(4)若將受害的情形公開，可能會使外界認為此家公司，對管理智慧財產權及營業秘密的專業度及努力不夠[29]。

發展新穎、更佳品質的技術產品及生產方法，成本十分昂貴，每年美國政府及私人機構投注以億萬美元的經費於研發工作，然而這些實驗成本所得到的成果卻常化為烏有，如果競爭者僅利用竊取的手段，而不需要投資任何研發成本，會使市場上產品的價格降低，而投注研發的公司不但無利可圖，亦造成研發性產品的投資意願盪然無存，同樣地，工作機會減少，投資成本增加，及其他附帶的客觀環境皆無法使既存的經濟體系更加強壯[30]。

---

[28] Ronald E. Yates, *Espionage Fight Shifts to Corporate Battlefield; Laws Offer Little Help; Cost From Spying is Put at $10 Billion a Year*, Chi. Trib., at C1 (Mar. 24, 1996).

[29] *Id.* at 7.

[30] Senator Arlen, Economic Espionage Act of 1996 (Senate - Oct. 2, 1996), the statement of Mr. Specter, http://thomas.loc.gov/cgi-bin/query/F?r104:4:./temp/~r1041fv7oB: 71874 (last visited 2003/8/15).

參、美國規範經濟間諜及營業秘密相關法規

　　參考經濟間諜法獨立立法的美國，既有成文法規中，與保障營業秘密或防治經濟間諜相關者，有已列於聯邦法典的法規，亦有由各州決定自行採用的州法。

一、統一營業秘密法

　　為提昇對營業秘密及專有資訊的保障於聯邦位階，美國聯邦法規對營業秘密有成文法的相關規定[31]，並在1948年的6月成為營業秘密法（Trade Secrets Act, TSA），其後歷經修正，為保障私人營業秘密科處刑責的規定[32]。營業秘密法的保障對於如銀行金融資料，提供安全的保護，只可惜TSA並無法幫助當事人在民事程序上，禁止對方揭露相關資訊，此外，TSA保障的內容，實務上亦受到自由資訊法（the Freedom of Information Act, FOIA）的保護，TSA為營業秘密的保障提供了一個基本的模範立法，亦為受僱人或代理人遵守的典範[33]。

　　1996年美國經濟間諜法施行之前，彙整美國營業秘密法規為營業秘密法，美國律師協會（American Bar Association）於1966年擬具「統一營業秘密法」（Uniform Trade Secrets Act, UTSA）[34]。其後美國法律協會所成立的統一州法全國委員會會議（National Conference of Commissioners on Uniform State Laws）於1979年8月9日通過

---

[31]　15 U.S.C. §1776, 18 U.S.C. §112, 19 U.S.C. §1335.

[32]　18 U.S.C. §1905 (2000)，本條文對於違法者可處以罰金或是一年以下有期徒刑。

[33]　Jerry Cohen, *Federal Issues in Trade Secret Law*, 2 J. High Tech. L. 1 (2003).

[34]　Uniform Trade Secrets Act, 14 U.L.A. 369 (1985 & Supp. 1989).

UTSA全文。1980年後，各州自行參考UTSA制定各州之法規，由於各州所持的理論依據有所不同，因此對於營業秘密保護尺度不一，造成不少公司及產業的困擾。統一營業秘密法主要針對民事程序的救濟，至於侵害營業秘密而造成的實際損害，或是達到遏止營業秘密竊賊之犯意及犯行上，並無有效的遏止作用，統一營業秘密法是目前美國各州對於營業秘密最重要的立法參考依據[35]。UTSA僅有民事救濟，往往緩不濟急且無法給予當事人足夠賠償，僅針對美國國內之經濟間諜違法洩漏或不當使用營業秘密之行為人[36]。

二、贓物法規

以往要竊取無論是軍事或商業上的機密，事實上並不容易，多半都用偷竊的方式，如Jose Lopez之前是通用汽車（General Motors，簡稱GM）行政職員，後來被定罪，乃因為在西元1993年自General Motors，偷取數盒裝滿機密的營業資料給新任職的福斯公司（Volkswagen）[37]。時至如今偷竊的技巧，並不需要實際從事任何具

---

[35] Brandon B. Cate, *Saforo & Associates, Inc. v. Porocel Corp.: The Failure of the Uniform Trade Secrets Act to Clarify the Doubtful and Confused Status of Common Law Trade Secret Principles*, 53 Ark. L. Rev. 687, 697-699 (2000); Robert Unikel, *Bridging the "Trade Secret" Gap: Protecting "Confidential Information" Not Rising to the Level of Trade Secrets*, 29 Loy. U. Chi. L. J. 841, 843 (1998).

[36] 美國公司根據UTSA提出民事賠償的請求，往往因財力或資源不夠力有未逮，即使獲得執行名義，被告無相當財富或資力可供求償，又缺乏政府機構在調查協力上的援助求償並不容易；採行UTSA的40餘州中，有24州的營業秘密法有刑則的處罰，單以州內的司法程序及力量往往無法有效調查及起訴此類案件，主要在於各州的營業秘密法無法制裁由外國政府或外國機構幕後所主持的經濟間諜活動。Sorojini J. Biswas, *The Economic Espionage Act of 1996,* htttp://www. myersbigel.com/ts_articles/trade_secet4.htm (last visited 2003/8/3).

[37] Christian Tyler, The Enemy Within, FIN. Times (London), FT Weekend, at 1 (Apr. 12,

體的行動，在1993年之前必須使用竊取手段，才能取得的資訊，目前都被儲存在電腦裡。

　　網際網路的盛行，使得資訊傳播無遠弗屆，亦成為洩漏營業秘密最佳利用工具，因為既存的聯邦法規無法有效保障高科技領域中竊取營業秘密的行為，以往企業遭受損失惟有經由民事訴訟請求賠償，美國國內的贓物法規（the National Stolen Property Act）在1934年由國會通過立法，本法主要是避免經由汽車運送贓物，但是政府必須要證明本法中的贓物乃是貨物、貨品或有體物（goods, wares or merchandise），而且還必須要證明被偷竊或是經由詐欺而為的運送（stolen, converted or taken by fraud）。

　　美國政府對竊取營業秘密之行為人採取嚴厲的刑責處罰，EEA通過前，各州州法保護營業秘密各自為政，雖依循聯邦「跨州贓物運送法（Interstate Transportation of Stolen Property Act of 1934, ITSP）」，然因智慧財產權無法構成該法定義中的[38]「貨物」。該法在西元1930年初期，為避免罪犯運送贓物於州際間，而以聯邦法規凌駕區域性及州法之執行力，規範限定貨物、有體物或商品的買賣，但因不包括被偷竊的「資訊」，導致該法對起訴聯邦經濟間諜並無實益[39]。該法對保護客體有金額之限制，依據第2314條條文內容，成立之要件有四：(1)以竊盜、詐欺或傳輸等方式取得物品；(2)被告不法傳送該竊取之貨物、商品或物品，且越過州際；(3)竊取物之價值必須在美金5,000元以上；(4)被告明知其為不法，經濟間諜法有別於此，並不要求該行為客體必有5,000美元以上之價值；多數司法機關

1997).

[38] 18 U.S.C. §2314.

[39] Caryl Ben Basat, *the Economic Espionage Act of 1996,* 31 Int'l Law. 245 (1997), http://web. lexis-nexis.com/universe/document?_m (last visited 2007/10/01).章忠信，「經濟間諜法簡介」，2002年2月20日，http://www.copyrightnote.org/crnote/bbs. php?board=8&act=read &id=10（上網日期：2007年8月12日）。

之判決認為此法適用對象僅限於有體物，不及於無法附著於形體之商業資訊。

　　因為各州檢警單位無足夠資源執行保護，各州法律亦難以有效保護營業秘密，並非各州對於營業秘密之侵害均定有刑罰規定，因此，各州難以貫徹執行跨州或國際性的侵害[40]。多數州雖然有針對不當洩漏營業秘密，得請求損害賠償為規定，然而無法限制當事人繳完罰金後不得繼續使用，或在繳罰金前已從使用得到莫大的利益，營業秘密的特質一旦公開即不再成為秘密，無從彌補當事人的損失，因此，ITSP實在無法解決經濟間諜存在的現象。

三、1996經濟間諜法

　　1992年12月17日，美國、加拿大及墨西哥制定了「北美自由貿易協定」（the North American Free Trade Agreement, NAFTA），NAFTA以美國的營業秘密法為主，遵循美國營業秘密法的規定；後於1994年4月15日主要的工業國家，包括美國，將烏拉圭回合談判作成了「GATT協定」（General Agreement on Tariffs and Trade, GATT），GATT建立世界貿易組織（the World Trade Organization, WTO），並且制定「與貿易有關之智慧財產權」協定（the Trade-Related Aspects of Intellectual Property Rights, TRIPs），TRIPs協定對於「未經揭露之資訊」（undisclosed information）加以界定，同時認為此類資訊必須有商業價值與秘密性才值得受保護。

　　1996年經濟間諜法（the Economic Espionage Act of 1996, EEA）[41]，EEA使美國保護營業秘密邁向國際化，除針對美國境內之

---

[40] 章忠信，同前註。

[41] 18 U.S.C.§1831-§1839.

犯罪行為外，亦追訴美國領域外犯罪行為，刑罰處罰針對經濟間諜活動及竊取營業秘密罪兩種[42]。以下將自EEA的規範內容探討經濟間諜行為及其罰則。

（一）經濟間諜行為

EEA立法前並未有刑事處罰，多數經濟間諜造成損害的案件僅能經由民事訴訟得到賠償[43]，如此無法避免未來犯罪行為人再度觸法，並杜絕此種不見容於社會的剽竊行為[44]。因為刑事及民事法規賠償結果不同[45]，民事法規僅能對於已發生的問題而給予金錢損害賠償，刑事法規則希望在犯罪發生之前，避免犯罪的產生，藉以改正行為人不當的行為，為達成前述目的，EEA不但加強刑責，同時在條文第1條及第2條[46]即明文規定經濟間諜行為。規範經濟間諜行為之行為人、行為態樣及內容，包括外國政府所支持之經濟間諜活動及美國國內營業秘密竊取行為。

行為人竊取營業秘密時，必須明知或可得而知，所竊取之秘密

---

[42] R. Mark Halligan, *The Economic Espionage Act of 1996: The Theft of Trade Secrets is Now a Federal Crime,* http://execpc.com/~mhallign/crime.html (last visited 2000/ 8/28).

[43] 企業通常有二種作法，進行民事賠償程序時，首先多數公司運用「競業禁止條款」、「保密契約」約束受雇人。David Cathcart, Contracts with Employees: *Covenants Not To Compete and Trade Secrets,* 36 Ali-Aba 87, 100 (1997). 而當違反此類合約時，公司可以違反契約或破壞忠實義務（fiduciary duty），針對受雇人提出違反保密義務的訴訟；其次，公司亦可選擇不當使用營業秘密，而在各州的侵權行為法下提起訴訟，目前已超過40州採行美國統一營業秘密法（UTSA），因此公司可請求民事禁制令或金錢上的損害賠償，此乃一般民事訴訟的優勢。Jonathan Band, *The Economic Espionage Act: Its Application in Year One,* Corp. Couns., at 1 (Nov. 1997).

[44] Kenneth Mann, *Punitive Civil Sanctions: The Middleground Between Criminal and Civil Law,* 101 Yale L.J. 1795(1992).

[45] Id.

[46] 規定於EEA第1條（18 U.S.C. §1831）及第2條（18 U.S.C. §1832）。

為具有專屬性的私有資訊不能公開[47]，至於所圖利的對象是自己或他人在所不論[48]。EEA不保障過失或非故意的洩漏機密，為避免競爭對手以充分的資金或資源提供內部人員，而竊取該公司或機關的重要文件、資訊或營業秘密，EEA第1條中所謂的外國政府及外國機構，包括任何外國政府的官方單位、研究單位，或其他由外國政府在幕後支持，而以營利社團法人或一般財團法人身分成立的組織。我國雖然與美國無正式外交關係，然而我駐美代表處的人員，仍可被定位為外國政府之代理人，而適用EEA第1條。

（二）竊取營業秘密

針對一般傳統性的經濟間諜，FBI調查時若發現並無外國政府支持，則可適用EEA第2條，即一般國內的商業機密竊取行為而加以偵查。EEA通過後，聯邦法規更能有效保障美國經濟間諜相關行為內涵，任何為所有人以外其他人之經濟利益，故意或意圖侵占相關或包括於州際或外國貿易所製造或儲存之營業秘密商品，企業之間的營業秘密竊盜行為動機，皆以經濟利益為主。犯罪行為固為法所不容，惟不如外國經濟間諜般影響國家安全，國會立法時特別要求檢察官對於國內之營業秘密竊盜案件，必須能證明被告不但有獲取經濟利益的企圖，並能實際獲得利益。

對於觸犯「經濟間諜」（Economic Espionage）罪，任何人意圖或知曉侵犯行為將裨益任何外國政府或機構[49]，即經濟利益（economic benefit）上的要件，不必涉及任何形式的商品，即使是策略應用上的優勢，或是任何對外國組織有利的行為，皆可依EEA第

---

[47] 18 U.S.C. §1831 (a).

[48] Pamela B. Stuart, *The Criminalization of Trade Secret Theft: The Economic Espionage Act of 1996,* 4 ILSA J. Int'l & Lonp. L. 374, 381 (1998).

[49] 18 U.S.C. §1831 & §1839.

1條加以處罰[50]；第2條竊取營業秘密罪[51]必須包括商品在內，第2條的起訴標準較高，因國會立法目的為遏阻外國政府所支持，嚴重影響美國經濟，進而危害美國國家安全之經濟間諜活動，相較於傳統的國內營業秘密竊盜行為，無論被告為美國籍或外國籍之個人或企業，對於美國之損害較不構成威脅性。

肆、EEA施行後所面對之難題

述及EEA制定的過程及立法背景，1996年EEA制定通過迄今之執行成效，是否一如當時預期解決既有的困擾與難題，或是有新衍生的情狀是當時未曾預期的，若單觀察防制中國大陸之經濟間諜部分，與外國經濟間諜所造成的威脅，EEA之施行成效似乎不彰，本文以下將由若干1996年後之案例予以說明[52]，當今歐巴馬政府如何因應以下所列舉的問題，值得觀察。

一、存在外國經濟間諜的威脅

早在西元1992年FBI即確認由外國資源所支持之商業間諜，造成美國國家安全極大的震撼[53]，FBI特別針對經濟間諜而展開數項

---

[50] H.R. Rep. No. 104-788, at 11 (1996).

[51] 18 U.S.C. §1832.

[52] 以下在案例部分以中國大陸經濟間諜為例，並參考Jonathan Eric Lewis, *The Economic Espionage Act and the Threat of Chinese Espionage in the United States*, 8 Chi.-Kent J. Intell. Prop. 189-235 (Spring, 2009) 一文見解。

[53] William T. Warner, *Economic Espionage: A Bad Idea*, Nat'l L. J. at 13 (Apr. 12, 1993).

的查緝行動[54]，如1994年[55]的經濟反情報活動（the FBI's Economic
Counterintelligence Program）；FBI同時發現經濟間諜以加倍地速度
成長[56]，來自23個國家，超過800件案例正在接受調查[57]。

隨著工商社會競爭日趨激烈，資訊技術的取得成為產業決勝的
關鍵，各國諜報工作逐漸轉移於竊取美國經濟機密，盜用無體智慧財
產權，損害美國國家經濟利益，既有之聯邦法規無法有效懲處經濟
間諜，因此EEA被認為是提供聯邦政府解決此類問題的絕佳武器[58]，
美國聯邦政府藉由EEA之立法，阻止外國政府或機構以不正當手段取
得美國商業機密，尤其是高科技機密，因此對涉及「圖利」外國機
構（instrumentality）或外國代理人的經濟間諜行為懲處最為嚴峻。
EEA對於國家政府所從事的合法行為或是經由合法授權者並不違反經
濟間諜法，只要該等政治實體就相關違反行為或任何美國政府、州政
府，或州政府行政單位，涉嫌違反本法之情形經合法授權者；EEA並

---

[54] 在矽谷超過二十年的FBI探員，被指派全天候的調查營業秘密被竊的相關案件。Norm
Alster, *The Valley of the Spies*, Forbes. at 200, 204 (Oct. 6, 1992).

[55] Clark, *supra note* 7, at 268, http://web.lexis-nexis.com/universe/document?_m (last visited
2003/8/12).

[56] 西元1994年發現的400個案例，至1995年已增加到800個。Dean Starkman, *Secrets and
Lies: The Dual Career of a Corporate Spy*, Wall St. J. at B1 (Oct. 23, 1997).

[57] Economic Espionage: Joint Hearing Before the Senate Select Comm. On Intelligence United
States Senate and the Subomm. On Terrorism, Tech., and Gov't Info. Of the Comm. On the
Judiciary United States Senate, 104th Cong. 12 (Oct. 2, 1996) (Herb Louis Freeh, Director
of the Federal Bureau of Investigation).

[58] 以參議院而言，EEA立法交由特定情報委員會（the Select Committee on Intelligence）
及防治恐怖份子科技及政府資訊小組（the Judiciary Subcommittee on Terrorism,
Technology and Government Information），眾議院方面則由司法委員會下的犯罪小組
（the Subcommittee on Crime of the Judiciary Committee）負責，聽證會過程中被邀請
來作證的成員，並不限於智慧財產權方面的專家，回顧當年的文獻，最常被引用的反
而是當時的聯邦調查局局長Louis J. Freeh的證詞。See S. Rep. No. 104-359, at 5 (1996);
H.R. Rep. No. 104-788, at 14-16 (1996).

不禁止任何其他美國政府，州政府，或州政府行政單位所從事之合法活動。

　　美國公司防止及阻止經濟間諜的步驟太慢，法律規範需要保障新的知識領域，智慧財產權必須要由法律予以涵蓋，才能真正被視為是智慧財產權，並得以保障美國本土之發明，美國產業界面臨智慧財產權被剽竊之內憂外患窘境。以往營業秘密的濫用，因缺乏一套針對經濟間諜的營業秘密法規，因此遇到外國商業間諜時，美國企業極難保障自身權益，EEA之制定目標首重既有智財權價值，而非開創更優質的工作環境，在鼓勵創造發明的同時，雖然以防禦的角度出發而層層考量法規的面相，相對地，亦有益於未來研發環境的締造[59]。營業秘密的洩漏對形成智慧資產及各種規模的企業都造成威脅，美國聯邦調查局和美國商會建立工商業防範間諜威脅的制度，並制定打擊經濟間諜的措施，成立美國商業與聯邦調查局集中資訊交流中心，同時與海外的所有商會合作，鼓吹全國共同打擊竊盜智慧財產權，不遺餘力。

二、EEA規範不足

　　科技文明的發達使傳統的商業間諜活動如虎添翼，利用電腦的網際網路，傳送資料的速度及攜帶的方便性與日俱增，相對地，機密洩漏的危險性及管道也隨之提高及增多。西元1995年，美國反情報中心（the National Counterintelligence Center）報告指出生物科技（biotechnology）、太空科技（aerospace）、無線傳播（telecommunications）、電腦軟體（computer software）、運輸（transportation）、先進材料（advanced materials）、

---

[59] Rochelle Cooper Dreyfuss, *How Well Should We Be Allowed To Hide Them? The Economic Espionage Act of 1996,* 9 Fordham Intell. Prop. Media & Ent. L.J. 1, (1998).

能源研究（energy research）、防禦系統（defense）及半導體（semiconductor）等相關資訊，皆為外國間諜的首要目標[60]。報告中亦指出至少有20種從事工業間諜的方法，傳統方式除偽裝成代理人，或以滲透侵入的方式，在目標公司從事情報蒐集工作，或違法進入被害人辦公處所，竊取硬體設備及資訊；目前方式包括電腦駭客侵入，利用無線傳播訊息及干擾私部門之間的通訊，而獲取相當的情報[61]，大部分的美國公司不但疲於應付此類情形，而且根本無法有周全的準備與其對抗[62]。

維持營業秘密保障的法規在州法位階實則減損經濟效益，如EEA制定為聯邦法位階，目前營業秘密所有人只能在其權益管轄權範圍內受到保障，以州法保障則權益範圍只在該州州內，若提昇至聯邦法層次，則權益保障可提高至全國——即美國境內皆可受保障，2007年美國工業安全協會（the American Society for Industrial Security, ASIS）的專業報導指出[63]，美國公司資產價值中的75%，是從該公司的智慧財產權資產而來，一個營業秘密或經濟間諜的案例自1萬元的

---

[60] *Annual Report to Congress on Foreign Economic Collection and Industrial Espionage (Annual Report),* p15, National Counterintelligence Center (1995), http://nsi.org/Library/Espionage/indust.html; Marc A. Moyer, *Section 301 of the Omnibus Trade and Competitiveness Act of 1988: A Formidable Weapon in the War Against Economic Espionage,* 15 Nw. J. Int'l L. & Bus. 178, 184 (1994); Karen Sepura, *Economic Espionage: The Front Line Of A New World Economic War.* 26 SYR J. Int'l L. Com. 127, 133 (1998).

[61] *Annual Report,* supra note, at 16.

[62] S. Rep. No. 359, 104th Cong., 2nd Sess. (1996).

[63] *ASIS Int'l, Trends in Proprietary Information Loss,* survey report, The National Counterintelligence Executive (NCIX) and the American Society for Industrial Security (ASIS) (August 2007), available at http://www.asisonline.org/newsroom/surveys/ spi2.pdf (last visited 2009/9/19); Also see Harvey Rishikof, *Economic and Industrial Espionage: A Question of Counterintelligence or Law Enforcement?* http:// nationalstrategy.com/Programs/NationalStrategyForumReview/SpringSummer2009NSFROnlineJournal/FeatureEssayEconomicandIndustrialEspionage/tabid/189/Default.aspx (last visited 2009/9/19).

價值至550萬元，同時造成一年美金數10億元的損失，不只對美國財務損失還包括企業的商譽、競爭力的影響。

西元1948年通過的營業秘密法（Trade Secrets Act）併入於聯邦刑事法規（Federal Criminal Code）[64]中，雖然其他有跨州贓物運送法（the Interstate Transportation of Stolen Property Act, ITSP）或是郵件及通訊詐欺法（Mail Fraud and Wire Fraud Acts）皆無法對營業秘密洩漏案件及營業秘密所有人提供強而有力的保障[65]，即使是其後的統一營業秘密法（Uniform Trade Secrets Act, UTSA）[66]通過，仍然發現許多公司無法對被告進行訴訟，一來乃因被告可能無資力，或是證據蒐集不足，甚至是原告公司並無足夠的財力資源進行民事訴訟，或者是握有的資料及調查過程很難證明營業秘密的竊盜案件。

三、中國大陸經濟間諜案例

EEA制定後尤其是中國大陸經濟間諜案件造成美國極大困擾，本

---

[64] 西元1948年6月25日納入聯邦刑事法規（Federal Criminal Code）中，此法（Trade Secret Act）對於受雇人若不當洩漏有關於雇用人或雇用人之公司，或其他組織之營業秘密或其秘密資訊，在僱傭期間中違背此法，將被罰款1,000美元或科處一年的有期徒刑，並造成僱傭關係的終止。但是依照此法而起訴的案件微乎其微。Sorojini J. Biswas, *The Economic Espionage Act of 1996,* http://www.myersbigel. com/ts_articles/ trade_secret4.htm (last visited 2003/8/3).

[65] 西元1995年曾經工作於二家主要大型電腦公司的離職員工，承認偷竊製造晶片的重要資訊，並且賣給中國、古巴（Cuba）及伊朗（Iran），以將近十年的時間，複製製造說明，此類資訊價值好幾百萬美金；中國人、古巴人及伊朗人因為這些資訊，而能縮短與美國之科技研發差距。在1995年FBI逮捕時依跨州贓物運送法及郵件詐欺加以懲處，但是困難在於行為人並沒有偷竊實際的財產，而是構想（ideas）。Herb Kohl, Statements on Introduced Bills and Joint Resolutions (Senate-1996/2/1), http://thomas.loc. gov/cgi-bin/query/F?r104:6:./temp/ ~r104xC3f7h:e27014 (last visited: 2003/8/15).

[66] 14 U.L.A. 369 (1985 & Supp. 1989).

文以為構成美國制定EEA或考慮再制定其他聯邦法規以為管轄,當然不全然皆因受到中國大陸經濟間諜案件的影響,然而在1996年後相當篇幅的新聞報導及實務案例,皆與中國大陸有關。

(一)電腦軟體

United States v. Fei Ye and Ming Zhong[67]案中,兩位矽谷工程師,葉費(Fei Ye)及鐘明(Ming Zhong)於西元2001年11月23日,在舊金山國際機場被逮捕時,正準備前往中國大陸,行李中裝滿了從Sun Microsystems Inc., Transmeta Corp., NEC Electronics Corp.及Trident Microsystems Inc.四家公司所竊取的營業秘密,被告二人之前曾任職於Transmeta、Trident公司,Fei Ye亦曾工作於Sun及NEC此二家公司,本案是EEA制定後第二個被定罪的案件[68]。

FBI發現被告等人竊取營業秘密的目的乃為圖利位於中國大陸屬於微軟系統的子公司——Supervision Inc.。被告二人抗辯因與中國浙江大學(Zhejiang University)教授共同進行高科技研發計畫,並接受中國資金援助,因而雙方進行接觸。西元2002年12月6日,面對聯邦政府指控從事經濟間諜,竊取營業秘密及陰謀將竊取之財產運送到

---

[67] U.S. v. Fei Ye, 436 F.3d 1117, 77 U.S.P.Q.2d 1942, 06 Cal. Daily Op. Serv. 1028, 2006 Daily Journal D.A.R. 1440, C.A.9 (Cal.), 2006.

[68] 第一個案件是2001年5月8日於俄亥俄州北區地區法院的 U.S. v. Okamoto & Serizawa一案,被告Serizawa居住於肯薩斯市,自1996年12月16日起至案發受雇於肯薩斯大學醫學中心(the Kansas University Medical Center, KUMC),另一名被告Okamoto自1997年1月至1999年7月受雇於the Lerner Research Institute (LRI),該機構隸屬於克利夫蘭診療基金會(the Cleveland Clinic Foundation, CCF)下,專門研究阿爾茨海默氏病,2001年此案發生時則居於日本。兩人為舊識被控自1998年1月至1999年9月竊取CCF研發的治療阿爾茨海默氏病的基因(DNA)物質。資料請見First Foreign Economic Espionage Indictment; Defendants Steal Trade Secrets from Cleveland Clinic Foundation (May 8, 2001), http://www. usdoj.gov/criminal/cybercrime/Okamoto_SerizawaIndict.htm (last visited: 2009/9/ 28).

國外共10項罪名，依據EEA法規，若能證明被告竊取營業秘密，乃為圖利外國政府或機構，即使外國政府並未事先知悉或實際從事共犯的行為，亦不能阻絕被告罪行的成立[69]。

本案被告Ming Zhong僅具有美國居民身分，未如另一名被告Fei Ye乃美國公民，EEA懲制的犯罪行為主體不限美國公民，亦懲戒外國行為人及其組織，包括非美國公民之外國人，由此可知美國維護其企業組織所擁有營業秘密之決心。本案被告從事經濟間諜行為，不當竊取營業秘密，並涉嫌將竊取之營業秘密運送到國外。因此違反經濟間諜法第1條a項第3款、第5款，及第2條a項第3款、第5款[70]之規定，另被指控違反美國民事法典第371條[71]及2314條[72]，期間被告於一審定讞後繼續上訴，至2006年12月前述被告上訴駁回，至此判決確定。

此外2009年4月31歲居住於北紐澤西的中國大陸人民，Yan Zhu被控偷竊前雇主之電腦軟體——原始碼資料[73]，這些原始碼資料乃專供該被竊公司之內部買賣，屬於十分機密的原始材料，被告持工作簽證自2006年4月至2008年7月，以資深環境工程師的身分任職於該公司，FBI經由調查證實被告出售上述物件到中國大陸，以改善空氣傳訊與水的品質，在與中國大陸——居住於河北及山西的兩名共犯從事犯罪行為時，被告扮演主導角色，而價值美金150萬元的軟體僅以十分之一的價格賣出。

---

[69] *Court Rules In (Settled) Secrets Case,* The Recorder 10 (2003/1/1), http://web.lexis-nexis.com/universe/document?_m (last visited: 2003/6/16). 負責本案的美國助理檢察官Ross Nadel說明自EEA通過後，本案為該州配合聯邦檢調單位對竊取營業秘密罪起訴偵查的第二件案例。See Laffert, *supra note.*

[70] 18 U.S.C. §1831 (a)(3), §1831(a)(5) and §1832(a)(3), §1832(a)(5).

[71] 18 U.S.C. §371.

[72] 18 U.S.C. §2314.

[73] Victor Epstein, Chinese man in NJ accused of trade secret theft (2009/4/10), http://www.usatoday.com/news/nation/states/newjersey/2009-04-10-725573065_x.htm (last visited: 2009/9/6).

　　Weysan Dun是FBI的特殊調查員，他指出自2001年迄今聯邦調查的案件中，中國大陸的經濟間諜數量以10%的比例增加，且幕後涉及中國政府部門、研究機構、組織等，美國軟體公司及製片商一再嘗試瓦解中國大陸的違法下載、製造經銷及偷竊……等行為，往往因為類似被告Yan Zhu的頂尖科學家，主謀、協助竊取美國企業辛勤研發、價值不斐的高科技營業秘密，不但使FBI疲於調查也使被告面對8項罪名的指控及超過20年的牢獄之災。

（二）高科技國防資訊

　　Boeing案[74]中被告Dongfan "Greg" Chung現年73歲，自1973年為止皆為Rockwell公司工作擔任工程師，直到1996年任職之防衛及太空基地部門被歸屬於Boeing公司，被告替中國大陸政府竊取該公司的高度保密資訊，包括太空船計畫及太空基地設置，2008年2月被告經FBI及美國太空總署（NASA）逮捕，如今面對八項指控並將於2009年11月9日宣判，被告違背當時任職時所簽署的保密條款，他於2002年退休後次年又應聘至波音公司至2006年9月，對工作期間所知悉的航太機密原本應善盡保密義務，提供給中國大陸不僅違背對波音公司的誠信原則，影響美國企業的商業利益，更嚴重的是對美國國家安全的威脅，因為中國大陸獲知此類資訊乃為其發展軍事佈局[75]。

　　根據調查證據顯示自1979年起，大陸當局開始指派任務給被告，包含要被告蒐集與太空船、軍機、民航機有關之特殊科技資訊，被告在回覆的信件中也一再表明已蒐集之型號內容與使用手冊，其中特別是Rockwell公司禁止外洩的資料，在1985年至2003年期間被

---

[74] For Immediate Release, U.S. Department of Justice, Former Boeing Engineer Convicted of Economic Espionage in Theft of Space Shuttle Secrets for China (2009/7/16), http://www. usdoj.gov/opa/pr/2009/July/09-nsd-688.html (last visited: 2009/9/27).

[75] 此為美國律師Thomas P. O'Brien的說法，同前註。

告重複往返中國大陸，並與大陸軍方人士密切來往，2006年9月11日FBI及NASA在被告家中，搜出多達250,000頁的Rockwell公司、波音公司及其他承包商與太空船有關的文件。FBI與NASA和波音公司在長達3年的調查合作中，使此案成為EEA制定通過後第一個定罪的案件，對EEA的執行而言成為一個十分有意義的里程碑。

另一個十分聞名的案件是潛艇靜音技術案[76]，被告Chi Mak（中文譯為麥大志）出生於中國，1978年移民香港，隨後來美國，1985年入籍為美國公民。從1983年起為中國大陸工作，直到2005年10月被捕之前被控偷竊上百份的軍事機密文件給中國大陸，其中包括武器、核子反應堆以及美國潛水艇上推進系統。麥大志被捕前是美國重要國防承包商Power Paragon的首席工程師，負責發展全球最先進的海軍武器系統科技，其中包括能夠讓潛艦無法被偵測的靜音推進系統，該套消聲設備可有效減低70%的噪音。

中國海軍一直想獲得美國潛艇的先進靜音電力系統，解決中國潛艇噪音量過大的問題，早在2000年就想透過發電廠的商業合同，取得適用於核潛艇的消音技術，但因為系統屬於美國軍事管制品而未能如願。2002年初，美國軍事機構發現中國潛艇已應用類似的消聲技術，增加美方對中國潛艇監視的困難，因而懷疑有洩密的可能性。2005年10月28日，美國聯邦調查局在洛杉磯國際機場逮捕準備前往香港的麥大泓夫婦，並在行李中搜出3張用特殊方式拷貝的加密光盤，內有潛艇推進系統等技術資料。隨後，麥大志夫婦在家裏被捕。

聯邦調查人員在麥大志家裡搜出一份中國大陸希望獲取的美國軍

---

[76] Press Release, United States Attorney's Office, Central District of California, Chinese Agent Sentenced to Over 24 Years in Prison for Exporting United States Defense Articles to China (3/24/2008), http://www.usdoj.gov/usao/cac/pressroom/pr2008/032. html (last visited: 2009/9/27).王珍，「美國潛艇靜音技術 洩密中國 美國重要國防承包商Power Paragon的首席工程師麥大志（華裔）被判有罪」（2007/5/24），http://mag.epochtimes.com/022/3129g.htm (last visited: 2009/9/27).

事技術清單，其中包括導彈防禦系統以及魚雷的資訊。美國聯邦政府亦控告麥大志的妻子趙麗華、弟弟麥大泓、弟媳李伏香、侄子麥銳等參與間諜活動。麥大志的律師在法庭上試圖說服陪審團相信，麥大志的弟弟麥大泓才是向中國出售情報的人，而麥大志本人並不知情。麥大泓及妻子於2001年5月通過麥大志以家庭團聚名義從中國移民到美國。FBI在經過詳細調查之後，發現麥大泓在移民美國之前是中共軍方技術研究人員，是標準的中共軍人，但其在移民資料上未完全披露其真正身分，特別是其具備某些敏感性的真實身分。此案在美國加州聖塔安那聯邦法庭經過一個半月的開庭審理，於2007年5月經大陪審團判決麥大志有罪，5項起訴罪名全部成立。

伍、制定美國聯邦營業秘密法之必要性探討

因為各州對營業秘密規定不一，加上為維護企業合理收益及研發意願，若能提升至聯邦位階的法規，可更增加各州對營業秘密保護的週延度，雖有如UTSA之既有法規，然而另外制定聯邦營業秘密法（FTSA）或於EEA現存法規中加入民事救濟條文，孰優孰劣則於以下段落予以探討。

一、能補強EEA之功能

美國經濟以創意與資訊流通為根基，工業時代暨後工業時代國際社會，對文化資產和創意產業寄予高度厚望，傳統工業只能透過原物料加工賺取勞工費用，當今產業則深深體認唯有結合智慧資產才能

提高收益[77]，企業亦藉智慧財產的保障維護其競爭利益，特別是營業秘密權益無需經由如申請、註冊、登記等程序確保，此種便利性使得以營業秘密保障新科技及新發明，有時間及手續上的優勢，目前提起EEA訴訟的案件太少（施行至今未超過100個案件）[78]；EEA未能提供民事損害賠償；非由受害人而是由檢察官決定全案的偵查與否；而且依據EEA進行時舉證證明刑事侵害責任遠高過民事侵害責任。

　　EEA雖有防範與制裁外國經濟間諜的目的，然而單以美國境內的營業秘密維護而言，並未達到其預期的功能性，若再制定FTSA並不影響EEA之位階與其目的性，且可補強其規範聯邦各州營業秘密法之一致性，營業秘密法未如著作權法、專利法受到更多重視[79]，使其聯邦化並不影響其他既有法規之功效，且有相輔相成的功效，目前將營業秘密法侷限在州法位階，對資訊的流動性及整體經濟的發達反而形成障礙，制定聯邦營業秘密法與契約、受雇人忠實義務、專利授權契約、競業禁止條款互為利用，更能兼顧企業之生存命脈──秘密資訊之維護。

　　EEA執行的困難度在於涉及外國政府或組織的經濟間諜案例，即使FBI擁有充分的偵查權，然而營業秘密的洩漏形成智慧資產及企業的重大威脅，FBI和美國商會建立工商業防範間諜威脅的制度及措施，成立美國商業與聯邦調查局集中資訊交流中心，並與海外的所有商會合作，鼓吹全國共同打擊竊盜智慧財產權不遺餘力。EEA立法後尚有其他立法規範電子通訊、電腦駭客、網路研發……等領域，如以下法規。

---

[77] Catherine L. Fisk, *Knowledge Work: New Metaphors for the New Economy,* 80 Chi.-Kent L. Rev 839, 857(2005).

[78] David S. Almeling, *Four Reasons to Enact A Federal Trade Secret Act,* 19 Fordham Intell. Prop. Media & Ent. L.J. 769,785 (Spring, 2009)

[79] 見EEA當時立法理由。H.R. Rep. No. 104-788, at 4 (1996), as reprinted in 1996 U.S.C.C.A.N. 4021, 4022-23; see also S. Rep. No. 104-359, at 5 (1996).

1. 愛國者法（Significant provisions of the Uniting and Strengthening America by Providing Appropriate Tools Required to Intercept and Obstruct Terrorism Act, USA Patriot Act[80]），2001年10月26日通過，主要為杜絕恐怖主義盛行，強化及聯繫美國法令，愛國者法擴張對恐怖主義的防禦，利用媒體監看我國人民或與外國人或組織之間的通訊內容，針對刑事案件的標準，特別是秘密偵查及謀取知識及資料而得到審判資訊的限制。

2. 網路安全研究及發展法（the Cyber Security Research and Development Act）[81]，針對電腦駭客惡意破壞網際網路，影響電腦系統及網路工作，為此相關的研發工作更為迫切，西元2001年12月4日眾議院制定本法，為促進公共利益，增進經濟成長與溝通，針對網路安全之研究及發展，更可解決為提昇高科技產業而投注鉅額之研究成果可得之保障。

3. 網路恐怖主義預防法（the Cyberterrorism Preparedness Act of 2002）[82]，為預防網路恐怖主義、網路犯罪及其他目的而設

---

[80] 2001年10月26日通過愛國者法（Significant provisions of the Uniting and Strengthening America by Providing Appropriate Tools Required to Intercept and Obstruct Terrorism A, 簡稱'USA Patriot Act', P.L. 107-56, signed (Oct. 26, 2001)）, http://www.nlada.org/DMS?Documents/1006186143.01/USA%20Patriot%20Act%20Summary.pdf (last visited 2003/8/6). USA PATRIOT Act, 814(1)(3), Pub. L. No. 107-56, 115 Stat. 272 (2001) [revising CFAA 1030(e)(8)].

[81] *Summary of H.R.3394, The Cyber Security Research and Development Act,* at 1, http://www.house.gov/science/cyber/summary.htm (last visited 2003/8/5). *Cybersecurity Bill Passes House, the statement of House Science Committee Chairman,* http:// www.house.gov/science/press (last visited 2003/8/17).

[82] *Sen. Edwards on Cybersecurity and Cyberterrorism, Congressional Report* (Feb. 13, 2002), http://www.uspolicy.be/Issues/E-commerce/edwards.021302.htm (last visited 2003/8/17; *Statements on Introduced Bills and Joint Resolutions,* Congressional Record: January 28 William Jackson, Bill calls cybersecurity best practices, Vol. 21, No. 3 (Feb. 4, 2002),

立，於2002年1月28日通過立法，所謂網路恐怖主義乃對於電腦系統的破壞，影響社會安全及經濟的穩定性，目前電腦在國家的電氣、石油、瓦斯、水、電話、緊急救助系統及銀行，或國家的防禦系統皆占有重要的地位。

4. 網路安全研究及教育法（the Cybersecurity Research and Education Act of 2002）[83]，2002年1月28日參議院一併提出本法，網路恐怖主義預防法（S.1900）與本法（S.1901）皆由參議員Mr. Edwards於國會第107次會期提出，並獲通過。通過之原因與網路恐怖主義預防法相同，主要區別乃在網路安全研究及教育法針對如何訓練訓練者，增進研究人員、教師及工作人員認知網路安全，惟仍無法取代EEA解決美國經濟間諜案件的功能與角色，我國更因為美國對於營業秘密的重視，而制定了營業秘密相關法規。

二、能兼顧美國各州之法規及經濟利益

各州在處理有關營業秘密保障的案件時，雖有UTSA可作為各州立法的範本，惟因各州仍可選擇遵循UTSA的精神，制定各州自行遵守的營業秘密法，制定EEA法規之必要性值得肯定，然而並未達到當時立法所預期的效率性與效果，科技發達的便利性使得目前從事經濟間諜行為者，不單是造成企業辛勤維護的營業秘密被竊取，更重擊美國整體科技發展及經濟損失。

---

http://www.gcn.com/21_3/news/17901-1.html (last visited 2003/ 8/17). Also see Brain Krebs, *Senator Introduces New Cybercrime Bills,* Newsbytes (Jan 29, 2002), http://www.securityfocus.com/new/317 (last visited 2003/8/17).

[83] *Sen. Edwards on Cybersecurity and Cyberterrorism,* Congressional Report (Feb. 13, 2002), http://www.uspolicy.be/Issues/E-commerce/edwards.021302.htm (last visited 2003/8/17).

FTSA使企業在維護其自身商業機密有更周全的保障，而聯邦法規可更進一步提昇智慧財產權的位階，依照目前各州規制不一，在統合經濟間諜法規方面，若能增加各州實質與程序的一致性，對案件的調查費用、程序配合、經濟利益皆有實益，因近年來技術更迭迅速、科技發展一日千里，智慧財產權之保護在國際貿易及國內產業發展環境均成為重點課題，竊取他人營業秘密圖利自己，從事經濟間諜行為的手段日新月異，造成經濟間諜之案件日益增加，以專法制定FTSA，使適用效果直接解決實務上制裁經濟間諜的爭端處理，藉此項專門的法律，達到保障營業秘密、懲治經濟間諜的目的。

三、我國可為借鏡之處

我國營業秘密法[84]自1996年公布施行，立法精神及目的皆參酌國外立法例，傳統的僱傭關係中，雇用人（資方）多屬經濟上之強者，為了維持其強勢地位，並保障重要資訊不被洩漏，應付出相當努力維持其營業秘密之安全性，如何以合理手段獲得知識上的隱密性及維持市場競爭力，絕不剽竊競爭者的營業秘密，皆是雇用人應當努力的方向。若有法規確實懲戒及遏阻當事人破壞職場倫理的不法行為更形重要。

我國營業秘密法單獨立法並定位為民事特別法，僅明定民事責任，因為民事請求對犯罪行為人約束力薄弱，當其以脫產、破產方式即可逃避強制執行，若行為人全無資力，毫無賠償被害人損失之可能，因此條文特別規範民事賠償部分[85]，至於刑事責任及行政責任，

---

[84] 西元2002年1月1日起，我國已正式成為WTO之會員國，我國加入WTO後，在智慧財產權方面最為重要者，乃是所謂TRIPs協定，全文參見：http://www.wto. org/english/tratop_e/trips_e/t_agml_e.htm。

[85] 民國84年規範民事賠償，只能以民法第184條「故意以背於善良風俗方法加損害於他人」為請求之依據，舉證甚為困難，且損害賠償額之計算，亦不容易。

仍適用現行刑法及公平交易法之規定[86]，因此至今仍無法有效解決經濟間諜產生的問題及困擾。與本法相關者，其他適用民法、刑法、公平交易法、公司法……等相關法令，至於犯罪行為客體若涉及智慧財產權規範內容，則須適用商標法、著作權法、積體電路電路布局保護法……，近來更新者，如電子簽章法、網路個人資料保護法。

　　然而經濟間諜行為觸及者所在多類，本文建議參考美國立法例於我國成立獨立法規，同時為強調其地位之獨特性，不和營業秘密法合而為一，如此不僅針對洩漏營業秘密，如離職後競業禁止行為，構成國內或國外從事經濟行為者之大宗，依賴如勞基法或勞委會公布之其他規則，無法使法官判決時有直接遵循的準則，僅依據之前如詐欺、背信……等罪刑科處刑責，對遏止經濟間諜等行為助益不大，未來以單獨立法方式作為我國規範經濟間諜之立法原則較為可行。

　　營業秘密法保障營業秘密，鼓勵產業之研究、開發或利用，並能維護商業倫理與競爭秩序，此可解決營業秘密有特別規定者，適用營業秘密法，從事經濟間諜行為者，則適用其他法律之規定；經濟間諜法亦定位為特別法，使企業透過公權力，可以快速並有效地保護私法上的營業秘密，企業主可向檢調單位反應，由其以國家資源進行查緝，參考美國或引以為鏡正可作為我國在立法時之經驗論證，並能保障我國在制定相關法規時之依據，檢視我國經濟、貿易、政治、科技……等各方面之重大變遷，探求一套兼具刑事制裁及民事救濟的法令，能在實質規範上產生重大意義。

---

[86] 依當時之院會紀錄，政府斟酌我國當時之產業競爭與經濟環境，參考外國之立法例，擬具「營業秘密法」草案，對於侵害營業秘密之行為，刑事責任上已有竊盜、侵占、背信、洩漏業務上工商秘密罪可分別適用論處，至於行政責任，公平交易法第36條，亦有處罰規定。

參考文獻

中文部分

1. 期　刊

羅麗珠，「美國的經濟間諜法案」，經濟部科技專案通報「技術尖兵」，第32期，頁12，1997年8月。

2. 其　他

王　珍，「美國潛艇靜音技術　洩密中國　美國重要國防承包商 Power Paragon的首席工程師　麥大志（華裔）被判有罪」（2007/5/24），http://mag.epochtimes.com/022/3129g. htm (last visited: 2009/9/27).

章忠信，「經濟間諜法簡介」，2002年2月20日，http://www. copyrightnote.org/crnote/bbs.php?board = 8&act = read&id = 10（上網日期：民國2007年8月12日）。

英文部分

1. 期　刊

Alster, Norm, *The Valley of the Spies*, Forbes. at 200, 204 (Oct. 6, 1992).

Almeling, David S., *Four Reasons to Enact A Federal Trade Secret Act*, 19 Fordham Intell. Prop.

Band, Jonathan, *The Economic Espionage Act: Its Application in Year One*, Corp. Couns., at 1 (Nov. 1997).

Berthelsen, John, *Friendly Spies*, Far E. Econ. Rev., at 28 (Feb. 1994).

Carr, Chris, *The Economic Espionage Act: Bear Trap or MouseTrap?* 8 Tex. Intell. Prop. L.J. 164-165 (2000).

Cathcart, David, *Contracts with Employees: Covenants Not To Compete and Trade Secrets,* 36 Ali-Aba 87, 100 (1997).

Cate, Brandon B., *Saforo & Associates, Inc. v. Porocel Corp.: The Failure of the Uniform Trade Secrets Act to Clarify the Doubtful and Confused Status of Common Law Trade Secret Principles,* 53 Ark. L. Rev. 687, 697-699 (2000).

Clark, Michael T,. *Economic Espionage: The Role of the United States Intelligence Community,* 3 J. Int'l Legal Stud. 253, 254-255 (1997).

Cohen, Jerry, *Federal Issues in Trade Secret Law,* 2 J. High Tech. L. 1 (2003).

Dreyfuss, Rochelle Cooper, *How Well Should We Be Allowed To Hide Them? The Economic Espionage Act of 1996,* 9 Fordham Intell. Prop. Media & Ent. L.J. 1, (1998).

Economic Espionage, Seattle Times, at A3 (Nov. 6, 1991).

Fisk, Catherine L., *Knowledge Work: New Metaphors for the New Economy,* 80 Chi.-Kent L. Rev 839, 857(2005).

Kenneth Mann, *Punitive Civil Sanctions: The Middleground Between Criminal and Civil Law,* 101 Yale L.J. 1795, (1992).

Lewis, Jonathan Eric, The Economic Espionage Act and the Threat of Chinese Espionage in the United States, 8 Chi.-Kent J. Intell. Prop., 189-235 (Spring, 2009).

L.A. Times, A10 (Feb. 3, 1993).

Mann, Jim, *Woolsey Cites Dangers in Economic Espionage, L.A.* Times, A10 (Feb. 3, 1993).

Media & Ent. L.J. 769,785 (Spring, 2009)

Moyer, Marc A., *Section 301 of the Omnibus Trade and Competitiveness Act of 1988: A Formidable Weapon in the War Against Economic Espionage,* 15 Nw. J. Int'l L. & Bus.178, 184

(1994).

Norton, Rob, *The CIA's Mission Improbable,* Fortune, at 55 (Oct. 2, 1995).

Sepura, Karen, Economic Espionage: The Front Line Of A New World Economic War. 26 SYR J. Int'l L. Com. 127, 133 (1998).

Stuart, Pamela B., *The Criminalization of Trade Secret Theft: The Economic Espionage Act of 1996,* 4 ILSA J. Int'l & Lonp. L. 374, 381 (1998).

Starkman, Dean, *Secrets and Lies: The Dual Career of a Corporate Spy,* Wall St. J. at B1 (Oct. 23, 1997).

Schweizer, Peter, *The Growth of Economic Espionage: America Is Target Number One,* Foreigh Aff., Jan./Feb. at 11 (1996).

Tyler, Christian, *The Enemy Within,* FIN. Times (London), FT Weekend, at 1 (Apr. 12, 1997).

Unikel, Robert, *Bridging the "Trade Secret" Gap: Protecting "Confidential Information" Not Rising to the Level of Trade Secrets,* 29 Loy. U. Chi. L. J. 841, 843 (1998).

Warner, William T., *Economic Espionage: A Bad Idea,* Nat'l L. J. at 13 (Apr. 12, 1993).

Virginia, *President's Remarks at Central Intelligence Agency in Langley,* 31 Weekly Comp. Pres. Doc. 1238 (Jul. 14, 1995).

Yates, Ronald E., *Cold War: Part II, Foreign Intelligence Agencies Have New Targets - U.S. Companies,* Chi. Trib., at C1, Aug. 1993.

Yates, Ronald E., *Espionage Fight Shifts to Corporate Battlefield; Laws Offer Little Help; Cost From Spying is Put at $10 Billion a Year,* Chi. Trib., at C1 (Mar. 24, 1996).

2. 其　他

Acohido, Byron, *Tech gadgets help corporate spying surge in tough times,* USA TODAY, http://www.usatoday.com/tech/ news/ computersecurity/2009-07-28-corporate-espionage-recession-tech_N.htm (last visited: 2009/9/6).

ASIS *Int'l, Trends in Proprietary Information Loss,* survey report, The National Counterintelligence Executive (NCIX) and the American Society for Industrial Security (ASIS) (August 2007), available at http://www.asisonline.org/newsroom/ surveys/spi2.pdf (last visited 2009/9/19).

Basat, Caryl Ben, *the Economic Espionage Act of 1996,* 31 Int'l Law. 245 (1997), http://web.lexis-nexis.com/universe/document?_m (last visited 2007/10/01).

Biswas, Sorojini J., *The Economic Espionage Act of 1996,* http:// www. myersbigel.com/ts_articles/trade_secret4.htm (last visited 2003/8/3).

Court Rules In (Settled) Secrets Case, The Recorder 10 (2003/1/1), http://web.lexis-nexis.com/universe/document?_m (last visited: 2003/6/16).

Epstein, Victor, Chinese man in NJ accused of trade secret theft, USA TODAY, http://www.usatoday.com/news/nation/states/ newjersey/ 2009-04-10-725573065_x.htm (last visited: 2009/ 9/6).

First Foreign Economic Espionage Indictment; Defendants Steal Trade Secrets from Cleveland Clinic Foundation (May 8, 2001), http:// www.usdoj.gov/criminal/cybercrime/Okamoto_ SerizawaIndict. htm (last visited: 2009/9/28).

Halligan, R. Mark, *The Economic Espionage Act of 1996: The Theft of Trade Secrets is Now a Federal Crime,* http://www. execpc.com/ mhallign/crime.html (last visited 2000/8/28).

Kohl, Herb, Statements on Introduced Bills and Joint Resolutions

(Senate - 1996/2/1), http://thomas.loc.gov/cgi-bin/query/F? r104:6:./temp/~r104xC3f7h:e27014 (last visited: 2003/8/ 15).

Rishikof, *Harvey, Economic and Industrial Espionage: A Question of Counterintelligence or Law Enforcement?* http:// nationalstrategy. com/Programs/NationalStrategyForumReview/SpringSummer200 9NSFROnlineJournal/FeatureEssayEconomicandIndustrialEspiona ge/tabid/189/Default.aspx (last visited 2009/9/19).

Senator Arlen, Economic Espionage Act of 1996 (Senate - Oct. 2, 1996), the statement of Mr. Specter, http://thomas.loc.gov/ cgi-bin/query/F?r104:4:./temp/~r1041fv7oB:71874: (last visited 2003/8/15).

Tucker, Dareen S., *The Federal Government's War on Economic Espionage,* 18 U.Pa. J. Int'l Econ L. 1113, http://web.lesix- nexis. com/universe/document?_m (last visited 2003/ 8/12).

U.S. officials eye N. Korea in cyberattack, USA TODAY, http:// www. usatoday.com/news/washington/2009-07-08-hacking- washington-nkorea_N.htm,(last visited: 2009/9/6).

U.S. Department of Justice, Former Boeing Engineer Convicted of Economic Espionage in Theft of Space Shuttle Secrets for China (2009/7/16), http://www.usdoj.gov/opa/pr/2009/July/ 09-nsd-688. html (last visited: 2009/9/27).

United States Attorney's Office, Central District of California, Chinese Agent Sentenced to Over 24 Years in Prison for Exporting United States Defense Articles to China (3/24/ 2008), http://www. usdoj.gov/usao/cac/pressroom/pr2008/032. html (last visited: 2009/9/27).

第五章　以專利法或著作權法保障電腦軟體之探討

曾勝珍

■摘要 SUMMARY

　　電腦的廣泛使用與網際網路的便捷，使得以電腦軟體程式設計申請專利，是專利權人確保其權益的積極做法，對於保障電腦程式中的設計程序，除開專利法外更可運用著作權法的保障，探討電腦軟體程式與專利法暨電腦軟體程式與著作權法的關聯及軟體使用契約與實務之間的運用，皆能提供以專利法或著作權法保障電腦軟體的具體建議。

關鍵詞

- 專利法
- 網際網路
- 電腦軟體
- 著作權法
- 間接侵害責任

Abstract

Both patent and copyright protection share several common features amenable to software protection. The damages available for copyright infringement are similar to those available for patent infringement. A number of recent patent disputes have involved important internet technologies, or concern the impact of the internet and related technologies on patentability.

Keywords: Patent Law, Copyright Law, Internet, Secondary Infringement Liability, Computer Software.

壹、導　論

2008年美國聯邦巡迴上訴法院（The United States Court of Appeals for the Federal Circuit, CAFC）在Bilski[1]案中，對於以專利法保障電腦程式中的設計程序（process），在探討定義時改變了以往十年中的解釋——自1988年開始的State Street Bank & Trust Co. v. Signature Financial Group, Inc.[2]案的標準，由「具備實用性、精簡及具體可見的結果」（useful, concrete, and tangible result），改變為所謂的程序也包含「商業方法與電腦軟體」（business methods and computer software），這樣的判斷標準其實更趨近於四十年前，由美國聯邦最高法院在Gottschalk v. Benson[3]案中所作的決定。

---

[1]　In re Bilski, 545 F.3d 943 (Fed. Cir. 2008).

[2]　State Street Bank & Trust Co. v. Signature Financial Group, Inc., 149 F.3d 1368, 1374 (Fed. Cir. 1998).

[3]　Gottschalk v. Benson, 409 U.S. 63, 70-71 (1972).

Bilski案亦闡明State Street Bank一案，永遠難以取代最高法院的見解，最高法院對主張可受專利法保障的程序，必須具備下述要件：(1)與特別的機器或設備有關；(2)將某種物體轉換成另一種狀態或物品[4]。值得探討的是若將為一般性使用目的的電腦，重新詮釋的軟體程式是否符合第一項要件，在Halligan[5]案中美國專利上訴及解釋委員會（the Board of Patent Appeals and Interferences），認為Bilski案中的機器轉換型態測試，應遠比一般性的電腦使用重新詮釋方法，需求標準更高[6]，因此一解釋的不確定性，造成軟體程式研發者思考除了專利法外，以著作權法進行保障是否也是另外一種選擇。

專利法或著作權法的保障都有其共通點，包括受到侵害的賠償請求態樣，不論專利法或著作權法的判斷標準，首先皆考量如被害人因為侵害行為而導致的收入及利潤之減少；其次，當被害人無法證明其所失利潤時，著作權法衡量侵害人因侵害行為而得到的利益，並依據法規的賠償倍數及比例計算賠償金額，專利法則提供相當比例的授權金作為補償。二者還有一項共通點，是經由間接侵害責任尋求賠償管道，即非經由直接侵害人（如使用人或購買者），而是向出售或製造、經銷該侵害商品的間接侵害人請求賠償。因此，越來越多的創作人及發明人會選擇以專利法之外，再以著作權法主張其權利的維護，二者之間的權衡將由下文依序探討。

貳、電腦軟體程式與著作權法間接侵害責任

電腦遊戲著作權人透過向出售盜版軟體商家的求償，比向不特定

---

[4] Id. at 954.
[5] Ex parte Halligan, No. 2008-1588, 2008 WL 4998541, at *13 (B.P.A.I. Nov. 24, 2008).
[6] Id.

的多數買受人求償更加方便，原告需證明：(1)其為合法著作權人，
(2)必須證明侵害人的違法行為[7]，當軟體程式被執行時，必須經由電
腦內的儲存記憶體（random access memory, RAM）才能複製備份，
而複製正是美國著作權法第106條規範中的侵害態樣，因著作權人擁
有對其著作的獨占權，本身可以主張權利或授權他人行使，由文意中
的「授權」字樣擴大解釋，包括輔助侵害人的侵害責任[8]，如果沒有
製造構成侵害裝置的第三人，使用人無法複製備份造成盜版的問題，
因此，著作權法允許被害人可以向非構成直接侵害的第三人求償。著
作權法並無明文規範間接侵害責任，而是在判例中得到法源依據[9]，
並因而延伸出不同類型的間接侵害責任。

　　無論是輔助、引誘、替代侵害責任，都必須存在於直接侵害責
任之後，才有成立的可能，以下將就其類型及定義說明如下；本文
以下先說明包括輔助侵害責任（contributory liability）及替代侵害責
任（vicarious liability），引誘侵害責任（inducement liability），
再論述美國2008年的相關案件及網路法律規定、重要判決見解（如
Napster[10]、Aimster[11]及Grokster[12]等案件），希冀對著作權法間接侵害
責任之範圍及內涵，有更新的解讀方式並藉由分析美國之法律及實務
提供予世人以為參考[13]。

---

[7] A&M Records, Inc. v. Napster, Inc., 239 F.3d 1004, 1013 (9th Cir. 2001). 35 U.S.C. § 271 (2006).
[8] H.R. Rep. No. 94-1476, at 61 (1976)
[9] 專利法則不同有明文規定，35 U.S.C. § 271 (2006).
[10] A&m Records, Inc. v. Napster, Inc., 239 F. 3d 1004, 1013-19 (9th Cir. 2001).
[11] In re Aimster Copyright Litig., 334 F. 3d 643, 646-47 (7th Cir. 2003).
[12] Metro-Goldwyn-Mayer Studios, Inc. v. Grokster, Ltd. 125 S. Ct. 2764 (U.S.S.C. 2005), 380 F.3d 1154 (9th Cir. 2004), 259 F.Supp.2d 1029 (C.D. Calif. 2003).
[13] 美國採用電子千禧著作權法，the Digital Millennium Copyright Act 1998, 簡稱DMCA, Pub. L. No. 105-304, 112 State. 2860 (1998) (codified in scattered sections of 17 U.S.C.)，偏向保障著作權人，RIAA即以此為對抗終端使用者的主要武器；英國則透過2003

一、輔助侵害責任

著作權法的輔助侵害責任和專利法的規定相同，當出售構成侵害的裝置或配件時，經銷商一樣具有輔助侵害責任，此項責任的要件是行為人「知情」（knowledge）及參與（participation），即輔助侵害人必須對侵害事實知情且誘使、幫助或參與其侵害活動[14]，當事人參與的情節輕重會與其責任多寡有關，侵權行為整編定義當事人知情且參與該侵害事實時，與侵害人連帶負責[15]，該侵害事實造成其他人的損害，且輔助侵害人給予主要侵害人相當協力或鼓勵以進行該當侵害行為，對於受到侵害的企業、組織或個人所遭受的痛苦，輔助侵害人與主侵害人應連帶負責。輔助侵權行為乃幫助（aiding）或鼓勵（encouraging）著作權侵害行為[16]，有三項要件：1.主要侵害人造成的直接侵權行為。2.明知侵害事實。3.有實質參與侵害事實的行為。關於知情（knowledge）不論實際或擬制知情，乃指被告應知或

年著作權暨其相關權利規範，Copyright Regulations, SI 2003 No. 2498, in effect as of 31 October 2003 ("Copyright Regulations")，補充2001年電子著作權規範，the EC Copyright Directive，簡稱Copyright Directive Directive 2001/29/EC on copyright in the information society ("Copyright Directive")，如美國的DMCA比起其他歐盟國家，對著作權有強效的保障；加拿大則仍處於觀望階段，即使美國方面不停給予修法壓力。

[14] Gershwin Publishing Corp. v. Columbia Artists Mgmt., Inc., 443 F.2d 1159 (2d Cir. 1971). Also see Sony Corp. of Am., 464 U.S. at 439; Metro-Goldwyn-Mayer Studios Inc. v. Grokster, Ltd., 545 U.S. 913, 930 (2005).

[15] Restatement of the Law of Torts (Second) §876(b) (1979).

[16] Metro-Goldwyn-Mayer Studios, Inc. v. Grokster, Ltd. (Grokster II), 380 F.3d 1154, 1160 (9th Cir. 2004).

可得而知侵害情事的情形[17]，提供場合與用具亦代表實際參與侵害事實[18]。

二、替代侵害責任

當一方有權利及能力掌控侵害行為並因此侵害而獲利時，則科予其替代責任。此種責任可能基於契約關係，即使實際未運作的權利，然而必須為「直接」的獲利，然而意指獲利和侵害行為間有直接或間接的關係，如收取侵害活動所在地的固定租金即不能構成替代責任的「利益要件[19]」，若收取行政管理費用、表演場地架設攤位販售商品的金額、停車費用及來自贊助人的經費……等則符合此要件[20]。

著作權法替代責任的發展始自於過去半世紀，音樂發行人對在演奏廳表演其作品的樂團收取權利金[21]，與代理責任之規範有關，即雇用人對其受僱人的侵權行為有連帶責任，法院科予雇用樂團公開演奏未經授權曲目的演奏廳所有人連帶損害賠償責任[22]，此乃雇用人責任理論（the doctrine of respond eat superior）[23]，引用此理論於非僱傭

---

[17] Sony Corp. v. Universal City Studios, Inc., 464 U.S. 417, 439-42 (1984), 然而後於西元2003年Aimster一案中，法官Posner卻不贊成此種Sony一案中，第九巡迴上訴法院的見解，認為第九巡迴上訴法院是錯誤的，必須對特定侵害事實實際知情才足判定為輔助侵害的成立要件。See Aimster, 334 F.3d at 649.

[18] A&M Records, Inc. v. Napster, Inc., 239 F.3d 1004, 1022 (9th Cir. 2001) (quoting Fonovisa, Inc. v. Cherry Auction, Inc., 76 F.3d 259, 264 (9th Cir. 1996)).

[19] Deutsch v. Arnold, 98 F.2d 686, 688 (2d Cir. 1938); Shapiro, Bernstein & Co. v. H.L. Green Co., 316 F.2d 304, 307 (2d Cir. 1963).

[20] Fonovisa, Inc. v. Cherry Auction, Inc., 76 F.3d 259, 263 (9th Cir. 1996).

[21] See Dreamland Ball Room, Inc. v. Shapiro, Bernstein & Co., 36 F.2d 354 (2d Cir. 1929). See also Shapiro, Bernstein & Co. v. H.L. Green Co., 316 F.2d 304, 307-308 (2d Cir. 1963) (citing cases).

[22] Shapiro, 316 F.2d at 307.

[23] Demetriades v. Kaufmann, 690 F. Supp. 289, 292 (S.D.N.Y. 1988).

或代理關係時，第三人須為行為人的侵權行為負連帶責任，如前述案
例中演奏廳的所有人因演奏的結果而得到經濟上的利益，相對地，作
曲人（音樂創作人）遭受其作品被侵權的結果，因此考慮公平性與合
理性，並比較其經濟地位的差異，若不科予演奏廳所有人責任，則著
作權人失去被補償的機會[24]。

當個人尋求利益，而利基建立於預期必將發生的損失時，通常合
理及公平的作法乃將損失歸致於得到利益的他方，以達平衡，「經濟
上獲利」（financial benefit）是替代責任最重要的要件，至於掌控演
出的權利與能力則為次要要件；使演奏廳所有人承擔如此責任，是否
有促使其為規避損失，增加對其演出內容監督的動力與功能，除了經
濟上的動機，企圖使承擔替代責任的所有人監督及避免侵權行為的前
提，乃所有人必須有能監督的權利與能力，同時必須在合理及公平的
範圍內才能為此項要求。

原告必須證明被告符合下述要件：1.主要侵害人造成的直接侵權
行為。2.被告享有因此侵害行為的直接經濟收益。3.被告有權限與能
力監督侵害人的行為[25]。與輔助侵權行為責任不同在於，替代侵權行
為責任並不以被告知情為要件，然而要件2及3則為必要條件，所謂
直接經濟收益包括營業量或顧客群的增加[26]。

上述替代責任與輔助侵害使著作權人在尋求救濟與節省索賠成
本方面產生極大意義，首先是除了主要（直接）侵害人外，著作權人
多了可以索賠的對象與管道，其次在補償之請求時，可節省時間與過
程，亦提高獲得賠償的機會[27]。

---

[24] See Aimster, 334 F.3d at 654. Cf. Dawson Chem. Co. v. Rohm & Haas Co., 448 U.S. 176, 188 (1980). 此理論亦相對應於專利法中的輔助侵權責任。

[25] Id. (quoting Fonovisa, 76 F.3d at 262).

[26] Napster, 239 F.3d at 1023.

[27] See Douglas Lichtman & William Landes, Indirect Liability for Copyright Infringement: An Economic Perspective, 16 Harv. J. L. & Tech. 395, 397-99 (2003).

三、引誘侵害責任

「引誘侵害責任」（inducement liability）[28]由Grokster[29]一案法院確立。原告必須證明被告明知並意圖幫助或教唆此類行為，原告提出證據1.Grokster明知或意圖分散其軟體，使使用者能散佈擁有著作權的內容（Grokster擁有的作品高達百分之九十為有著作權）。2.Grokster確知其使用者乃為下載其他擁有著作權的資訊內容才會使用其產品，如Grokster接收的電子郵件乃有關詢問如何播放有著作權的電影[30]，以Oak Industries v. Zemith Electronics一案為例[31]，以產品本質判斷，若有侵權可能之性質存在，則有導致發生侵權結果的可能[32]。

---

[28] 法院檢視Grokster一案中是否構成實質侵害的使用。Grokster I, Metro-Goldwyn-Mayer Studios, Inc. v. Grokster, Ltd., 259 F. Supp. 2d 1029, 1041 (C.D Cal. 2003). Grokster II, MGM Studios Inc. v. Grokster , Ltd., 380 F.3d 1154, 1162 n.9 (9th Cir. 2004). Grokster III, Metro-Goldwyn-Mayer Studios, Inc. v. Grokster, Ltd, 125 S. Ct. 2764 (2005)一案自西元2003年至2005年間，歷經地院至最高法院的數次判決結果，使著作權人擁有另種嶄新保護依據。再討論實際的幫助行為上，Grokster並未提供實質的從事侵害的設備與網路位置，而由使用人利用軟體系統，互相連結創造出網路內涵及提供相關途徑，第九巡迴上訴法院最終並未判定Grokster的輔助侵害責任，Grokster, 380 F.3d at 1164；至於Grokster是否負擔監督之責任，法院以為Grokster並無權終止或關閉使用者的路徑及相互之間的連結，Id. at 1165.原告引用第七巡迴上訴法院所言「明知的故意」（willful blindness），然而，本案第九巡迴上訴法院認為Grokster根本無從管理與監督使用人間直接的侵害行為，最高法院最終適用間接侵害責任-引誘侵害責任。

[29] 本案被告Grokster（使用Fast Track P2P系統）及StreamCast Networks（使用Grnutella P2P系統），並未使用中央集中管理目錄系統，而是運用Fast Track「超級點」（Super nodes）進行「目錄」的功能，Gnutella則使用全部分散式的目錄系統，本案被告最主要功能乃在改良及分配系統軟體的部份，使使用者能更方便使用，Grokster, 259 F. Supp. 2d at 1039-41, 1043.

[30] Grokster III, 125 S. Ct. at 2772.

[31] Oak Indus., Inc. v. Zenith Elec. Corp., 697 F. Supp. 988-992 (1988).

[32] Grokster III, 125 S. Ct. at 2779.

　　法院最終以下述三點認定Grokster承擔侵權責任，1.被告嘗試吸收之前Napster的使用者，除了Grokster及Napster名稱相類似，二者提供的內容也有許多類似之處[33]，且被告怠於阻止及限制侵權行為之發生，並從中取利。2.法院發現被告未曾嘗試或盡力發展過濾或使用其他工具、技術以終止因運用其軟體而造成的侵權行為[34]，第九巡迴上訴法院未曾考量此點，最高法院則以此更加肯定被告意圖使使用者更易於從事侵權行為。3.更多人使用被告之軟體，被告獲取更多廣告收益。

　　本案判決結果在技術革新及資源分配方面並未達到正面助益，因為內部或公共的分享皆會引致侵權行為的產生，因此判決結果，可能導致新發明的事論，然而不論此案判決，網際網路上檔案的分享與時俱增，即使不透過前述系統，僅以電子郵件寄送方式或即時訊息（MSN）即可。著作權法的引誘侵害責任和專利法的規定環環相扣，引誘侵害責任課予侵害人更高度的責任，因為若沒有侵害人鼓勵直接侵害的行為，侵害結果不一定發生，這是和輔助侵害責任最大的區別[35]。

參、電腦軟體程式與專利法

　　電腦軟體的相關發明可以申請專利，如電腦化的商業方法（computerized business methods）是最明顯的例子。1981年美國最高法院改變之前電腦軟體發明被視為是數學計算程式，還不能被認定

---

[33] Id. at 2881.

[34] Id. at 2781.

[35] MEMC Elec. Materials, Inc. v. Mitsubishi Materials Silicon Corp., 248 F. App'x. 199 (Fed Cir. 2007).

可申請專利保障的見解[36]，1998年7月聯邦巡迴法院則對電腦化的商業方法，賦予專利法上保障做了重要的詮釋[37]，即電腦系統可將資料轉換成可供利用的、精簡具體的方法結果，可以申請專利的保障，包括貨幣值、價目表、財務資料等，也造成無論在金融界、保險、會計行業上，對其計算或計量方式上的突破[38]。

　　2010年6月28日美國最高法院公告Bilski v. Kappos案判決結果，九位大法官一致認為Bilski案主張發明依法不得授予專利，判決結果以為需考量整體主張發明，若為不得授予專利的抽象概念，即使以限定使用環境、增加非重要後解決活動（insignificant post solution activity）等手段迴避，也不會因此轉變為35 USC 101適格方法發明。抽象原理本身是基礎事實、原始動機，不得授予專利[39]。Bilski案第1、第4項所描述的避險相關操作、數學公式皆屬抽象概念，一如Benson、Flook兩案之演算規則，不得授予專利。而其餘各項描述商品及能源市場的避險操作應用例，就像Flook（Diehr）案所說的限定使用環境、增加非重要後解決活動，一樣非35 USC 101規範可授予專利的方法發明[40]。

---

[36]　Diamond v. Diehr, 450 U.S. 173 (1981).

[37]　State Street Bank & Trust Co. v. Signature Financial Group Inc., 149 F.3d 1368 (Fed. Cir. 1998), cert. denied, 525 U.S. 1093 (1999).

[38]　Jeffrey D. Neuburger, Technology, the Internet and Electronic Commerce: Staying Interactive in the High-Tech Environment, A Summary of Recent Developments in the Law, 927 PLI/P 755(2008).

[39]　但抽象概念、自然法則、數學公式本身雖不得授予專利，在既知結構或方法上應用自然法則或數學公式所產生的發明，仍有可能成為可授予專利之客體。黃蘭閔，美國最高法院：Bilski案主張發明屬抽象概念故不予專利，北美智權報，2010年9月8日，http://naipo97.pixnet.net/blog/post/22084773（上網日期：9/22/2010）。

[40]　Bilski案的影響未必只限於美國境內。澳洲專利局（IP Australia）7月21日公告編號2009201212號申請案聽證（Hearing）程序最後決定，其內容即引用Bilski案此次判決，認定該申請案主張的「發明商業化方法」（Method for Commercialising Inventions）並非可授予專利之發明。黃蘭閔，同前註。

　　此類方式或公式是否具備專利法上所要求的新穎性，也造成質疑與討論，反對者以為並不足以創新到可以用專利保護的程度，2000年3月美國專利與商標局（Patent and Trademark Office, PTO）做出回應，將提供商業方法申請專利的檢驗準則，並加強由資深的審查人員審查該類申請案，同時PTO亦延聘具備商業背景與專業技術的新進審查人，負責金融、銀行、保險及電子商務商業方法的案件審查，解除外界對此議題的疑惑[41]。

一、專利法實務

　　專利與網路的應用關係日趨密切，如下說明與網路有關的專利申請案[42]與訴訟案件。

　　Ethos Technologies, Inc.公司於2007年3月27日取得專利（專利編號—Patent No. 7,197,144）[43]，此專利有關避免電腦檔案與程式被入侵及盜用的系統；2.發明人James B. Kargman於2007年3月27日取得專利（專利編號—Patent No. 7,197,478）[44]，此專利有關網路上進行電子商務交易的系統；3. Yahoo! Inc.公司於2007年3月27日取得專利（專利編號—Patent No. 7,197,544），此專利有關網站上連結個人廣告及祝賀的系統[45]。

　　In re Comiskey[46]案則有關主張以商業方法申請專利一案，聯邦巡迴法院支持專利上訴及爭議委員會的決定，維持該委員會決定拒

---

[41]　Jeffrey D. Neuburger, 927 PLI/P at 756.

[42]　僅以2007年3月27日當日獲准取得的數例說明。

[43]　Jeffrey D. Neuburger, 927 PLI/P at 757.

[44]　Jeffrey D. Neuburger, 927 PLI/P at 757-58.

[45]　Jeffrey D. Neuburger, 927 PLI/P at 758.

[46]　In Re Comiskey, No. 2006-1286, 2007 U.S. App. LEXIS 22414 (Fed. Cir. Sept. 20, 2007).

絕申請人的專利，並將該案撤回至專利商標委員會（USPTO）請求重新審議，因其中電腦與數據機的溝通裝置包含不具專利的金屬程序（mental processes?），而不接受其專利之申請；雖然此商業方法涵蓋的溝通裝置具備顯著性，單純以溝通裝置申請專利，因為當中所使用的技術，若是擁有一般性技術的人也非顯而易見，反而能獲得專利核可的機率會高很多；但本案法院仍判決維持原議。

　　Yodlee, Inc. v. Cashedge, Inc.案[47]，對之前判斷被告所主張依據網路科技，將先前藝術加入專利事項的內容，允許被告將其網站設計加上先前藝術（prior art）的索引標籤，因為單純以先前既有的學術論文與專利索引，對先前藝術的資料搜尋十分緩慢，因此被告申請加入新的補充內容，使其專利事項更加完備；Crutchfield New Media, LLC v. Hill & Assoc., Inc.案[48]，有關一個網路零售商申請針對專利權人所提出侵害請求的確定判決，法院審查專利權的專利事項內容後，進而引用最高法院判決，Medimmune, Inc. v. Genetech, Inc.[49]案的結果，確認此零售商提出的無侵害事實合理，並同意其確定判決的請求成立。而Microsoft Corp. v. AT&T Corp.案[50]，從美國出口的主機磁片中可以進行複製功能的軟體密碼，雖然是在美國國外經過組裝至電腦主機後再販售，並未構成美國專利法中出口零件侵害情事[51]，因為被告的程式設計師並非直接將該軟體出口，所以不符合專利法之侵害規範。

---

[47] Yodlee, Inc. v. Cashedge, Inc., No. C 05-01550 SI, 2007 U.S. Dist. LEXIS 58872 (N.D. Cal. Aug. 6, 2007).

[48] Crutchfield New Media, LLC v. Hill & Assoc., Inc., No. 1:06-cv-0837, 2007 U.S. Dist. LEXIS 33264 (S.D. Ind. May 4, 2007).

[49] Medimmune, Inc. v. Genetech, Inc., 127 S.Ct. 764 (2007).

[50] Microsoft Corp. v. AT&T Corp., No. 05-1056, 2007 U.S. LEXIS 4744 (U.S. April 30, 2007).

[51] 35 U.S.C. §271(f).

二、著作權法與專利法規範的比較

雖然著作權法可以提供類似專利法的保障，但仍有差異如下[52]：

表5-1

比較內容	著作權法	專利法
保護客體	保障著作權人A具備原創性著作的專有權，即不允許任何未經過著作權人同意或授權的複製行為。	除了相同於著作權法的保障外，保護客體還包括創意本身，範圍更加寬廣。
權利的專屬性	美國著作權法§106使著作權人對其著作有獨占的專有權，可以複製、散佈、公開發表，公開展示其作品，但無法禁止如其他人B在獨立創作（independent creation）下所完成之相同或類似於A的作品；亦即A及B分別擁有對其作品的著作權，有可能作品相類似但存在兩個著作權。	專利法則不同，即使B在完全不知情的情況下，作出和A相同或類似的產品，以先取得專利的A優先且專屬，B無法再主張專利權的取得。一項發明或設計只能有一個專利權。
權利的取得	著作權不須經由申請及註冊而取得，採「創作主義」，在被害人主張損害賠償的請求時，無法由條文中明定的賠償倍率與律師費用等做為依據；當糾紛發生時，待爭訟結果確定才能計算賠償的數據。	專利法又不同，因為專利的申請程序與取得不易，專利權人必須經由相當準備與努力才能取得專利權，因此，美國專利法中明定賠償的依據。

---

[52] 本表由作者自行整理並參考 Lauren Katzenellenbogen, Charles Duan &James Skelley, Alternative Software Protection in View of In Re BilskiSKI, 7 Nw. J. Tech. & Intell. Prop. 332(2009)一文。

肆、軟體使用契約

　　當出賣人販售軟體時會附上一份或數份的「消費者使用契約」（End User License Agreement），契約內容成為對著作權人最大的保障，無論契約中的用語、定義、規定及解釋，都將是著作權人主張權益受損時的重要依據，因此有關電腦軟體的銷售，如何制定出一份完整的軟體使用契約，將由下述相關案件作出探討。

一、MDY v. Blizzard[53]案

　　亞利桑納州地方法院（the District Court for the District of Arizona）審理此案時，將電腦遊戲的買賣契約違約情事，考量以著作權法或契約法做為依據，視為本案爭點，並斟酌契約用語的合法性。Blizzard出售及授權一種電腦遊戲，「消費者使用契約」中載明限制使用人利用「bot」程式，使未經取得授權的其他使用人，也能進入遊戲現場加入遊戲，造成對合法購買此遊戲軟體的使用人不利，MDY販售針對Blizzard設計的「bot」程式，干擾到使用合法遊戲軟體的買受人[54]。

　　MDY則主張無侵害事實，Blizzard同時提出對MDY侵害其著作權的反訴聲明，有關「bot」程式部分是屬於契約名詞（contractual term）或授權狀態（license condition），法院判斷有關Blizzard著作權的複製、修改及散佈[55]，是授權狀態。本案法院引用1999年第九巡

---

[53] MDY Industries, LLC v. Blizzard Entertainment, Inc., No. 06-2555, 2008 U.S. Dist. LEXIS 53988, at *18-19 (D. Ariz. July 14, 2008).

[54] Blizzard, 2008 U.S. Dist. LEXIS 53988, at *4.

[55] Blizzard, 2008 U.S. Dist. LEXIS 53988, at *18.

迴上訴法院在Sun Microsystems, Inc. v. Microsoft Corp.[56]一案中的見解，認為當著作權人對於其著作給予非專屬授權的使用時，意味著被授權人是合法妥善的行使被授予的權利，也就是正常運作的情形下，著作權人不會對被授權人主張侵害其著作權的請求，除非被授權人違背了授權契約的內容，因此，授權契約的用語、範圍、權利及義務的界定，都必須明確而審慎，在一般的軟體買賣契約中通常已涵蓋，而不需要另外再制定一份獨立的契約，第九巡迴上訴法院在Sun Microsystems一案中，判定被告Microsoft的行為確實違反授權契約的內涵，因而決定原告勝訴。

亞利桑納州地方法院審理Blizzard案時，針對案件中兩造簽訂的「使用者同意契約」（the End User License Agreement, EULA）詳加審閱，如前所述，雙方的權益事項皆依契約明文為準。合約內容既已載明是有限度且非專屬的授權範圍，買方必須完全同意合約內容及限制條件下才能使用[57]，專屬於著作權人Blizzard的權利，如複製、散佈或修改該遊戲軟體等事項，買方MDY都被限制行使[58]，最終法院判定本合約的限制規定，是形成契約有效成立的狀態，而非單純契約用語，Blizzard勝訴。

前述MDY v. Blizzard案中MDY即主張著作權法第107條對使用人的合理使用限制，然而該案法院則以為，即使是經由合法授權後的軟體使用者，也不能違背買賣契約中對違法複製及轉讓的限制，一味限縮使用者的自由，使著作權人擁有更大的主導權，實務上不見得能運作得宜，以下仍由案例探討作出結論。

---

[56] Sun Microsystems, Inc. v. Microsoft Corp., 188 F.3d 1115, 1121 (9th Cir. 1999).

[57] Blizzard, 2008 U.S. Dist. LEXIS 53988, at *14.

[58] Blizzard, 2008 U.S. Dist. LEXIS 53988, at *17.

二、相關案例

（一）Krause v. Titleserv案（2005年）

　　第二巡迴上訴法院對此案中由公司出資聘僱程式設計師設計的軟體，何者為著作權人作出決定[59]，檢視名義上的所有人（如程式設計師）、出資公司或軟體購買者，採取綜合判斷的標準如下：(1)此公司是否對該軟體之設計有付出相當對價，(2)該軟體是否是為此公司而設計，(3)該軟體是否因應此公司客制化之需求而設計，(4)該軟體是否儲存在此公司的伺服器中，(5)著作權人是否保留複製該軟體的權利，(6)著作權人是否同意此公司擁有及使用該軟體，(7)此公司是否有可隨意放棄或銷毀該軟體的自由。

　　法院更指出與其考量該軟體名義上的所有人，不如判斷實際能產生影響的因素與條件，因為Titleserv.公司符合[60]上述七項要件，出資請Krause為公司營運而設計的軟體，軟體儲存在公司的伺服器中，即使與Krause的聘僱關係結束後，仍由其擁有及使用該軟體的權利，Titleserv.公司有放棄或銷毀該軟體的自由；因此法院判決被告Titleserv.公司勝訴。

（二）DSC Communications v. Pulse Communications案（1999年）

　　原告DSC是一家專為製造電話網路轉換設備的公司，被告Pulse則是專為搭配原告軟體而製造相容硬體的公司，本案爭點有關向被告購買硬體設備的電話公司，如RBOCs（Regional Bell Operating

---

[59] Krause v. Titleserv, Inc., 402 F.3d 119 (2d Cir. 2005).

[60] Krause, 402 F.3d at 124.

Companies）公司，對購買後的軟體使用是否擁有複製的權利[61]，聯邦巡迴法院認為軟體所有權的檢測標準，在於授權契約是否有明確的限制範圍，而RBOCs對所購買的軟體，不但不能如同著作權人般有複製的權利，也不能在除了DSC所製造以外的其他機器上使用，而這些規定在購買契約上的授權條款裡，都有明確記載[62]。

買受人即使主張「第一次銷售理論」（first sale doctrine），也無法排除DSC在契約裡的限制條文，包括：(1)著作權人擁有對複製品的所有權利，(2)嚴格禁止將軟體的內容轉讓或公開給任何第三人，(3)嚴格禁止將軟體使用於非經過授權的其他機器上；因此法院判決原告DSC Communications.公司勝訴。

（三）Stuart Weitzman v. Microcomputer Resources案（2007年）

本案法院認為在保障電腦軟體的案件中，前述Krause v. Titleserv.案和DSC Communications v. Pulse Communications.案，都是具備指標性的判決，但本案則只有尚未簽署的契約[63]，未如同前述案件已有書面明文規範，因此，認為本案中可以主張美國著作權法第107條，單純為儲存或與其他電腦裝置相容的複製並不構成對著作權人的侵害。

---

[61] DSC Communications v. Pulse Communications.,170 F.3d 1354 (Fed. Cir. 1999).

[62] DSC Communications, 170 F.3d at 1361-62.

[63] Stuart Weitzman v. Microcomputer Resources, 510 F. Supp. 2d 1098 (S.D. Fla. 2007).

伍、結　論

從近年來案例法的推衍，偏向著重於對著作權人的保障，著作權人可以在軟體買賣的授權使用契約中，對買受人的使用限制重重，但2007年Stuart Weitzman案，則因契約不明確進而推翻此種認定，一般而言，如買賣手機或其他機器時，因為軟體程式往往就在該機型之內，買受人對購買的手機擁有「物」的所有權，但對其中配置的軟體必須視買賣契約上，有關的著作權權益行使及移轉的規定。

Bilski一案對專利物件僅從專利法的保障外，提供了著作權法的考量，尤其是間接侵害責任的部分，而哪種規範對當事人有利，則必須衡量相關情狀後再做出決定，軟體使用契約（software end-user license agreements）的內容將是審酌雙方權益的主要依據，因此買方（使用人）同意將購買後的軟體安裝在其硬體設備上，只能在買方本身所持有或能操控的其他電腦，依據契約內容行使有限度且非專屬的權利，買方的使用行為必須是為個人且非商業性質的娛樂用途，所有的使用皆在購買人同意本合約的前提上才能進行[64]。

有關複製他人電腦程式，造成對著作權人的侵害情形時，美國著作權法第107條條文內容，排除單純為儲存或與其他電腦裝置相容的複製行為，亦即此類複製並不構成對著作權人的侵害[65]；通常啟動一個電腦程式後在主機的記憶體中，自動會儲存此程式的備份資料，購買軟體或電腦遊戲的使用者，有別於該軟體或電腦遊戲的著作權人，雖然擁有此物件所有權，但如何使用及使用範圍等，皆應遵循購買時的使用者同意契約為主。

網路盛行對傳統商標法產生莫大影響，音樂、影片檔案下載的便

---

[64] Blizzard, 2008 U.S. Dist. LEXIS 53988, at *13.
[65] 17 U.S.C. § 117 (2006).

利性及即時通（MSN）、電子郵件的使用使資訊傳遞的速度如風馳
電掣，傳統侵害責任對著作權、專利權的保障範圍造成衝擊，特別是
電子商務及網路商店盛行，科技進步研發神速使法規面的保障力有未
逮，本文參考美國相關判決，盼望大眾採納與引進新科技的同時，對
於國際社會法令的維持與規範共同努力。

參考文獻

中文

黃蘭閔，美國最高法院：Bilski案主張發明屬抽象概念故不予專利，
　　北美智權報，2010年9月8日，http://naipo97.pixnet.net/blog/
　　post/22084773（上網日期：9/22/2010）。

英文

　　Articles

Douglas Lichtman & William Landes, Indirect Liability for Copyright
　　Infringement: An Economic Perspective, 16 Harv. J. L. & Tech.
　　395, 397-99 (2003).

Jeffrey D. Neuburger, Technology, the Internet and Electronic
　　Commerce: Staying Interactive in the High-Tech Environment,
　　A Summary of Recent Developments in the Law, 927 PLI/P
　　755(2008).

Lauren Katzenellenbogen, Charles Duan &James Skelley, Alternative
　　Software Protection in View of In Re BilskiSKI, 7 Nw. J. Tech. &
　　Intell. Prop. 332(2009).

　　Cases

A&M Records, Inc. v. Napster, Inc., 239 F.3d 1004, 1013 (9th Cir.

2001). 35 U.S.C. § 271 (2006).

Crutchfield New Media, LLC v. Hill & Assoc., Inc., No. 1:06-cv-0837, 2007 U.S. Dist. LEXIS 33264 (S.D. Ind. May 4, 2007).

Demetriades v. Kaufmann, 690 F. Supp. 289, 292 (S.D.N.Y. 1988).

Dawson Chem. Co. v. Rohm & Haas Co., 448 U.S. 176, 188 (1980).

Deutsch v. Arnold, 98 F.2d 686, 688 (2d Cir. 1938).

Dreamland Ball Room, Inc. v. Shapiro, Bernstein & Co., 36 F.2d 354 (2d Cir. 1929).

Diamond v. Diehr, 450 U.S. 173 (1981).

DSC Communications v. Pulse Communications.,170 F.3d 1354 (Fed. Cir. 1999).

Ex parte Halligan, No. 2008-1588, 2008 WL 4998541, at *13 (B.P.A.I. Nov. 24, 2008).

Fonovisa, Inc. v. Cherry Auction, Inc., 76 F.3d 259, 263 (9th Cir. 1996).

Gottschalk v. Benson, 409 U.S. 63, 70-71 (1972).

Gershwin Publishing Corp. v. Columbia Artists Mgmt., Inc., 443 F.2d 1159 (2d Cir. 1971).

In re Aimster Copyright Litig., 334 F. 3d 643, 646-47 (7th Cir. 2003).

In re Bilski, 545 F.3d 943 (Fed. Cir. 2008).

In Re Comiskey, No. 2006-1286, 2007 U.S. App. LEXIS 22414 (Fed. Cir. Sept. 20, 2007).

Metro-Goldwyn-Mayer Studios, Inc. v. Grokster, Ltd., 259 F. Supp. 2d 1029, 1041 (C.D Cal. 2003).　MGM Studios Inc. v. Grokster , Ltd., 380 F.3d 1154, 1162 n.9 (9th Cir. 2004).

Metro-Goldwyn-Mayer Studios, Inc. v. Grokster, Ltd, 125 S. Ct. 2764 (2005)

MEMC Elec. Materials, Inc. v. Mitsubishi Materials Silicon Corp., 248

F. App'x. 199 (Fed Cir. 2007).

Medimmune, Inc. v. Genetech, Inc., 127 S.Ct. 764 (2007).

Microsoft Corp. v. AT&T Corp., No. 05-1056, 2007 U.S. LEXIS 4744 (U.S. April 30, 2007).

MDY Industries, LLC v. Blizzard Entertainment, Inc., No. 06-2555, 2008 U.S. Dist. LEXIS 53988, at *18-19 (D. Ariz. July 14, 2008).

Oak Indus., Inc. v. Zenith Elec. Corp., 697 F. Supp. 988-992 (1988).

Krause v. Titleserv, Inc., 402 F.3d 119 (2d Cir. 2005).

State Street Bank & Trust Co. v. Signature Financial Group, Inc., 149 F.3d 1368, 1374 (Fed. Cir. 1998) , cert. denied, 525 U.S. 1093 (1999).

Shapiro, Bernstein & Co. v. H.L. Green Co., 316 F.2d 304, 307 (2d Cir. 1963).

Sun Microsystems, Inc. v. Microsoft Corp., 188 F.3d 1115, 1121 (9th Cir. 1999).

Stuart Weitzman v. Microcomputer Resources, 510 F. Supp. 2d 1098 (S.D. Fla. 2007).

Yodlee, Inc. v. Cashedge, Inc., No. C 05-01550 SI, 2007 U.S. Dist. LEXIS 58872 (N.D. Cal. Aug. 6, 2007).

第六章　The Critique of Negative Knowledge and Unfair Competition in Taiwan

曾勝珍

目次

摘要 SUMMARY

營業秘密保護之目的在於維護產業競爭倫理，調和經濟競爭秩序，鼓勵產業技術之創造與維新，並提供消費者更佳的消費環境與選擇。我國為配合及尊重國際上的共識，已將營業秘密視為智慧財產權的一環，國際潮流中如TRIPs協定，對我國相關立法有極大影響，其他如外國立法例，亦為我國參考立法的重要藍圖。電腦化的社會型態，產生許多秘密資訊洩漏或被竊取的危機，如何妥善運用科技工具及網際網路的便利，又能有效保障企業體系視為命脈的營業秘密，是當今資訊時代值得重視與探討的主題。

本文將先行說明我國在營業秘密保障上相關立法之規定；其次考察美國法規；再就實務上電腦化對營業秘密保障產生的影響進行分析；最後提出對我國相關法制的建議，公司保存機密資訊對研發成果的保護及利潤的追求，達到一體兩面的功效，分為營業戰略、智慧財產權的維護等部分說明。

確保智慧財產權的取得、讓與或內容，在實務上可採取書面契約及確認程序等方式進行。我國營業秘密法雖於民國八十五年一月十七日公布施行，惟其中並未因應經濟間諜罪刑、科技型態更新而有修訂，因此本文考察美國法，斟酌我國現況，提出立法論之建議以供參考。

關鍵詞

▪ 智慧財產權	▪ 網際網路	▪ 電腦化
▪ 營業秘密	▪ 經濟間諜	

Abstract

Trade secret cases pose special problems distinct from other intellectual property lawsuits because alleged trade secrets are rarely defined in advance of litigation. Perhaps the strangest theory of trade secret law is the concept of negative know-how, a theory under which an employee who resigns and joins a different business can be liable for not repeating the mistakes and failures of his or her former employer. The boundaries of the negative knowledge concepts have not been well articulated in the case law. This article first reviews the Taiwan (ROC) Statutes and theories, especially in Fair Trade Law. There is a growing debate between the proponents of negative knowledge and unfair competition. Broad application of the negative know-how theory then would create new restrictions on employee mobility and allow employers to obtain court-created non-competition covenants against former employees based on their knowledge of failures and errors.

Keywords: Intellectual Property Rights, Trade Secret, Internet, Negative knowledge, Unfair Competition, Post-Employment Non-Competition.

I. Introduction

In recent years, the protection of trade secret has been greatly concerned. Usually, employees who leave their companies are asked to sign a non-compete agreement, since employers may worry that those employees may disclose the confidential information or business strategies of the company against the policy. If "negative knowledge" is disclosed, it may be amended, added or deleted by other competitors for R&D of competitive products, it would result in threat to the original company. Therefore, asymmetric treatment of positive and negative knowledge may affect the investor's assessment on corporate value, which may lead to unfair competition.

Before the establishment of specific laws concerning the protection of trade secret, countries tend to punish the violation of fair competition[1]; there are studies criticizing such a theory in the United States[2]. This paper aims to explore the following issues: the definition of the term "negative knowledge", its impact on protection of trade secret, whether it is unfair competition when the doer

---

[1] Other countries such as both Germany and Japan have "Unfair Competition Prevention Law"; China has "Anti-Unfair Competition Law." Article 4, Paragraph 9, 2004 Germany Unfair Competition Prevention Law provides that, any person engages in the following acts would constitute the unfair competition: the provision of imitation goods or services of competitors, and (a) arising from the consumers' confusion about the source of goods or services; (b) inappropriate use of or impairment of the imitation goods or services' good comment (good reputation), or (c) obtain the knowledge or basis necessary to imitation with dishonest methods. Also, according to the provisions of in Article 17 and 18 of the Law, any who impinges on the other's trade secret should bear the criminal responsibility. Based on the U.S. Trade Secret Protection Act and Germany Unfair Competition Prevention Law, Japan took one cultural policy for the Japanese economy and the environment, but Japan did not upgrade trade secret as the right, only as the benefits of business, which are protected with Unfair Competition Prevention Law. Japan adopted similar laws from the U.S. and three elements in TRIPS Article 39, and known as (1) secret management; (2) usefulness; (3) non-publicity, which are not essentially different from those of the United States. See Huang, "New system of trade secret protection," Taiwan Bar Journal, Issue 11, Vol. 8, 2007.

[2] See Charles Tait Graves, "The Law of Negative Knowledge: A critique", 15 Tex. Intell. Prop. L. J.387-416 (Spring 2007). This paper explored the problem proposed by above author mainly; however, the implications, definitions and language were finished by the author of this paper, who will take the responsibility of them. The following are cited the legislative cases of other countries as well as practical cases in the United States for illustration.

improperly using non-trade secret business information[3], servant's right to choose job and public benefits, in order to encourage corporate innovation and development, trade-off employer's information by former employees in an employment relation. According to the maintenance of fair competition and protection of intellectual property rights, both should be balanced. The next sections will discuss the legislative cases in Taiwan and the United States, as well as the latest practical developments in the United States. Finally, conclusions and suggestions to industrial application in Taiwan are proposed.

II. Negative Knowledge

At present, practical trade secrets leak and commercial espionage often occur among staffs, especially those who are job hopping or head hunted, causing competition against the original company. If an employer questions the staff's loyalty and exit movements, he would be reluctant to exert great efforts to train or provide better welfare and promotion, in turn, the staffs' efforts in R&D of new technologies or products would be relatively reduced, as well as the job opportunities, which is more unfavorable for the employer. Also, if the leaving employee does not report the prior knowledge or experience to the new

---

[3] Tait Graves, "Non public Information and California Tort Law: A Proposal for Harmonizing California's Employee Mobility and Intellectual Property Regimes under the Uniform Trade Secrets Act," UCLA J. L. & Tech. 1 (2006). This paper noted the California tort law and adopted Uniform Trade Secrets Act (UTSA), which are the scope and limitations for the people of California using non-public information.

employer, he may be blamed by the new company for not informing; but if he reports fully, he may face lawsuit from the former employer for violating the intellectual property rights, that is, leakage of related trade secrets.

As to prohibition of leaving employee turnover to competitors, apart from preventing positive trade secrets being leaked, but also may be worried about "negative knowledge" has been fully interpreted, and thus develop into an adverse business strategy to the original employer; even it is through the modification[4] by leaving employee, it may still be classified as "misappropriation of trade secrets", so it would be a serious threat to the leaving ones. If the aforementioned theory is implemented, whether positive or negative knowledge, whether report to the new employer, he would still have the responsibility, and the employer may be bound to restrict leaving ones' occupation freedom.

Broadly speaking, when negative knowledge is related to R&D of new products or technologies, it is difficult to measure the value, as most are private with a high degree of uncertainty. Moreover, the company managers would avoid or not repeat the above-mentioned shortcomings, as they know company's R&D plan, which affects the company's cash flow or net profit manipulation, resulting in a direct impact on company value. Therefore, it not only can avoid the unnecessary waste of money and human resources in the R&D process or outcome, but also accelerate the R&D products.

When a leaving employee with the negative knowledge which is not publicly accessible, as his employment relationship ends, he

---

[4] See Charles Tait Graves, "The Law of Negative Knowledge: A critique", Tex. Intell. Prop. L. J., 15, 388(2007). that paper called this modification as "the modification rule".

would have the fiduciary duty in fiduciary relationship[5]. The employer should remind him the confidentiality obligations periodically, usually a confidentiality contract is signed. However, the employee often did not carefully read, or even forgot about the terms, so the periodic reminding would help avoiding future problems, particularly when his new job has close correlation with the previous company's secrets. Such contract can remind both the employer and employee, while trade secret cases often have serious consequences through unintentional disclosure. The nature of the trust relationship is: one party places trust in the other party who is in dominant position[6], it is difficult to define "negative knowledge" known by employee and its scope, the following explained the case in California Court of Appeal.

In Courtesy Temp. Serv., Inc. V. Camacho case[7], the plaintiff had "negative knowledge" failed to attract buyers. In the discussion on the reason that the client cannot become the buyer; if seller made his utmost efforts to provide services, but not be able to attract buyers, that cannot be included in "customer list", but also bet a lot of effort of the plaintiffs. Therefore, the plaintiff may argue that such information should be protected trade secrets. Cinebase Software, Inc. v. Media Guar. Trust, Inc.[8], which also cited the opinion from Camacho case, considered the "negative research" could be regarded as trade secrets

---

[5]　This paragraph referred to Graves's text, and personal opinions of the authors were collating.

[6]　See Restatement (Second) of Torts § 874 (a) (1978), and trans. By Chao, HW, Yang, CJ, (2006) Anglo-American Tort Law, 204, Taipei: Wunan. The translation version cited lawyers and clients relations, the relationship between doctors and patients, this paper thought that the employee had the faithful secrecy obligations for employee.

[7]　222 Cal. App. 3d 1278, 1287 (Cal. Ct. App. 1990).

[8]　No. C98-1100EMS, 1998 WL 661465, at*12 (N.D. Cal. Sept. 22, 1998).

and be protected, that is, it could be made available to the industry to avoid business failure. UTSA was enacted in 1979, the definition of trade secrets continues to apply the explanation in Article 757 of the U.S. Restatement of Torts[9].

The protection of private information is applicable to unfair competition theory, which is built on the concept of common law and tort restatement. Restatement of Torts[10] provided the responsibility of improper possession of trade secrets, that is, if a natural person receives the trade secrets from the third person, regardless of knowing that it is a secret, this natural person should not be punished according to the Restatement, unless it is in bad faith knowingly; if the natural person is ignorant of the situation, or not knowing it contains trade secrets, he does not bear the responsibility until informed of confidentiality matters and continue to use the secret[11].

---

[9] See Restatement (First) of Torts, 757 cmt.b.(1939). Restatement of Torts was completed by The American Law Institute in 1939. The notes from paragraph 757 to 759 of Chapter provide the definition of trade secrets and torts, which had high reference value. According to Note B, Restatement of Torts, 757 (1939), the definition of trade secrets is: "trade secrets can cover any formula, model, design or data compilation, which give the competitors the opportunity to obtain an advantage; it can be the formula of a chemical mixture; methods to treat and preserve materials; the mechanical model or customer lists. Unlike other trade secret information, trade secrets are not single or short-lived information for dealing with business, e.g. a secret tender's amount of bid or other conditions, specific servant's salary, securities investments, the date of announcing a new policy or sample. Trade secrets, refer to procedure or method continuously used by business operation, and it usually associates with goods production, such as the machine or formula; or involves the sale or operation of goods, such as the price decision or directory of discounts or other concessions code, the list of specialized customers, bookkeeping or other office management methods.

[10] Restatement (Third) of Unfair Competition (1995).

[11] The Restatement (Third) of Unfair Competition and Potential Impact on Texas, at 5, http://www.utexas.edu/law/journals/tiplj/volumes/vol14iss3/meier.html (last visited 2003/8/6).

Earlier, the protection of trade secrets or confidential information may use unfair competition theory, which is provided in Article 759 of the Restatement[12]: if an individual (natural person) obtains or knows the secret information through improper means or methods for reap commercial benefits, he should take the responsibility; the focus lies in access to and use of the property of the person involved, leading to competitive practices. The legislative intent is to avoid theft or unauthorized abuse, crime does not necessarily subject to trade secrets.

Restatement of Unfair Competition amended in 1995 regarded trade secret as the information for business or operation management, it was valuable and secret, which could provide actual or potential economic benefits to others[13]; The main purpose of using such information is to compete with competitors, not simply for their own profit or creating business opportunities, for example, in the same industry, in order to combat the competitors, some steal raw materials, ingredients, recipes and even business methods, business plans, customer lists... and other related information.

However, as Restatement of Torts was completed in 1939, which was summarized from the early case and law, its normative content is too abstract and cannot cope with the rapidly changing business activities; therefore, when ALI of the United States passed the Restatement of Torts in 1978, the above-mentioned provisions relating to trade secrets were deleted, but the court still cited them, as they are of highly legal value[14].

---

[12] Restatement (First) of Torts §759 (1939) & §759 cmt. b.

[13] Restatement (third) of Unfair Competition 39 (1995).

[14] Feng, C.Y., About trade secret - theory and practice of trade secrect, 309, 1997.

American Bar Association formulated Uniform Trade Secrets Act (UTSA) in 1966[15]; before that, in order to upgrade the protection of trade secrets and proprietary information, the United States Code of Federal Regulations had relevant provisions of statute law on trade secret[16], and Trade Secrets Act (TSA) was collocated in June, 1948; after subsequent amendments, in the Section 18, Code of Federal Regulations, Article 1905, 1906, 1907 and 1909[17] were provisions for the protection of private trade secrets and criminal responsibility[18]. TSA is different from the other legislative norms, but it still provides a basic model legislation for the protection of trade secrets, which is also servants or agents' model to comply with[19].

Before the mid-1960s, the states of the U.S. still remained in the stage that protect trade secrets with common laws, followed by the Law Association of the United States established the National Conference of Commissioners on Uniform State Laws, and it passed full text of UTSA in 9, August 1979. Until 1980, the states adopted UTSA by way of legislation[20], thus the common laws of all states had to recognize and protect trade secrets, but because of the states are based on different theories, therefore the protection of trade secrets are of varying degrees, causing a number of companies and industrial

---

[15] Uniform Trade Secrets Act, 14 U.L.A. 369 (1985 & Supp. 1989).

[16] 15 U.S.C. § 1776, 18 U.S.C. § 112, 19 U.S.C. § 1335.

[17] 18 U.S.C. § 1905, 1906, 1907 & 1909.

[18] 18 U.S.C. § 1905 (2000), in this provision, the offender will be punishable by fine or limited imprisonment of less than one year.

[19] Jerry Cohen, "Federal Issues in Trade Secret Law", 2 J. High Tech. L. 1 (2003).

[20] Yeh, M.L, Su, H.W., Li, D.H., Protection of trade secrets and tactics - practice and examples of contract applications, , 29, Yung Rang, 1996.

problems. UTSA targets mainly at civil procedure relief, it had no effective prevention from the physical damage from violations of trade secrets or cannot inhibit the theft of trade secret; UTSA is now the most important legislative reference for trade secret in the United States[21].

UTSA has been amended in 1985, it is not standardized by all states, only enacted by the National Committee on Uniform State Laws; the states according to their specific circumstances to take its definition[22]; although there are only 12 provisions in UTSA, it defined and provided trade secrets, violation patterns and civil relief, which also affected certain provisions in the Economic Espionage Act, we can see its importance; for the information that is still under laboratory or in development, UTSA lists it in trade secrets with "potential independent economic value"; even for the market survey used once, or

---

[21] Brandon B. Cate, "Saforo & Associates, Inc. v. Porocel Corp.; The Failure of the Uniform Trade Secrets Act to Clarify the Doubtful and Confused Status of Common Law Trade Secret Principles", 53 Ark. L. Rev. 687, 697-699 (2000); Robert Unikel, "Bridging the "Trade Secret" Gap: Protecting "Confidential Information" Not Rising to the Level of Trade Secrets", 29 Loy. U. Chi. L. J. 841, 843 (1998).

[22] Article 1, Paragraph 4 in UTSA states: "Trade secret means information, including prescription, model, compilation, program, design, methods, techniques or processes, and (1) its independent real or potential economic value is not public way and others cannot know easily, and its leak or usage can make others obtain economic value. (2) has made reasonable efforts to maintain its secrecy ". See Yang, CS, "United States law of trade secret protection", Chung Hsing Law Review, Issue 23, 306, 1986. After analysis, its elements are as follows: 1) novelty; 2) materialization of elements; 3) independent substance or potential value; 4) cannot be easily achieved; 5) reasonable efforts to maintain secrecy. See Hsu, YL, "the protection of trade secrets - the Fair Trade Law and Intellectual Property Law II", 24-27, 1993, the Act only provided the civil liability of violating trade secrets, criminal responsibility is still provided by the states on their own.

still under development, the new products of pilot phase, are all have legal protection as trade secrets.

As to the past trade secret disputes in UTSA and unfair competition law, the most commonly used is the Restatement of Torts, after several amendments, although the definition in current provisions on trade secrets is different from the past, it still includes that: any disclosure of process, method, device, formula and other information owned by individuals or enterprises can increase the advantage over our competitors [23], however, UTSA did not expressly pointed out the definition of "negative knowledge"; in one article, it defined that it must have independent economic value; in 1985 legislative advice discussion, the information with commercial value was considered from the negative perspective, e.g. a certain manufacturing process or method is proved to be no use through long-term efforts and spending, if the competitors know that, they will reduce R&D time and money, of course, this can be considered one of trade secrets [24].

Ⅲ. Formation and Countermeasures of Unfair Competition

Patent, copyright or trademark rights can be achieved through the registration, as long as obtain registration protection, even if the secret is lost due to public, it will continue to enjoy the registration protection

---

[23] Restatement (first) of Torts, 757 cm. b (1982).

[24] See Unif. Trade Secrets Act § 1, Commissioners' Comment (amended 1985).

and not miss the "technology value"; when the company's technology has not yet achieved the registration protection, but it is leaked by leaving employee, the potential economic value and competitive advantage of the technology may be soon lost[25]; and trade secret claims often depend on the victim's (plaintiff) defense counsel against the leaving ones, allegation not to use confidential information; therefore, the protection of the rights is totally different from general intelligence property rights[26], something not included in UTSA is: if people deliberately make use of litigation against impinging trade secret by competitors, through such malicious litigation, employees have to struggle with such litigation and strike a balance when transferring to a new post or launching a new career, the plaintiff take this to fight against the defendant to achieve the purpose of unfair competition [27], which is not reasonable.

In diversified management subjects of intellectual property rights, take what law to regulate is worth looking into, whether it is market research or the definition of market demand, from the R&D flow, definition of user requirements, or design specifications, to logic design and testing, which are all related to trade secrets. As a commercial competition means, it must be able to directly create corporate profitability, or else the costs of a huge intellectual property rights management system will make most companies hesitate; a good

[25] Wang, CC, "choice of trade secrets and patents", MOEA Intellectual Property Monthly, Issue 111, 127, 2008.

[26] Charles Tait Graves & Brian D, Range, "Identification of Trade Secret Claims in Litigation: Solutions for a Ubiquitous Dispute", 5 NW. J. Tech. & Intell. Prop. 68 (2006).

[27] supra note, at 83.

planning of the intellectual property rights management system should be able to control the cost in a reasonable scope, and it can inhibit and eliminate the possibility of crime in advance, avoiding the enormous litigation costs and caseloads in future.

At present, as the general use of the Internet and related information technology, competitions among industries become more seriously; in order to maintain competitive edge, avoid other know the relevant information and become competitors, defense and information industries[28] request for confidentiality strictly, including foreign visitation of process-related projects or access to any confidential information, they must sign confidentiality clause; so the domestic industry exhibition will take some measures as restrictions on visits, but it ignores the necessary confidentiality measures at source of the production design; once the secrets are open, they are no longer secrets, therefore, other relevant intellectual property, such as trademark law, patent law, copyright law, or Integrated Circuit Layout Protection Act and other laws ... to protect their products, or otherwise legal means, such as use litigation or customs procedures to prevent plagiarism and counterfeit products from listing [29].

---

[28] E.g. before launch of Intel's Pentium II chip, all companies and manufacturers cooperated with were required to sign confidentiality agreements, until the public of the product. Feng, Understanding of trade secrets law - theory and practice of trade secrets law , pp. 23-24, 1997.

[29] E.g. Japanese popular electronic pet tamagotchi is an example. The product was listed in November 1996 in Japan, because the structure core was just a circuit board, LCD and control procedures, it is not difficult to imitate, so domestic manufacturers launched similar chickens, dogs, dinosaurs and so on through reverse engineering in April 1997 in Taiwan. Feng, same as above, pp. 25-26.

Because of technology updates and special nature of the industry, the traditional intellectual property rights cannot respond to new objects, such as micro-organisms patents, chip design, software, and trade secrets; and therefore avoiding the destruction of economic espionage before obtaining such patents or trademarks, expanding the protection of intellectual property are necessary, so as to let the industry be willing to bet money and effort, including technical personnel, research and development or experiment, also to solve the obstacles to industrial upgrading.

With the advent of the information age, a wide range of information, including technology and R&D information, production and manufacturing information, quality control and maintenance information, marketing and sales information, as well as internal financial and operating information, are likely to have unlimited economic value, thereby affecting the success or failure of an enterprise.

Therefore, at present practical operation proposed that, the non-compete agreements both in employment contract or leaving the company should set out the definition of trade secrets, such as high-tech industries' R&D results, the original raw materials and formula which can be analyzed through the reverse engineering; so a detailed description, definition and connotation of the types of trade secrets is necessary; also, the penalties in leakage of trade secrets, including relevant provisions on criminal liability or a fine should be detailed, so as to achieve prevention function. As to the employee's information or skills, which is known or learned during employment, if the employer consider it belonging to confidential, then the former shall take the responsibility not to tell others.

1. Laws and Regulations in Taiwan

The 548th interpretation of Council of the Grand Justice in Taiwan, is about the principle in prohibition from the abuse of power being used to the field of intellectual property rights, the Fair Trade Law Article 45 stipulates that "proper conduct to exercise rights in accordance with copyright law, trademark law or patent law is not suitable for the provisions of this Act." Do the above contain trade secrets law? What conduct is proper, and which belongs to the abuse of power[30]? In mandatory provisions, leaving employees must not only comply with the norms of competition, even "negative knowledge" is also protected the interests of original employers, which deters the competitors and restricts competition, is it feasible? How to judge with Taiwan laws, the following examined the Taiwan Trade Secret Act, relevant provisions of non-compete and the Fair Trade Law, followed by re-examined whether the laws of the United States can be reference in theory and practice.

(1) Trade Secret Law

Taiwan's trade secrets law was announced for implementation by the President on January 17, 1996, its legislative intent is "to protect trade secrets, maintain industry ethics and competitiveness order, and reconcile the social and public interests"[31]; according to the provisions of Article 2 in the Law, trade secret means methods, techniques, processes, formulas, procedures, designs or other information can be

---

[30] See Feng, C.Y., "Digital content protection and technology protection measures - considerations of law, industry and policy", The Taiwan Law Review, Issue 105, 92, 2004.

[31] See Article 1, Trade Secret law.

used for production, marketing or business, and they conform to the following:

①Not known by common people involved in such information;

②With actual or additional economic value because of its secrecy;

③Owner has taken reasonable security measures.

So the "invention", "creation" in patent protection, "the meaning of the expression" in copyright protection, as well as the "layout" in Integrated Circuit Layout Protection Act[32], even the so-called know-how and the production and marketing information, were covered, including all of the information from design, production, sale, sales management, operation in industry and commerce. Therefore, the Law may cover more fields, like services, manufacturing industries.

As the scope of trade secret is very wide, therefore the most important key is to take appropriate measures to maintain secrecy, that is, must take reasonable security measures; and the trade secrets with legal protection must have actual or additional economic value, that is, trade secret itself can be directly or indirectly input to industrial and commercial activities, and generate economic benefits[33]. Industry person can prompt the development of high-tech for Taiwan's industrial upgrading, and no longer rely on foreign technical assistance, so as to enable Taiwan's economy be more developmental.

---

[32] "Integrated Circuit Layout Protection Act" was worked out by the Bureau of Standards, Metrology and Inspection, enacted on February 11, 1996

[33] See Attorney Feng, B.S., "How to effectively use trade secrets and ensure the rights and interests", 14th edition of "intellectual property rights column series (2)"

(2) Fair Trade Law

Taiwan Fair Trade Law was announced by the President on February 4, 1991, went into effect on February 4, 1992, had a latest amendment until February 6, 1992, the legislative intent was "to maintain trading order and the consumers' interests, ensure fair competition, promote economic stability and prosperity."[34] Fair Trade Law Article 19, paragraph 5[35], provides the type of coercion, inducement or other improper methods to obtain the trade secrets, the type is clearly inadequate; when consumers dealing with different types of information, If they are involved in negative knowledge, causing negative efforts, and so extend the time for consumers to judge, making opportunities for competitors.

If A is both Company A's salesman and the shareholder of Company B, when he represents Company A and negotiates with potential new customers, he deliberately increases the prices, and introduces the Company B to the customer, is this behavior reasonable in a fair trade? When the client does not know A, B Company's actual prices, A Company's higher price is a negative effect, through "business judgment", the customer will choose Company B, resulting in unfair competition[36].

The Fair Trade Law only protect "business" trade secrets (Trade

---

[34] See the Fair Trade Law Article 1.

[35] Fair Trade Law Article 19, paragraph 5, the conduct that obtain others' secrets of production and marketing, the transaction data or other relevant technical secrets through coercion, inducement or other irregular methods

[36] Wang, WY, "Directors' non-compete obligation", The Taiwan Law Review, No. 61, 20, 2000.

Secret Law, paragraph 2), the trade secret of a natural person without "business" of is not protected, it is significantly insufficient to maintain the foregoing fair competition, business ethics, and other purposes; Article 36 and Article 41 of the Fair Trade Law provide the criminal penalty and administrative penalty, the Fair Trade Commission didn't impose sanction against the first time infringing trade secret, which was not appropriate[37].

In Article 15 of Administrative Penalty Law announced on February 5, 1995, if private legal person's director or other person with representation right infringes the Administrative Penalty Law when doing the director's duties, the doer should be subject to punishment if there is intent or gross negligence. If legal person's staff, servants or employees are against the Law due to duties, both the legal person and staff should be subject to punishment due to willful or gross negligence. The fines are not more than $ 1 million NTD. But for the one with benefits more than $ 1 million NTD, impose a fine according to the amount.

In Article 19, paragraph 5 of Fair Trade Law, obtaining the business secret of others is prohibited, trade secret protection is limited to the "business" referred to in Fair Trade Law Article 2, such as companies, wholly-owned or partnership commerce and industry enterprises, trade associations, and others group of people providing goods or services transaction; and the "counterparty" of transaction in Article 3 is relatively inferior to natural person engaged in research

---

[37] See Wen, YC, "Infringement of trade secrets and its legal responsibility", master's thesis, Graduate Institute of Law, National Chung Cheng University, p. 2, 1994.

and invention simply[38].

The criminal penalty and administrative penalty provisions take cease and desist orders from Fair Trade Commission for violations as the elements, not imposing sanction against the first time infringing trade secret is not appropriate[39]. As to the protection object, the Article lists "marketing secrets, transaction counterparty data" as protection objects, and "other relevant technical secrets act" is regarded as a general protection matters, the definition or the scope of trade secret is not detailed, only limited to literal explanation; "technical secrets" and other related matters as the scope of protection, which is narrower than the scope of the Trade Secret Law later.

(3) Criteria of Negative Information

Taiwan's definition[40] of trade secret targeted at economic espionage or theft of trade secrets in the past, which was in accordance with Fair Trade Law Article 19, paragraph 5: "get other's production and marketing secrets, counterparty data or other relevant technical secrets through coercion, inducement or other improper methods." That is, the behavior against fair competition is prohibited, hide "negative knowledge" and not report, that should belong to the Fair Trade Law

---

[38] See Hsu, Y.L., The protection of trade secrets, San Min Books, p. 54, 1993.

[39] See the Fair Trade Law Article 36 and Article 41

[40] Some commentators believe that "negative knowledge" is the trade secret, but according to the definition of trade secrets in the U.S. Restatement of Torts in P757 of 1939 Version, it should conform to (A) information owner has taken reasonable measures to ensure its secrecy; (B) Not known by common people involved in such information; (C) has some independent economic value; "negative knowledge" in this paper can be summarized into a broad sense of business secret. See Tzeng, SC, "Discussion on attribution of trade secret rights (Part II), The Law Monthly, Vol. 56, Issue 2, 94-95, 2005.

Article 24, within the scope of acts prohibiting unfair competition. E.g. Company A restricts its leaving employee, that he cannot disclose any relevant Company A's "negative knowledge" during working in Company B, is it reasonable?

If the acts that are of the nature of unfair competition cannot be regulated in accordance with the provisions in Fair Trade Law, view the availability of the provisions in Article 24. The so-called unfair competition, means the act has the criticism of commercial competition ethics, and commercial competition is in violation of social ethics, or against the central essence of fair competition on price, quality and service; usually, the leaving employee is required to comply with non-compete agreement is reasonable, whether Company A's restrictions are in line with the situation in Fair Trade Law Article 24, however, the actual violations are judged by the Fair Trade Commission.

According to "Reference manual for signing non-compete"[41] announced by Council of Labor Affairs, the non-compete agreement is in the principle of contract freedom, the employer shall not forced or coerce new labor to sign, as the new one has job need and without experience. Worse still, except the period in-service, even the period after the employment relationship is restricted, it is true that "negative knowledge" in Taiwan may be relatively a new concept; this paper argued that "negative knowledge" may be attributed to the broad trade secrets.

---

[41] Published by Council of Labor Affairs, Executive Yuan, 2003.

2. Taiwan's Cases[42]

Non-compete agreement in general is to protect business interests without jeopardizing the restricted one's economic viability, which is within the scope of legal norms, e.g. as semiconductors, wafer industries, and other high-techs are the core of Taiwan's economic development, enterprises often invest a lot of money in human capital for R&D, so the protection of trade secrets and talents retention are of extreme importance; employers fear the leaving one disclose business secrets on manufacturing technology and so on, so they reach an agreement of non-compete, if there is a violation, leaving one shall hold liable for damages.

To avoid increasing the transaction costs and maintain workplace ethics, when employers and employees enter into employment contracts, they usually sign a non-compete agreement, so as to protect trade secrets and avoid acts of economic espionage. However, if non-compete agreement only protects employers' interests, although the future ownership of trade secrets could avoid, for the vulnerable employee in economically weak, or even the new grads, they would easily sign the employment contract (including the non-compete agreement) for a new job, but their future developments are often restricted to the original signed contract, which even leads to a very high compensation, such cannot achieve the original purpose of dispute settlement of non-compete agreement, but arises more disputes and disputes between the two sides.

---

[42] Here thanks Mr. Ren-bang Chian at Graduate Institute of Finance, Ling Tung University (Taiwan) for collecting and collating documents

In general, Taiwan business owners often provide a non-compete agreement in the employment contract:"agree not to join any competing until one year after leaving, if in violation of the provisions, refund any training costs of the company before leaving and all year-end bonuses as the minimum amount of damages"[43]. It is generally believed that: such non-compete provisions are because labor has the obligation not to use or reveal the trade secrets or confidential information in former employment, so as to avoid the competitors have the opportunity to crack down on the original company; however, it limits the employee's employment and freedom of occupation, therefore, there must have some "compensation clauses"[44], or else it will have an impact on the economy.

The existing laws regarding non-compete mainly relate to managers and directors in civil law and company law[45], even if the non-compete agreement has compensation clauses already, under the existing procedural law framework, proof should be given that employee has a significant breach of trust or breach of good faith acts, so as to claim damages based on non-compete agreement; otherwise,

---

[43] Taiwan Taipei District Court Judgment (2002) Lao-Su-Tze-Di#129.

[44] According to the former case, Taipei District Court thought the non-compete compensation provisions were: "if party A's (the defendant) reasonable employment opportunities are affected due to this non-compete restrictions, A should inform of party B (the plaintiff), which considers lifting restrictions, or providing a proper compensation." However, the above situation is too subjective, the violation of the principle of integrity and fairness is easy; in accordance with Civil Code, Article 247, paragraph1, 2 to 4 and 72 provide that the one with violations of public order should be invalid provisions. Although the compensation exists, in form, its essence lies in the employer's arbitrary. So it is invalid; and there is no other term of compensation, the original stability and fairness should be maintained

[45] Please refer to the Companies Act Article 32, 54, 108, 115.

the non-compete agreement will have no use. When determining whether the non-compete agreement is valid, the court will consider whether the leaving employee has a significant breach of trust or breach of good faith, so that employers face a high threshold of the burden of proof, the non-compete agreement may be tantamount to dead letter[46], and thus restricting and impacting their employment opportunities.

Whether to pay compensation is determined by former employer, one-sided increase the responsibility of a employee, which is disadvantageous, in violation of the principle of good faith, public order and good customs; in the absence of other compensation provisions, the effectiveness of non-compete agreement has no reason. At present, enterprises non-compete agreement must be signed by both parties, and then goes into effect, the reasonable limits should take into account the competitiveness of both enterprises and employees; it is necessary to stress that this consideration is already included in salary or special allowance, or in exceptional circumstances, agree to pay non-compete compensation. If the leaving one deliberately steals company's customers and intelligence substantially, he is out of protection, of course without compensation.

(1) Syscom Case

April 2007, the Supreme Court entered a judgment: Sysmcom asked for its business manager to compensate the damages of $ 2.25

---

[46] Song, YM, the protection of trade secrets in the court decision, the protection and use of intellectual property rights in cross-strait, pp.458, 2002.

million NTD[47]; in this case, the manager held Imperva's shares and served as its representative during his term of office, which was not in line with Article 32 of the Company Act: manager shall not act as business manager of other companies at the same time, it is obvious that he was in violation of non-compete agreement.

As Syscom's business manager was in breach of its faithful labor obligations, he didn't inform the company of the bid from Feng Chia University, resulting in failure to tender, so the company asked for damages, the Supreme Court decided that although Imperva won the $ 7.5 million NTD bid, even it got a net profit of $ 2.25 million NTD from it, it didn't mean that the manager could earn the net profit of $ 2.25 million NTD. So it could not confirm whether the computer indeed had a loss of $ 2.25 million NTD net profit, and therefore could not determine the manager's substantial harm to the company, the damages were considered as invalidated.

When signing a contract, it is clear that if employee violates non-compete agreement and causes damages to, he shall hold the liability.

---

[47] Supreme Court Judgment(2007) Tai-Shang-Tze-Di # 923. Syscom Taichung branch company business managers, who engaged in the design of computer software programs, system design engineering, computer hardware maintenance and other related business marketing and customer visitation, signed a contract with the company on November 1, 1996, if there was violation of non-compete agreement causing damage to the company, they would take the damages. However, its business manager privately held 41 thousand, 2500 shares of Imperva without the company's approval, his term was from March 8, 2000 to March 7, 2003, he has already operated or invested in similar business affairs before leaving, forming the violation of the non-compete agreement. Imperva won the bid of Feng Chia University with $ 7.5 million NTD, Syscom believed that the manager had in breach of its faithful obligations, concealed the bid messages and did not report, causing the company a loss of about $ 2.25 million NTD.

Standing on a business perspective, the manager was not responsible, there was a clear violation of non-compete agreement, so he should hold liable for damages. However, that manager had his labor obligations, hiding the bid and not informing just lost the bid, without causing substantial damage to the company, it is not sure whether the case is fair according to Fair Trade Law Article 24, this case illustrates the cognitive difference between two sides.

(2) Atergi Technology Case

On May 1, 2007, the Taiwan High Court entered a judgment: Atergi Technology required its assistant manager and Chun Yi Co. to compensate damages[48], in that case, there were not reasonable compensatory measures (compensation measures) when signing non-compete agreement, which was in the violation of property rights, public order, good customs and the spirit of the Constitution, it should be null and void. Even if the non-compete agreement in job contract was considered as a valid, but the assistant and engineering manager set up their own company and had never used working time to operate it, there were no breach of trust, so no need to hold the responsibility. Again, Chun Yi Co. directors' investment was purely personal conduct,

---

[48] Taiwan High Court Judgment(2005) Shang-Tze-Di # 124. Atergi Technology accused its business assistant and engineering manager against the contract clauses 8, 9, 11 in non-compete agreement during serving the company after signing a work contract, the agreement provided: within one year after leaving, he shall not engage in the same business with the company or employed by competing companies. But he founded Chun Yi Co. with other factory during that period, which engaged in the same electronic components manufacturing, it was a clear breach of trust act. Based on work contract, the manager shall compensate Atergi $ 1.5 million NTD, and the directors of the company should be held jointly and severally liability as unfair means and competition.

without any prejudice to Atergi.

After signing the non-compete agreement in job contract, Atergi Technology's assistant manager and engineering manager' salary or allowance was improved, and Atergi Technology defended that its compensatory measures were included in the wages, but there was no real evidence. This showed that the company did not compensate the staff's loss for the non-compete provisions, so the non-compete agreement was invalid.

3. Discussion on the relevance of case and the compensation amount[49]

In pursuit of economic interests, enterprises often resort to all means to achieve; proper ways enable the industry has healthy competition, but there are many unfair competitions infringing servant's job freedom and survival right; when enterprises unilaterally restrict employees with high break-up fees and contract, more disputes between companies and employees are caused; through the discussion on relevance of case and the compensation amount, this paper illustrated the impact of unfair competition on the society.

(1) Case data and descriptive statistics

Case data sources were from the Law Bank website, data type was yearly data, mainly aimed at relevance of non-compete case and compensation amount in Taiwan, the study period was from January 1, 1996 to February 29, 2008, a total of 421 pieces.

---

[49] Study on the relevance of case and the compensation amount, the documents were also provided by Mr. Ren-bang Chian at Graduate Institute of Finance, Ling Tung University

Table 6-1   Number of non-compete related cases

	Non -compete	Payment of liquidated damages	Damages	Total
Number of related cases	22	151	248	421
%	5.2%	35.9%	58.9%	100%
	Local court	High court	Supreme court	
Non-compete	16	5	1	
Payment of liquidated damages	104	39	8	
Damages	166	66	16	
Total	286	110	25	
%	67.93%	26.13%	5.94%	

Source: Plotted based on the historical data of the Law Bank website.[50]

According to Table 1 about the proportion of non-compete cases in Taiwan, non-compete cases were 22 pieces, accounting for 5.2%; 151 cases were payment of liquidated damages, accounting for 35.9%; 248 cases were damages as high as 58.9%; after signing non-compete agreement, when enterprises or employees' rights and interests are jeopardized, the damages claimed are the main dispute, which originally is company costs to protect the enterprise and employees' freedom of contract, but now damages arising from disputes, in which the unfair competition would result in waste of business and social costs.

---

[50] The cases and resources were found on the website of The Law Bank, the study period was from January 1, 1996 to February 29, 2008, http://db.lawbank.com.tw/Eng/List.asp.(

Table 6-2   Distribution of court for non-compete related cases

Unit: piece

	Local court	High court	Supreme court
Non-compete	16	5	1
Payment of liquidated damages	104	39	8
Damages	166	66	16
Total	286	110	25
%	67.93%	26.13%	5.94%

Source: Plotted based on the historical data of the Law Bank website.

Based on Table 2 about the distribution of court for non-compete related cases, as unfair competition is derived from the non-compete cases, litigation disputes are often appealed, including appeal to the High Court, which is 110 pieces of cases, accounting for 26.13%; and the Supreme Court were 25, accounting for 5.94%, which indicates an average of 32.07% disputes arising from unfair competition will result in a waste of social resources due to continued litigation costs. In the legal theory, it is for the sake of fairness and justice, but it cannot make efficient use of social resources, which should be taken into account thoroughly.

(2) The relevance of case and the compensation amount

In view of the analysis on non-compete Taiwan-related cases, usually the one appeal to the High Court and Supreme Court mainly dissent from the amount of compensation; after the verdict from High Court and the Supreme Court, most cases are dismissed or defeat suits, so the appeal case and compensation amount were done the correlation analysis.

According to Figure 1, starting in 1997, among the non-compete cases in the Supreme Court, to the amount of damages is highest, with a total of $ 46914677 NTD, and the payment of liquidated damages is $ 25243748 NTD, which yearly increases; the amount of non-compete is $ 2250000 NTD, it shows that it has been noticed in recent years. Based on the case content analysis, when the amount of damages requested by unfair competition is too high, its judgments are rejected and become defeat suits.

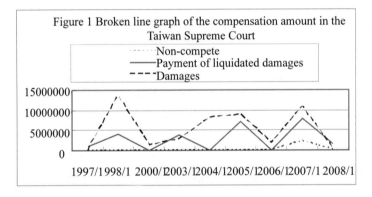

Figure 6-1   Taiwan Supreme Court

Source: Plotted based on the historical data of the Law Bank website.

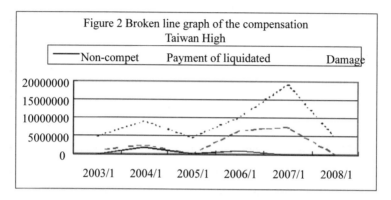

Figure 6-2　Taiwan High Court

Source: Plotted based on the historical data of the Law Bank website.

According to Figure 2, as the Copyright Law, Intellectual Property Law and other relevant laws and regulations were implemented in Taiwan in 2002, the amount of relevant cases appeal to the High Court has gradually enhanced, the number of domestic-related cases and compensation amount show increasing rising trend from 2003 to 2006, it means that enterprises attach rising importance to unfair competition and damages gradually.

IV. Practices in the United States

In the restatement of unfair competition amended in 1995, trade secret is regarded as the information, which can be used for business or operation and management, it is valuable and of secrecy, providing other actual or potential economic benefits[51]; the main purpose is to beat the competitors mainly, not simply for one's own profit or to create business opportunities, one will even take improper means like theft or leakage of business secrets, such as raw materials, ingredients, recipes and even business methods, business plans, customer lists and other related information. The doer obtains and knows others' secret information through improperly ways, so as to obtain the benefits, such as the case of Rehabilitation Specialists, Inc. v. Koering [52], the Court held that unfair competition was not narrow-defined infringement act. The theory of unfair competition prevention is based on stopping the doer looting the victim's property, such as the case of Roy Export Co. Establishment of Vaduz v. Columbia Broadcasting Sys., Inc.[53] The scope of Unfair Competition Law is broader than that of Trade Secret Law, even if the information content does not constitute a trade secret, it can still be protected, such as the case of Flexitzed Inc. v. Nat 'l Flextized Corp[54].

---

[51] Restatement (third) of Unfair Competition 39 (1995).

[52] 404 N. W. 2d 301, 305 (Minn. Ct. App. 1987).

[53] 672 F. 2d 1095, 1105 (2d Cir. 1982), others such as Computer Assocs. Int'l, Inc. v. Computer Automation, Inc., 678 F. Supp. 424, 429 (S.D.N.Y. 1987). In the theoretical basis of unfair competition in New York state law, the doer should maliciously use others' services or property results, leading to consumer's confusion with the original products, affecting the purchase wishes; Advanced Magnification Instruments, Ltd. V. Minuteman Optical Corp., 522 NYS 2d 287, 290 (App. Div. 1987), employee's invalid use or reproduction of employer's confidential information or documents also constitutes unfair competition; Another example, EI DuPont DeNemours & Co. v. Christopher, 431 F. 2d 1012 , 1016 (5th Cir. 1970), rampant industrial espionage make American business and industry unable to grow in free competition trade and good faith of employment relations.

[54] 335 F. 2d 774, 781 (2d Cir. 1964). The past norms of unfair competition must have competitive behavior of property or merchandise, but today's scope is broader, including

There are different standards to determine whether it constitute trade secrets in different cases, there is general knowledge or public information or combination on trade secret; for example, recipes of fried chicken are very similar, the composition and raw materials are feasible by everyone, trade secret protection is for the unique proportion, the order or special ingredients[55]; although most are not regarded as the trade secrets in practice[56], it is necessary to integrate individual elements in the public domain into trade secrets, unlike the generally known, and likewise the protection of "negative knowledge", otherwise the servant's motive of invention and innovation will be restricted.

In California, the United States, the leaving employees are prohibited to serve in similar work-so the secret information not constitute trade secrets; different from the past California tort law, Business and Professions Code section 16600 was expressly enacted; unlike the aforementioned UTSA, this law protects the secret information which not forms trade secrets yet, so as to strengthen the protection of his former employer; so legislation stipulates that a servant has the freedom to choose a job and use their professional knowledge and technology, but the former employer should not be

---

the labor of others, technology improper abstracting. Ecolab Inc. v. Paolo, 753 F. Supp. 1100, 1111 (EDNY 1991), even if the information content does not constitute a trade secret, but a servant leak, unauthorized use internal documents and information for the future development, also forming unfair competition.

[55] See Hutchison v. KFC Corp., 833 F.Supp.517, (D. Nev. 1993), aff 'd Hutchison v. KFC Corp,. 51F.3d 280 (9th Cir 1995).

[56] See Tait Graves & Alexander Macgillivary, Combination Trade Secrets and the Logic of Intellectual Property, 20 Santa Clara Computer & High Tech. L. J. 270 (2004).

harmed or be faced to unfair competition.

In the case of Novell Inc. V. Timpanogos Research Group Inc. (TRG[57]) by Utah District Court in 1998, the court accepted the plaintiff's request to grant the injunction. In that case, the defendants were employed by the plaintiff, working as procedures design, project planning and dismantling the secret information, so they were required to sign a confidentiality contract; the plaintiff bet quite a substantial amount of money and manpower to develop relevant technologies, and it made reasonable efforts to protect its trade secrets; and secondly, the plaintiff strictly controlled the channels and means to obtain trade secrets by the general people.

According to Utah Supreme Court's verdict[58], value of trade secrets lies in - cannot open, that is, once open, the value is lost, the plaintiff will suffer irreparable damage[59]; to prohibit the defendant to use secret business information relevant to the plaintiff, and do not violate the protection of the public "know" right[60]; in this case, "negative knowledge" application was involved, the defendant had cleared the mistakes made by plaintiffs, of course, he avoided repetition in the new company, so "negative knowledge" played an important role in this case, not to mention the goods of two companies will form competitive relationship; ultimately, the Court issued an injunction to the plaintiff, so as to prohibit the defendant to use any

---

[57] 1988 WL 177721 (Utah Dist. Ct.), 46 U.S.P.Q. 2d 1197.

[58] Microbiological Research Corp. v. Muna, 625 P. 2d 690, 696 (Utah 1981).

[59] See Autoskill v. National Educ. Support Sys., Inc., 994 F. 2d 1476, 1498 [26 USPQ 2d 1828] (10th Cir. 1993).

[60] Above had referred to UTSA as Model Act, its contents are adopted and deleted by the states themselves, Utah has adopted UTSA also.

secret information related to plaintiff in the nine-month period, so it didn't not prejudice the defendant's freedom to use his professional and technical knowledge, nor his choice of employment was not affected.

The use of non-compete agreement can protect the industry person from the unauthorized use of secrets, but the duty of confidentiality may be ended because of the termination or discharge of the employment contract, and employees will no longer be bound by the confidentiality clause, or the staff uses the secrets from his original career, resulting in damages. As confidentiality clause cannot prevent the damage from employee turnover, the valid and effective non-compete clause can be able to further ensure the original employer's competitive advantage, and prevent malignant job-hopping and headhunt, so as to further protect secrets and the competitive advantage effectively.

In recent years, the enforcement power of restrictive clauses is no longer regarded as a matter of course by the Court of the United States; currently, whether servant's right of choice and signing non-compete agreement are respected, taking into consideration the reasonableness of the agreement[61], in general, "good faith" or "fiduciary duty" is used to restrain persons in employment, but often limited during the period of employment, especially in high-tech industries, the employer has invested huge capital in the plant, hardware equipment and personnel training, if the servant switches to rival companies with

---

[61] See Huntington Eye Assoc., Inc. v. LoCascio, 553 S.E.2d 773, 780 (W. Va. 2001), the prohibition terms in this case were invalid, because the intention of impeding a employee was larger than protecting the interests of employer.

his professional knowledge, it is not only unfair for the former one, but also forming unfair competition[62]; so it is appropriate to sign non-compete agreement.

Non-compete agreement is to protect the employer's interests, which are worthy of the protection, namely to maintain the original employer's goodwill, confidential information or trade secrets. Pennsylvania courts consider such as customer lists[63], pricing information and delivery information[64], chemical process, manufacturing process, machine, operation mode[65], customer credibility[66], special training methods, recipes or other mechanical data or related knowledge, system operation mode[67], all belonging to the interests of employer worth protection; while others such as the information derived from reverse engineering, workers' attitude, technology or general knowledge, or messages provided by the general

---

[62] See William Lynch Schaller, Jumping Ship: Legal Issues Relating to Employee Mobility in High Tech. Indus., 17 Lab. Law 25 (2001) ; for the technology update or reform are often costly, employer invests numerously, but if the competitor easily steals and transfers trade secrets, he will not spend any R&D costs, so his costs are lower, leading to low prices, which is unfair competition; as to more serious results, one will have no motive betting new inventions and providing job opportunities, and ultimately be of no help on the economic development of the United States.

[63] Bohler-Uddeholm, Am. Inc. v. Ellwood Group, Inc., 247 F.3d 79, 107 (3d.Cir. 2001). However, if the servant himself edits a client list through his own service, the Court didn' t consider constituting trade secret, as another case in Pennsylvania: Renee Beauty Salons, Inc. v. Blose-Venable, 652 A.2d 1345, 1349 (Pa. Super. 1995).

[64] Id.

[65] SNA, Inc. v. Array, 51 F. Supp. 2d 554, 567 (E.D. Pa. 1999).

[66] Vector Sec., Inc. v. Stewart, 88 F.Supp.2d 395, 400 (E.D. Pa. 2000).

[67] SI Handing, Inc. v. Heisley, 753 F.2d 1244, 1258 (3d Cir. 1985).

supplier, are not within the scope of protection[68]. In different cases, Courts are often faced with the definition problem, so the Pennsylvania Court held that:

(1) The information constitutes a secret for all in essence, and can have a competitive value.

(2) Whether it is of technical value, or simply commercial information, may constitute benefits worthy of protection.

(3) On a case-by-case basis[69]. This paper considered that "negative knowledge" consistent with the above-mentioned elements, the following described its use in Taiwan.

V. Reference Value for Application of "Negative Knowledge" in Taiwan

There is no standardized written law on "negative knowledge" in Taiwan at present. The laws of the United States can make judgments based on the facts of individual cases, in the case of Pepsi Co, Inc. V. Redmond[70], it pointed out that "If leaving employee should inevitably use the trade secrets before in new job employment, then it cannot be regarded that he works for the competitor." This ruling has affected the subsequent employment relationship deeply, as the leaving one knows the mistakes made by the former company and its process,

---

[68] Christopher M's Hand Poured Fudge, Inc. v. Hennon, 699 A.2d 1275 (Pa. Super. 1997).

[69] *Id.*

[70] 54 F. 3d 1262 (7th Cir. 1995).

even beverages such as Coca-Cola's ingredients may be weighed, its formula is still the trade secrets; "negative knowledge" from the leaving servant may also constitute the former employer's trade secrets inevitably[71]; when converting work, if in the same fields, it is almost impossible to avoid the use of skills and experience from its previous work, even if the employee has no intention of misappropriation of the former employer's trade secrets, they can easily be exposed, this is the so-called inevitable disclosure theory[72].

At present, trade secrets to become an important asset of each company, which bet a large sum of money, manpower and R&D to accumulate competitive advantages, when the employee leaves, the company has faced the threat of leakage of trade secrets. Practically, if the former employer wishes to restrict leaving employees, who may not work in the relevant field with their professional skills, an appropriate compensation must be given; if restricting with non-compete agreement, "compensatory measures" should be given in employment period, so as to take care of employees' job choice, and without prejudice to their trade-off measures for livelihoods.

Government should not restrict any use of the general knowledge,

---

[71] For the same viewpoint, see Nathan Hamler, "The Impending Merger of the Inevitable Disclosure Doctrine and Negative Trade Secrets: Is Trade Secrets Law Headed in the Right Direction?" 25 *J. Corp.* L. 385 (2000)

[72] As early as 1980 in the cases of FMC Corp. V. Varco International Inc., 677 F. 2d 500 (5th Cir. 1982) and Union Carbide Corp. V. UGI Corp., 731 F. 2d 1186 (5th Cir. 1984), this theory was proposed; if the plaintiff can prove that the defendant's new employer will inevitably invoke the trade secrets misappropriated by defendant, the court will agree to issue an injunction against the defendant, the burden of proof lies in the proof of (defendants) willingness to misuse.

skills, or experience known during tenure, as well as job-hopping willing, or else hurt the overall economic development. Therefore, when the employer hope to hire competitors' leaving employees, he inevitably may involve the trade secrets, employer can reach an agreement with the staff not use and expose former trade secrets, and inform of that is illegal, otherwise he would hold civil liability for damages.

If the secret is very valuable, and the employee's job is the same or similar with the former one, employer should be very cautious in some related activities involved in trade secrets, let servant deliberately avoided, a cautious company should be all of its reasonable efforts, and make sure the inevitable danger will not lead to exposing trade secrets. He may even recognize with the servants' former employer which secret deserve to be protected, and his good faith to avoid infringement of trade secrets; servant's manager all has the responsibility, he must remind that not easily use the trade secrets belonging to others.

The points can be used for reference and learned by Taiwan in the application of the United States were discussed here. In the case of FMC Corp. V. Varco International, Inc. [73], the defendant served as a mechanical manager in the plaintiff company, which had high-tech industrial technologies, he was also asked to sign a confidentiality contract; and then he switched to the plaintiff's competitors, which had many similar products with the plaintiff, wanted to dismantle products through reverse engineering, so the defendant was hired; followed by the considerations from Fifth Circuit Court of Appeals for the case: 1) the reason for the defendant employed was to restore and dismantle

---

[73] 677 F.2d 500(5th Cir. 1982).

plaintiff's products; 2) the new company didn't limit the defendant using secret of the former company [74], the defendant and the plaintiff did not sign any "non-compete clause", the court decision implemented the "inevitable exposure theory", the plaintiff lost.

As the leaving employee knows the mistakes made by the former company in R&D and the reasons for them, if competitors aware of this knowledge, they may reduce their time and financial resources in that project, so the negative knowledge constitutes trade secrets, such as the case of Winston Research Corp. V. Minnesota & Manufacturing Co.[75]: the plaintiff was a tape manufacturer, the defendant and other people were employed by the plaintiff company originally, the latter left and worked at plaintiff's competing company, which developed similar products with technology informed by the defendant[76]; in the first instance, the court held that the accused persons known well about errors and problems in manufacturing process of plaintiff company, so competing company's problems and obstacles were avoided, production time, costs and R&D expenditures were reduced, and therefore the knowledge can be attributed to the plaintiff's trade secrets[77]; however, the Court of Appeal did not consider negative knowledge may constitute a trade secret[78].

In the Case Hurst v. Hughes Tool Co. in 1981[79], the Court

---

[74] Id. At 505.

[75] 350 F.2d 134 (9th Cir. 1965), the case had long controversy, but the court investigated the trade secrets posed by negative knowledge directly, so it is also useful.

[76] Id. at136-37.

[77] Id. at 143.

[78] Id.

[79] 634 F.2d 895, 899 (5th Cir. 1981).

considered the plaintiff's failure reason and experience only made one not repeat the same mistakes, not enough to form a trade secret. Additionally, in the case of SI Handling Sys., Inc. V. Heisley[80], the Court questioned Pennsylvania law used the Restatement of Torts to define trade secrets[81], whether also admitted negative knowledge was trade secret, the attitude was uncertainty, because there were not many practical cases, more space was left for future development and discussion.

In the discussion of restrictions on the use of "negative knowledge", employer's biggest concern is: leaving staff uses the message derived from work experience to form competitive advantage, which greatly reduce new company's depletion and expenditure; therefore, if the new employers take availability investigation of such information in advance, the compensation and disputes can be reduced in future; however, the employer eagers to let the new staff show up, and even through head hunting, this makes the new one be more dependence on the past work experience; how to make the new staff use his talent fully, but also avoid the "unfair competition " created by new employer deliberately, it is very important for high-tech or biochemical industries, which relies on specialized technology and professional performance; it is recommended to avoid the use of highly sensitive "negative knowledge" or take the initiative to inform, so as to reduce the time in prevention and investigation.

Advocating that "negative knowledge" is the "common knowledge" easily know by general people or industry-specific people,

---

[80] 753 F.2d 1244, 1262 (3d Cir. 1985).

[81] The Restatement (First) of Torts (1939).

which may be used for defense by the new employer[82], so as not to infringe the former employer's trade secrets; it is difficult to classify trade secrets into single, individual or combination trade secret, if it is public information, any person have the right to use it; it is recommended that new employer do proper information classification for "negative knowledge", so as to clarify the scope and authority, and avoid the burden of proof and caseloads.

VI. Conclusions

People exert themselves actively in introducing advanced technology of science and technology, including computer information, medical and biochemical aspects, or through technology licensing, technical cooperation, corporate mergers and acquisitions, as well as cash purchase, etc., with a view to strengthen the existing level of technology R&D, enhance business profitability and operating pattern. After this effort, it poses a threat to competing countries in international markets; with an increasingly competition in industrial and commercial society, information technology acquisition has become the key to winning; enterprises suffer serious losses due to the unauthorized use of intellectual property rights, the past non-performance of contract, unfair competition, infringement act or UTSA only requests civil damages, no special provisions of civil penalties;

---

[82] See Tait Graves & Alexander Macgillivary, Combination Trade Secrets and the Logic of Intellectual Property, 20 Santa Clara Computer & High Tech. L. J. 269 (2004).

if the employee leaves the original company, switching to competitor, whether he should be punished criminally, so the employer with strong economic status will easily bring charge against employee turnover and fight against competitors.

This paper proposed to view whether "negative knowledge" would create unfair competition through following means: 1) whether the leaving employee's "negative knowledge" can cause competition, namely, the causal relationship between the two must be clear and specific; 2) assess the value constituted by "negative knowledge" and its impact on the overall benefits; 3) whether the information owner prohibit to use "negative knowledge" is a malicious idea, that is, his main motivation is for exclusive use of information and forming unfair competition; 4) whether the leaving employee can prove that his "negative knowledge" was known through hard work and personal experience, which has nothing to do the former employer's secret information; even if there is connection, the sources and methods for independent access to information are not affected. If want to prove that the use of "negative knowledge" by leaving one affects the former enterprise's competitive advantage, the burden of proof is on former employer, which calculates the value of trade secret cases, including R&D technology, time, relative manpower input; therefore, burden of proof must be done by the former employer indeed[83], this paper

---

[83] In the mixed composition of trade secrets, such as A, B, C respectively is establishment element of trade secrets, then the value of combination trade secret should be higher than their respective values, that is, $(A + B + C)$ must be greater than $(A) + (B) + (C)$, see Keystone Plastics, Inc. v. C & P Plastics, Inc., 506 F.2d 960, 964 (5th Cir. 1975). Employer should prove that employee uses "negative knowledge" in new company, which significantly reduces its costs, or prove the development costs and funding invested, so as to demonstrate

considered that the most difficult to clarify was the burden of proof in such proceedings.

Before the victim (plaintiff) sues, first he should confirm his loss is a trade secret, or be consistent with the elements of trade secret; and secondly, the information contents of "negative knowledge" advocated not to use should be described in detail. When the court makes the decision in favor of the plaintiff, of course it will request the defendant to stop using information content proposed by the plaintiff; the court is based on the plaintiff's request, so the plaintiff's claim for damages must be in good faith, if it is malicious and only for monopolizing the market and information, it naturally should not be protected, so as to avoid unfair competition, affecting the overall interests of the society.

The attention to the protection of trade secrets in today's society is far more than the past; the implementation and practice of the concept should usually go through years of accumulation and the test of time, with the needs of diversification of industry and information-based society, plagiarism of others wisdom essence reduces R&D costs, even the time and process of theft can be shortened through scientific and technological tools; in the past, trade secret protection issues are mostly positive business messages, which can create wealth, such as customer lists, raw material, manufacturing process, formula, recipes and trade secrets; the protection of "negative knowledge" is the new direction of thinking now and the future. This paper discussed the status of Taiwan laws and the practices in the United States, with a view to protect intellectual property rights, and at the same time, to avoid unfair competition, so that competitors can start trading based on

the value of "negative knowledge ".

fairness and mutual benefits, so as to reach fairer deal and activate the market, protect the investor and consumer's demands specifically, and stimulate the economy toward virtuous circle.

References

Chinese

Wen, Y.C. (1994), "Infringement of trade secrets and its legal responsibility", master's thesis, Graduate Institute of law, National Chung Cheng University

Wang, W.Y. (2000), "Directors' non-compete obligations", The Taiwan Law Review, Issue 61, 20.

Wang, C.C. (2008), "Choice of trade secrets and patents", MOEA Intellectual Property Monthly, Issue 111, 127.

Song, Y.M. (2002), "The protection of trade secrets in the court decision", the protection and use of intellectual property rights in cross-strait, 458.

Hsu, Y.L. (1993), "The protection of trade secrets", 54.

Hsu, Y.L. (1993), "The protection of trade secrets — Fair trade law and Intellectual Property Law Series II", 24-27.

Tzeng, S.C. (2005), "Discussion on attribution of trade secret rights (Part II)", The Law Monthly, Vol. 56, Issue 2, 94-95.

Feng, C.Y. (1997), Understanding of trade secret law —theory and practice of trade secret law, 23-24.

Feng, C.Y. (2004), "Digital content protection and technology protection measures —considerations of law, industry and policy ", The Taiwan Law Review, Issue 105, 92.

Huang, C.D. (2007), "New system of trade secret protection", National Lawyers Journal, Issue 11, Vol. 8.

Yang, C.S. (1986), "US laws on trade secret protection", Chung Hsing Law Review, Issue 23, 306.

Yeh, M.L., Su, H.W., Li, D.H. (1996), "Tactics of Trade Secret Protection — practice and application of contract examples", Yung Ran Publishing, 29.

Trans. by Chao, H.W., Yang, C.J. (2006), Anglo-American tort law, Taipei: Wu Nan Books, 204.

English

Brandon B. Cate (2000), "Saforo & Associates, Inc. v. Porocel Corp.; The Failure of the Uniform Trade Secrets Act to Clarify the Doubtful and Confused Status of Common Law Trade Secret Principles", Ark. L. Rev., 53(687), 697-699.

Charles Tait Graves & Brian D, Range (2006), "Identification of Trade Secret Claims in Litigation: Solutions for a Ubiquitous Dispute", NW. J. Tech. & Intell. Prop., 5, 68.

Charles Tait Graves (2007), "The Law of Negative Knowledge: A critique", Tex. Intell. Prop. L. J., 15, 387-416.

Jerry Cohen (2003), "Federal Issues in Trade Secret Law", J. High Tech. L., 2, 1.

Nathan Hamler (2000), "The Impending Merger of the Inevitable Disclosure Doctrine and Negative Trade Secrets: Is Trade Secrets Law Headed in the Right Direction?" J. Corp. L., 25, 385.

Robert Unikel (1998), "Bridging the "Trade Secret" Gap: Protecting "Confidential Information" Not Rising to the Level of Trade

Secrets", Loy. U. Chi. L. J., 29, 841, 843.

Tait Graves & Alexander Macgillivary (2004), "Combination Trade Secrets and the Logic of Intellectual Property", Santa Clara Computer & High Tech. L. J.,20, 269.

Tait Graves (2006), "Non public Information and California Tort Law: A Proposal for Harmonizing California's Employee Mobility and Intellectual Property Regimes under the Uniform Trade Secrets Act," UCLA J. L. & Tech.

William Lynch Schaller (2001), "Jumping Ship: Legal Issues Relating to Employee Mobility in High Tech. Indus." Lab. Law., 17, 25.

第七章　稅不稅有關係——談著作財產權課徵遺產稅與鑑價問題

曾勝珍、黃鋒榮[*]

目次

[*] 本文作者分別為嶺東科技大學財務金融研究所教授，加拿大英屬哥倫比亞大學法學院訪問學者暨博士後研究員；嶺東科技大學財經法律研究所碩士，台灣省政府專門委員。

▋摘 要 SUMMARY

　　知識經濟時代已來臨，透過人類智慧的創造，無形之智慧財產越形重要，從較具有強制排他性與市場流通性的專利權、商標權等，到較消極被動的著作權、營業秘密等，其價值均潛在著無限想像空間，本文將分析說明著作財產權繼承時之遺產稅課徵，遺產總額之範圍、著作財產權價值之估算及以著作財產權抵繳遺產稅之相關內容，再就其衍生之著作財產權鑑價問題，進一步分析著作財產權評價問題，最後探討鑑價師制度之導入是否可就此類問題提供解決方案。

壹、前　言

　　依我國著作權法規定，著作權分為著作人格權與著作財產權，著作人格權專屬於著作人所有，不得轉讓，亦不得繼承；著作財產權得轉讓，當被繼承人死亡時所擁有之著作財產權，則與一般財產同樣列入遺產，除遺贈外，由繼承人依民法規定繼承，同時，亦面臨遺產稅之申報與核課問題。依遺產及贈與稅法（以下簡稱遺贈稅法）第8條規定，遺產稅未繳清前，不得分割遺產、交付遺贈或辦理移轉登記。故本文擬先就著作財產權繼承時之遺產稅，及以著作財產權抵繳遺產稅之相關內容加以分析說明，再就其衍生之著作財產權鑑價問題，進一步分析探討。

貳、著作財產權繼承時之遺產稅課徵

　　我國遺產稅之客體，採屬人主義兼採屬地主義，凡經常居住國內[1]之國民死亡時，不論其在國內或境外之所遺全部財產[2]（即遺產），均須課徵遺產稅。而經常居住境外之國民及外國人，死亡時在國內遺有財產者，應就其在國內之遺產，課徵遺產稅[3]。

　　由於著作財產權內容繁雜，辨識本不容易，遺產稅之納稅義務人[4]於申報限期內對繼承財產負有完整申報之責任，亦不得以稽徵機關未提供遺產資料為由而免其短、漏報之責[5]；又遺產稅納稅義務人對於遺產全部為公同共有，就遺產稅亦應負連帶債務責任[6]。如此加諸納稅義務人之責任甚大，宜對計入遺產總額之範圍及其價值之估算等，予以探討釐清之。

---

[1]　依遺贈稅法第4條第3項規定，被繼承人或贈與人有：死亡事實或贈與行為發生前2年內，在中華民國境內有住所者；或在中華民國境內無住所而有居所，且在死亡事實或贈與行為發生前2年內，在中華民國境內居留時間合計逾365天者。（但受中華民國政府聘請從事工作，在中華民國境內有特定居留期限者，不在此限。）之情形，即屬於經常居住中華民國境內者。依同法同條第4項規定，如不符合經常居住中華民國境內之規定者，即為經常居住中華民國境外者。

[2]　遺贈稅法第4條第1項規定：「本法稱財產，指動產、不動產及其他一切有財產價值之權利。」

[3]　遺贈稅法第1條規定。

[4]　依遺贈稅法第6條第1項規定：有遺囑執行人者，為遺囑執行人；無遺囑執行人者，為繼承人及受遺贈人；無遺囑執行人及繼承人者，為依法選定遺產管理人。

[5]　財政部1984年11月21日台財稅第63352號函解釋。

[6]　財政部網頁，財政部2007年4月2日新聞稿，http://www.mof.gov.tw/fp.asp?xItem=37072&ctNode=657（上網日期：2009年9月11日）。

一、計入遺產總額之範圍

（一）規範原則

　　被繼承人死亡時，其著作人格權為著作人本身之專屬權，不得讓與或繼承，自非遺產稅之客體；而著作財產權為其遺產之一，但不全為遺產稅課稅之客體，遺贈稅法係依取得方式而不同之規範：

1.被繼承人自己創作之著作權不計入遺產總額[7]，故於遺產稅之計算時，此部分並不計入課稅。

2.被繼承人係以買賣、受贈或互易等受讓方式取得之著作財產權，則仍應與被繼承人之其他財產計入遺產總額中[8]，核算遺產稅額。

3.共同著作或因讓與而產生之共有著作財產權，則依權利歸屬之應有部分比例，認定其財產及計算其價值。

4.職務期間之著作財產權，遺贈稅法並未明文規定；本文以為，依上揭第16條第5款所規定「被繼承人自己創作之著作權」之精神，應為：

　　(1)被繼承人如係以受雇人或受聘人身分，而依約定取得之著作財產權，並以雇用人或出資人為著作人之場合，應准其不計入遺產總額課稅。

　　(2)被繼承人如係以雇用人或出資人身分，而依約定取得之著

---

[7]　遺贈稅法第16條第5款規定；另同條第4款規定「遺產中有關文化、歷史、美術之圖書、物品，經繼承人向主管稽徵機關聲明登記者。但繼承人將此項圖書、物品轉讓時，仍須自動申報補稅。」所稱之「遺產中有關文化、歷史、美術之圖書、物品」，應指著作之原件或重製物，為物權之範圍，並非指其著作財產權。

[8]　依遺贈稅法第1條規定，遺產總額範圍應包括被繼承人死亡時依同法第1條規定之全部財產，及依同法第10條規定計算之價值。但同法第16條規定不計入遺產總額之財產，不包括在內。

作財產權之場合，不論該著作之著作人約定為何人，均非
被繼承人自己創作之著作權，仍應計入遺產總額中，始為
適法。

5.製版人本身並無創作之行為，故製版權應列入遺產中。

至於遺贈稅法第9條第1項第4款有關「著作權及出版權依其登記
機關之所在地為準」，以認定被繼承人之國內或境外財產之規定，因
著作權及出版權已不須再聲請登記[9]，因此，本文建議予以刪除或將
「著作權及出版權」修正為「製版權」。另為免個案核定之繁複與行
政作業成本之經濟考量，建議財政部得依同法同條第2項規定，以通
案方式規定：「被繼承人死亡時或贈與人贈與時之著作財產權，除可
證明其為中華民國境外之財產者外，餘推定為境內之財產。」[10]

（二）死前贈與視同遺產

為防止被繼承人利用生前贈與以規避死後之遺產稅，遺贈稅法第
15條有「視同遺產」之規定，亦即被繼承人於死亡前2年內[11]，贈與

---

[9] 按著作權法於1985年修正後，採創作主義，著作人於著作完成時享有著作權，並不須
再向登記機關註冊登記；而出版權於1999年1月25日出版法廢止後，新聞紙、雜誌、
書籍及其他出版品等亦不須再聲請登記。

[10] 我國國民於境外依他國之法律登記取得之著作財產權，或有得據本規定以認定被繼承
人死亡時境外之著作權及出版權，惟其在實務上發生之情形不多。

[11] 本條文第1項原規定為「被繼承人死亡前3年內」，但為避免被繼承人死亡前3年內
贈與之財產，併課遺產稅後，已納之贈與稅、土地增值稅於依遺贈稅法第11條規定
（1998年6月26日公布修正生效）核計扣抵稅額時，僅限於死亡前2年內贈與財產部
分之贈與稅、土地增值稅，始可扣抵遺產稅之不合理現象，而於1999年7月15日修
正第1項為「被繼承人死亡前2年內」。又為避免1998年6月26日遺贈稅法第11條公
布修正生效後，至本條修正公布生效（1999年7月17日）前發生之繼承案件，發生
前述不合理現象，爰於第2項增訂追溯適用規定。參考1999年7月15日遺贈稅法第
15條修正之立法理由，法源法律網，http://db.lawbank.com.tw/FLAW/FLAWDOC01.
asp?lsid=FL006067&lno=15（上網日期：2009年10月13日）。

其配偶[12]或其依民法第1138條及第1140條規定之各順序繼承人及其配偶之財產，應於被繼承人死亡時，視為被繼承人之遺產，併入其遺產總額徵稅[13]。其法律效果應僅及於該贈與之財產應併入被繼承人之遺產總額核課遺產稅而已，自不因法律規定「視為被繼承人之遺產」，應併入其遺產總額徵稅，致該贈與之財產於「贈與後至被繼承人死亡時」之期間，其所有權應「視為被繼承人所有」[14]。換言之，本項規定僅係遺贈稅法課稅計算時，名目上之調整，對於被繼承人死亡前2年內所為贈與行為，並不發生任何實質上之影響。受贈人並不因此規定，而需將已取得之贈與財產歸還被繼承人或將之納入遺產，故亦不影響被繼承人遺產中之應繼財產及各繼承人之應繼分與應取得財產。此與生前特種贈與之歸扣不同，僅歸納二者之差異，如表7-1。

表7-1　被繼承人死亡前2年內贈與視同遺產與生前特種贈與歸扣之差異

	死亡前2年內贈與視同遺產	生前特種贈與歸扣
適用法規	遺贈稅法第15條	民法第1173條
適用範圍	被繼承人於死亡前2年內贈與其配偶或其依民法第1138條及第1140條規定之各順序繼承人及其配偶之財產[15]，範圍較廣，但僅追及被繼承人於死亡前2年內之贈與。	僅限繼承人[16]中有在繼承開始前因結婚、分居或營業，已從被繼承人受有財產之特種贈與，範圍較窄，但不論特種贈與時間多久均被追及。

---

[12] 配偶相互贈與之財產，依第20條第1項第6款規定，不計入贈與總額，但如被繼承人於死亡前2年內所贈與其配偶之財產，視為被繼承人之遺產，併入其遺產總額。

[13] 乃將實質上已為「贈與」之財產，在法律擬制之範圍內，仍併入遺產總額，課徵遺產稅；但其法律效果應僅及於該贈與之財產應併入被繼承人之遺產總額核課遺產稅而已，自不因法律規定「視為被繼承人之遺產」，應併入其遺產總額徵稅，致該贈與之財產於「贈與後至被繼承人死亡時」之期間，其所有權應「視為被繼承人所有」。最高行政法院94年判字第178號判決及高雄高等行政法院94年度訴字第878號判決。

[14] 最高行政法院94年判字第178號判決。

	死亡前2年內贈與視同遺產	生前特種贈與歸扣
贈與價額	被繼承人死亡時之時價估算。	依贈與時之價值計算。
適用時點	申報遺產稅時，遺產分割前。	歸扣效力於繼承開始時即發生，遺產分割時，由其他共同繼承人主張歸扣，如無人主張者，為歸扣權之拋棄。
免除規定	無。	被繼承人於特種贈與時有反對之意思表示者，得免歸扣[17]。
適用效力	僅為遺產稅課徵時之計算，並不影響被繼承人遺產中之應繼財產及各繼承人之應繼分與應得財產。	特種贈與財產歸入被繼承人之遺產中，而擴大應繼財產之總額，影響共同繼承人之應繼分與應取得財產[18]。

　　再者，此項視同遺產而併入遺產總額之著作財產權，如係被繼承人自己創作之著作權，仍不計入遺產總額。若屬製版權以及被繼承人因買賣、繼承、受贈或互易等受讓方式取得之著作財產權之部分，則須計入遺產總額課稅。

---

[15] 凡條列之人受被繼承人於死亡前2年內贈與之財產，均視為遺產。不論渠等是否為遺產之實際繼承人，故繼承人雖為拋棄繼承之表示，其受被繼承人於死亡前2年內贈與之財產，仍視為遺產。亦不問其贈與之原因。

[16] 以被繼承人於死亡時期為標準，指同一順序之共同繼承人與代位繼承人均包括在內。戴東雄，繼承法實例解說，自版，2003年3月，增修再版，頁90。

[17] 依民法第1173條第1項但書規定之文義，似應以被繼承人於特種贈與之當時，有反對之意思表示者為限。但關於遺產繼承，首應尊重被繼承人之意思，故宜認為被繼承人在贈與後或以遺囑，亦可作免除歸扣之表示。陳棋炎、黃宗樂、郭振恭合著，民法繼承新論，三民書局，2009年3月，修訂4版，頁149。

[18] 我民法貫徹財產處分之自由，尊重受贈人之既得權，並避免法律關係之煩雜，多數說及實務見解，特種贈與價額超過應繼分之部分，無庸補出，返還其他共同繼承人。郭振恭，論歸扣之標的及效力，收錄於林秀雄主編，民法親屬繼承實例問題分析，五南書局，2003年9月，初版，頁350-351。最高法院90台上字2460號民事判決。惟亦有少數學者主張特種贈與價額超過應繼分之部分，應為返還。而學者陳棋炎，則認為受特種贈與之繼承人雖可「獨享」其特種贈與之權利，而其他共同繼承人在其特留分為限，可「分享」歸扣利益。陳棋炎、黃宗樂、郭振恭合著，民法繼承新論，三民書局，2009年3月，修訂4版，頁154-163。

（三）繼承財產之排除

　　為避免同一筆財產[19]，因短時期內連續繼承而一再課徵遺產稅，加重納稅義務人之負擔，遺贈稅法16條第10款規定，被繼承人死亡前5年內，繼承之財產已納遺產稅者，不計入遺產總額。本項規定之適用前提，自以5年內繼承之財產完納遺產稅者為限。而所稱「同一筆財產」或「繼承之財產」應係指繼承之「特定財產」而言，與繼承人之固有財產應分離，且須就該「特定財產」之資產與負債先行清算[20]。

　　準此，被繼承人死亡前5年內繼承之財產中，製版權以及因買賣、繼承、受贈或互易等受讓方式取得之著作財產權，因於被繼承人繼承該財產時，已計入遺產總額課稅，其繼承人得將該財產排除，而不計入遺產總額[21]。

（四）最終計入遺產總額之範圍

　　綜上，遺產中著作財產權計入遺產總額之範圍者，歸納為下列二項：其一，為被繼承人死亡時仍為其所有之製版權，以及買賣、繼承、受贈或互易等受讓方式取得之著作財產權。但應減除被繼承人死亡前5年內所繼承並已納遺產稅之部分。其二，為被繼承人死亡前2年內，所贈與其配偶或其依民法第1138條及第1140條規定之各順序繼承人及其配偶之財產，為製版權以及被繼承人以買賣、繼承、受贈或互易等受讓方式取得之著作財產權部分。

---

[19]　「同一筆財產」或「繼承之財產」應係指繼承之「特定財產」而言，與繼承人之固有財產應分離，且須就該「特定財產」之資產與負債先行清算。最高行政法院95年度判字第01399號判決。

[20]　最高行政法院95年度判字第01399號判決。

[21]　但如於被繼承人繼承時，不計入遺產總額者，因非屬於已納遺產稅之財產，於本次繼承時，則須計入遺產總額課稅。

二、著作財產權價值之估算

依上述最終計入遺產總額範圍之著作財產權，應依被繼承人死亡時之時價估算其價值[22]；而著作財產權為無形資產之一，其價值之計算，依遺贈稅法施行細則第35條準用同法第34條礦業權、漁業權之價值估計規定，應以其額外利益額[23]，就其賸餘年數所依規定倍數估計之[24]。

（一）著作財產權鑑價之賸餘年數

著作財產權之賸餘年數如何認定，遺贈稅法並未規定。如從最終計入遺產總額之著作財產權以受讓方式取得者為限，與所得稅法第60條營利事業之無形資產相當[25]，係以15年為計算著作權攤折（類似賸餘年數）之標準，較為簡便。惟被繼承人之遺產並非營利事業之資產，無法適用此規定。

---

[22] 參見遺贈稅法第10條第1項前段規定。

[23] 遺贈稅法施行細則第34條第2項規定，額外利益額謂由各該權利最近三年平均純益減除其實際投入資本，依年息百分之十計算之普通利益額後之餘額，未經設權之土法礦窯及未經領證之漁業，本無期限，不能認為享有礦業權、漁業權者，應就其營業利得，依週息百分之五還原計算其價額。

[24] 遺贈稅法施行細則第34條第1項所定之倍數如下：
　1.賸餘年數為1年者，以其額外利益額為其價額。
　2.賸餘年數超過1年至3年以下者，以其額外利益額之2倍為其價額。
　3.賸餘年數超過3年至5年以下者，以其額外利益額之3倍為其價額。
　4.賸餘年數超過5年至7年以下者，以其額外利益額之4倍為其價額。
　5.賸餘年數超過7年至12年以下者，以其額外利益額之6倍為其價額。
　6.賸餘年數超過12年至16年以下者，以其額外利益額之7倍為其價額。
　7.賸餘年數超過16年者，以其額外利益額之8倍為其價額。

[25] 依所得稅法第60條規定，著作權限以出價取得者為資產。其估價以自其成本中按期扣除攤折額後之價額為準。而著作權之攤折額，以其成本照15年為計算攤折之標準，攤折年數按年均計算之。

　　從著作財產權之存續期間來看，攝影、視聽、錄音及表演等類型之著作，以及以別名或不具名之其他類型著作，其著作財產權之存續期間係以著作公開發行日起算50年，繼承時即得以確認其存續期間之賸餘年數，應無疑義。而其他之著作，在著作財產權為受讓取得情況下，由於被繼承人並非著作人，依著作權法第30條或第31條規定，須以著作人或共同著作人最後一位死亡者死亡後起算50年。如繼承時，該著作之著作人已死亡，其著作財產權之存續期間即能明確認定；如該著作之著作人仍生存時，其著作財產權之存續期間雖存有未確定之狀態，但其賸餘年數應可合理推估均超過50年，而適用遺贈稅法施行細則第34條第1項第7款所定之8倍規定。

（二）著作財產權鑑價之額外利益額

　　依遺贈稅法施行細則第34條第2項規定，額外利益額謂由各該權利最近三年平均純益減除其實際投入資本，依年息百分之十計算之普通利益額後之餘額，其認定：

1. 對於被繼承人受讓取得之著作財產權而言，其實際投入資本即是被繼承人受讓取得之成本，較為確定。
2. 著作財產權如有授權使用者，收取授權金或版稅者，可推估其最近三年平均純益，並依規定作著作財產權之估價。
3. 如係無償供他人使用或並無人使用其著作者，即無純益可言，其額外利益額為零，從而該著作財產權鑑價結果為沒有價值。

　　此一規定雖在稅法課稅上，或有其方便性；但充其量僅適用在稅務會計，財務會計是否準用，也成為疑問[26]。尤其是無償供他人使用之著作，其估算之價值不應以其額外利益為基礎，故著作財產權其價值之估算，與其他無形資產一樣，需要一套合理的鑑價制度，並須發

---

[26] 詹炳耀，智慧財產估價的法制化研究，臺北大學法律研究所博士論文，2003年，頁30。

展成為一種市場機制；如此，不但可活絡著作財產權之交易流通，促進知識文化之利用發展，亦可為著作財產權在訴訟（如侵權之損害賠償金額或訴訟費用計算）與非訟事件（如強制執行或遺產分配）中，提供客觀的評價資訊，這個議題是極須解決之問題，此部分將留待下文再予討論。

參、以著作財產權抵繳遺產稅之探討

稅捐債務之本質為金錢給付之債務，本應以現金繳納，惟遺產稅之發生，納稅義務人因無法事先知悉[27]，且遺產稅係以課稅遺產淨額課徵百分之十[28]，其金額不小，對納稅義務人而言，是一筆具有時限性的龐大支出，況且所繼承之遺產，以不動產或動產為大宗，其變價耗時，為舒緩一次繳納巨額現金之壓力，除可於繳納期限內申請稽徵機關核准延期外，如遺產稅應納稅額在30萬元以上而以一次現金繳納確有困難時[29]，以實物抵繳稅額，得於納稅期限內，亦得申請分期繳納或就現金不足繳納部分，申請以在我國境內之課徵標的物或納稅

---

[27] 鍾鳳娥，以公共設施保留地及未上市（櫃）股票抵繳遺產及贈與稅問題之研究，淡江大學會計學系研究所碩士論文，2003年6月，頁2。

[28] 我國遺產稅稅率以往採累進稅率，依課稅遺產淨額（即遺產總額減除遺贈稅法第17條規定之各項扣除額及第18條規定之免稅額後之淨額）不同之級距，就其超過額課徵2%至50%不等稅率（1995年1月13日修正）。惟2009年1月13日修正後，改採單一稅率，並大幅調降率為10%。

[29] 依司法院釋字第343號解釋意旨，遺產稅本應以現金繳納確有困難，始得以實物抵繳。是以實物抵繳，既有現金繳納確有困難之前提要件，稅捐稽徵機關就此前提要件是否具備，及其實物是否適於抵繳，自應予以調查核定，而非謂納稅義務人不論在何種情形下，均得指定任何實物以供抵繳。

義務人所有易於變價[30]及保管之實物一次抵繳；而課徵標的物屬不易變價或保管，或申請抵繳日之時價較死亡或贈與日之時價為低者，其得抵繳之稅額，以該項財產價值占全部課徵標的物價值比例計算之應納稅額為限[31]。

被繼承人死亡時，其著作財產權為遺產之一部分，惟如納稅義務人如欲以著作財產權抵繳遺產稅，除必須符合「應納遺產稅額在30萬元以上」與「現金繳納確有困難」之前提要件外，並須分別就「著作財產權為遺產稅課徵標的物」及「納稅義務人所有之著作財產權」，是否符合相關規定，以決定之。

至於被繼承人自己創作之著作財產權，依遺贈稅法第16條第5款規定，不計入遺產總額，即非為遺產稅課徵標的物，繼承人（納稅義務人）則無法以此著作財產權抵繳遺產稅。

一、遺產稅課徵標的物之著作財產權

在著作財產權為遺產稅課徵標的物之場合，依上述之討論，納稅義務人以此著作財產權申請抵繳遺產稅時，稅捐機關不得以著作財產

---

[30] 我國遺贈稅法於1985年修正前，僅以易於變價或保管之實物抵繳為限，修正後放寬範圍至「課徵標的物」或「納稅義務人所有易於變價及保管之實物」。以實物抵繳遺產稅關係納稅義務人與國家稅制間之公平合理性，如任由納稅義務人以實物抵繳（尤其是不易變價或保管之財產），不但增加實物變價與財產保管等稅務稽徵或行政管理之成本，亦可能因跌價而造成稅收之損失，故有學者認為不應以實物抵繳。如納稅義務人以易於變價或保管之物抵繳稅款，較無爭議；惟對於不易變價或保管之實物抵繳，則多持否定之看法。周玉津，實物抵繳遺產稅似開倒車，中國稅務旬刊，1995年1月20日，第1559期，頁20。羅友三，新修訂遺贈稅法評析，中國稅務旬刊，1995年1月31日，第1560期，頁9。以及江敏雄，現行遺產稅稽徵問題淺論，中國稅務旬刊，1995年6月20日，第1574期，頁7-9。謝益良，遺產及贈與稅實物抵繳之研究，財稅研究，1997年3月，第29卷第2期，頁43。

[31] 參見遺贈稅法第30條第4項規定。

權不易變價或保管為由，否准其抵繳，但其得抵繳之稅額，以該項財產價值占全部課徵標的物價值比例計算之應納稅額為限。

　　本文以為，稅捐機關如准許並收取抵繳之著作財產權後，該著作財產權即成為國有財產，而著作權法第42條將「著作財產權人死亡，其著作財產權依法應歸屬國庫者」，規定將其著作財產權歸於消滅，使其成為公共領域著作，任何人均得自由利用，二者似乎背道而馳。故以此論點觀之，稅捐機關如准予此等著作財產權抵繳，其執行之結果，恐難認為符合代物清償之目的。故本文以為，稅捐機關應否准其抵繳，惟目前實務上尚無案例，猶待主管機關之解釋或行政法院於個案上判決，以進一步釐清。

二、納稅義務人所有之著作財產權

　　納稅義務人所有之著作財產權，屬於納稅義務人所有之財產，納稅義務人以此著作財產權申請抵繳遺產稅時，尚須符合「易於變價及保管之實物」之要件。著作財產權種類繁雜，除部分之語文、音樂、錄音或視聽等類著作，稍有授權市場外，大多數著作財產權並無買賣或授權之交易市場，其變價及保管應屬不易。在現有環境與市場體制下，納稅義務人申請以自己所有之著作財產權抵繳遺產稅，並不可行。

　　被繼承人已經受讓取得或納稅義務人所有之著作財產權，雖得申請抵繳遺產稅，惟獲准抵繳遺產稅之可能性並不高。此須稅務機關或行政法院依個案確認外，建立一著作權之交易市場，有助於此問題之改善[32]。惟如繼承人未繳納遺產稅，而遭稅捐機關聲請強制執行時，

---

[32] 傳統見解認為評（估）價是事實問題，應由法官自行解決，楊建成，智慧財產權審判中專家鑑定問題研究，收錄於「兩岸智慧產權保護與運用」，政治科技政策與法律研究中心，2002年7月，初版，頁41。但法官在做成法律評價前，因為專業知識受

除尚未發表之著作不得查封之情況外[33]，其餘之著作財產權仍可成為
強制執行之對象。

肆、著作財產權評價問題之探討

　　傳統上，著作權係屬狹義的智慧財產權（intellectual property
rights, IPR）[34]，世界貿易組織（WTO）之「與貿易有關之智慧財
產權協定」[35]（Trade Related Aspect of Intellectual Property Rights;
TRIPS）與世界智慧財產權組織[36]（World Intellectual Property
Organization, WIPO）亦將著作權列舉或歸類在智慧財產權之範圍
中。財團法人中華民國會計研究發展基金會與美國財務會計準則委員

限，不得不委託專家鑑定，故法律針對著作財產權之評價，始終未有明確規範。惟學
者亦有認為此不僅是事實問題，因鑑價師選任、其依據評價技術規則之客觀性、鑑價
師公正性與保密責任、評價資訊公開，以及評價程序等，亦甚至有可能是法律問題。
詹炳耀，同前註26，頁55-56。

[33] 參見強制執行法第53條第1項第6款規定。

[34] 劉江彬、黃俊英，智慧財產管理總論，華泰書局，2004年2月，初版，頁20。

[35] 係由世界貿易組織（WTO）中包括美國、歐盟及日本等124國，於1994年所簽署「與
貿易有關之智慧財產權協定」，1996年1月1日起生效，是目前國際保護與貿易有關之
智慧財產權種類最完整之多邊協定，主要內容可分訂定智慧財產權之最低保護標準、
智慧財產權保護之執行與爭端解決等三部分。劉博文，智慧財產權之保護與管理，揚
智出版社，2002年7月，初版，頁155-159。

[36] WIPO concluded in Stockhold on July 14, 1967 (Article 2 viii)。巴黎公約、伯恩公
約及馬德里協定等各有關智慧財產權之國際公約組織，原先各自設有「國際局」
（International Bureau），以管理暨執行該公約之相關業務，為加強國際合作及提高
行政效率，於1970年將各國際局合併而成立「世界智慧財產權組織」，並成為聯合國
所屬之專門機構，總部設於瑞士日內瓦，目前會員國超過140個，設有國際局之常設
機構，負責執行智慧財產權國際間保護工作。同前註，頁141-145。

會則將著作權列為無形資產之一種[37]，在我國相關法規中亦作如是規範[38]。無論是智慧財產權或無形資產，在學界及實務界尚未有統一之用語與定義；而有學者則認為智慧資本（intellectual capital）＝知識資本（knowledge capital）＝非財務資產＝無形資產＝隱藏資產＝不可見資產＝意味達成目標[39]，更顯現出其範圍之廣泛，亦隱含著對其評價之挑戰性。

由於不同的時間、對象，彼此認知與專業能力程度的差別，將造成對於此項無形資產價值的認知差異，也將形成知識性商品價格（price）與價值（value）間之價值差距（value gap），「相同的知識或技術，於不同對象與目的，所達成的價值並不相同」，亦即取得參考標準困難。且其價值需要透過專業知識與技術服務的過程始能創

---

[37] 無形資產之會計處理準則，財團法人中華民國會計研究發展基金會，財務會計準則公報第37號，第2段至第8段。此定義與美國財務會計準則委員會（FASB）的定義相同，可參考FASB，Statement of Financial Accounting Standards NO.141，Business Combinations（June 2001），P124。無形資產須同時符合可辨認性、可被企業控制與具有未來經濟效益等三個要件。另一般公認會計原則彙編(1984年10月18日修正)，財團法人中華民國會計研究發展基金會，第 23 條第1項亦規定「無形資產如商譽、商標權、專利權、著作權、特許權等，均應分別列示。」

[38] 相關法規計有：
1.商業會計法第50條第1項「購入之商譽、商標權、專利權、著作權、特許權及其他等無形資產，應以實際成本為取得成本」。另同法第27條第1項係將無形資產明定為資產類之會計科目的法源基礎。
2.所得稅法第60條第1項「營業權、商標權、著作權、專利權及各種特許權等無形資產估價，均限以出價取得者為資產」。
3.營利事業所得稅不合常規移轉訂價查核準則第4條第1項第9款「無形資產：指營業權、著作權、專利權、商標權、事業名稱、品牌名稱、設計或模型、計畫、秘密方法、營業秘密，或有關工業、商業或科學經驗之資訊或專門知識、各種特許權利、行銷網路、客戶資料及其他具有財產價值之權利。」

[39] 林大容譯，Leif Edvinsson & Michael S. Malone著，智慧資本—如何衡量資訊時代無形資產的價值（Intellectual capital-realizing your company's true value by finding its hidden roots），麥田出版社，2001年9月，初版，頁33。

造出價值，因此有學者認為無形資產評價應朝「該項無形資產運用或使用後所創造的價值」為評估依據，而非此項知識與技術本身的單一價值[40]。易言之，對於不同的無形資產，因其認知與目的之不同，須建立不同的價值認定標準；同時，對於相同的無形資產，也因環境與使用者等差異，所創造之價值不同，自然也需不同的評價標準[41]。

依美國布魯金斯研究院在其「布魯金斯工作小組的無形資產報告」中[42]，依企業掌控程度與能否獨立出售移轉，將無形資產分為三級，而著作權被列為第一級「可擁有及出售者」[43]，則代表著作權在諸多智慧財產權或無形資產中，屬於較易評價者之一。而著作權法第88條與遺贈稅法施行細則第34條已規範可供評價之方式，本文以為若能提高對著作權重視程度，則著作權亦能如商標權或專利權般具市場價值，智慧財產權終會取代傳統有形資產，而成為國家社會經濟活動或財富衡量的指標。

[40] 張孟元、劉江彬，無形資產評估鑑價之理論與實務，華泰書局，初版，2005年1月，頁9-10。

[41] 學者認為，智慧財產權的鑑價是在侵權行為、授權契約、稅務規劃、管理策略、擔保、權利讓與、投資評估與清算執行中，實踐保護智慧財產權的基礎所在，在著作權繼承中，無論是前文已探討之遺產分割、遺產稅核課與抵繳，或是後文將敘及之強制執行，都須面臨著作財產權之評價問題，實有待建立一套評價制度。詹炳耀，同前註26，頁41-42。

[42] 戴至中譯，約翰‧貝瑞（John Berry）著，最無形的、最核心—有效衡量並管理企業六大無形資產、讓競爭優勢極大化的具體策略，美商麥格羅希爾公司台灣分公司，2005年5月，初版，頁25-26。

[43] 第二級：可掌控但不具個別性而無法獨立出售者—研發、獨特的營運流程或良好的管理系統。第三級：不是由一家公司能完全擁有或掌控者—如人員、相關人際關係（合夥研發、供應鏈或共同設計產品）及網路效應。同前註。

一、著作財產權評價考量因素

　　著作財產權無論由市場機制或法律規範來決定其價值，其評價所需考量因素，有學者認為主要有：作者、內容、範圍、題材、體裁、篇幅、市場與同類作品數量等因素[44]；亦有學者從成本面看，主要有：使用人力、薪資、邊際福利與固定費用之攤銷等[45]。而在數位科技與網際網路時代，對著作財產權之衝擊影響最大，尤其是重製與散布成本低，速度又快，一方面可提昇著作權之使用流通價值，另一方面亦由於使用的便利性，造成著作權的侵害；因此，科技發展與環境變遷等非經濟因素[46]亦須納入考量。

　　又著作人格權雖專屬於著作人，不得讓與或繼承，惟其權利之行使亦關係著作財產權之價值。如前文所探討，在國內出版界「影子作家」生態下，著作人姓名表示權消極不行使，反而促使其著作價值提昇。在美國之日本卡通動畫影集之著作權授權交易中，美國被授權公司為文化差異或市場因素，嚴重修改日本卡通動畫影集作品內容，而漠視著作人同一性保持權之保護[47]，亦引起動畫影迷的批評，與學界對合理使用重新定義的探討。在日本法院則已有侵害著作人格權的賠償遠高於著作財產權之判決[48]。故著作人格權亦是著作財產權本身評價時，應考量之另一重要因素。

---

[44] 周林，版權價值評估，收錄於「知識產權價值評估中的法律問題」，法律出版社（大陸），1999年12月，初版，頁131。

[45] Robert F. Reilly & Robert P. Schweihs, Valuing Intellangible Assets, (1999), P369.

[46] 有關智慧財產權或無形資產鑑價考量因素，大致可分為經濟因素與非經濟因素，惟其內涵學者間各有不同之研究結果與看法，詳細情形可參考詹炳耀，同前註26，頁143-147；以及邱永和，國有智慧財產鑑價之研究，財團法人工業資訊促進會88年度委託學術機構研究計畫期末報告，1999年6月30日，頁118。

[47] Joshua M. Daniels, "Lost in Translation: Anime, Moral Rights, and Market Failure", Boston University Law Review (June 2008), P709-742.

[48] 參閱日本東京地方裁判所1999年（平成10年）8月18日第11575號判決。

二、著作財產權評價之方法

有關智慧財產權鑑價國內外有諸多文獻探討，可能評價之方法亦不少[49]。學者劉博文認為無形資產之評價，宜從交易、使用與賠償等三種價值評估的目的來選擇評價之方法[50]。以下即依此三面向，探尋著作財產權評價之方法：

（一）著作財產權交易價值的計算

將著作財產權當作買賣或交換之交易標的物，而予以評價，一般採「持續使用價值」（going concern value）原則，又可分三種計算方式[51]：

1. 成本法（cost approach）

係在假設「無形資產之價值不低於成本」之前提下，直接以自行投入研發或購置取得之成本（或成本加成法）為衡量基準，一般企業最常用於未上市的產品；其優點為簡化轉移或交易的過程與價值評估的困難，且有客觀之成本資料作佐證，在研究機構與政府部門常使用。其缺點為研發成本經常與其經濟價值不成正比，且非以收益作評價，亦未納入市場及競爭環境等客觀因素及條件，常會是單方價值判斷的標準，缺乏經濟價值的判斷基礎。

由於著作權法對於「原創性」之要求並不高，著作完成時即享有著作權，雖經公開發表，然多為未出版上市，性質上頗適合採用成本法，商業會計法第50條第1項、所得稅法第60條第1項及一般會計中

---

[49]　詹炳耀，同前註26，頁156-158；邱永和，同前註46，頁18。

[50]　劉博文，同前註35，頁232-235。

[51]　以下係本文自國內學者詹炳耀、邱永和及劉博文等人論述，綜合整理而成，文字用語已有不同，文責由本文自負。

歷史成本原則均採之。惟因著作類型不同及利用數位科技輔助工具，其成本資料舉證並不容易，又將同一著作之成本分攤至其各種著作財產權中，缺乏理論依據；而且著作財產權多由其權利行使，始產生其價值，以成本法評價，實不合理。

2. 市場法（market approach）

必須建立在正常的市場機制基礎上，在市場上取得其他相類似的智慧財產權交易價格之同質參考樣本，作為評價之依據，以進行企業整體價值的評估與分析。大部分以「市場殘值法」（residual method）、「資本資產評價法」（CAPM）、「套利理論」（APT）或「投資市場溢價理論」（valuation premium in the capital market）等為理論基礎，將企業整體獲利能力與有形資產獲利值間之差異，作為企業無形資產總體評估之價值，為目前最廣泛使用的評價模式之一。其優點是反映供需法則，可評估實際市場價值，並對於未來之風險與利潤進行分析。缺點則是很難找到與本身完全類似的交易實例，當樣本失真或取樣錯誤，將造成評價的偏誤。

雖然著作財產權利用市場法評價，較成本法更能反映市場價值，亦為美國內地稅局（Internal Revenue Service, IRS）明定為最優先選擇之智慧財產權評價方案[52]。其關鍵仍在類似市場交易價格之取得不易。國內著作財產權仍以授權市場為主，鮮有直接以著作財產權交易之市場，縱使語文（出版）、音樂或電腦程式等著作之買賣交易，多為個別議價方式進行，資訊並不公開，更難符合市場法之有效率之完全競爭市場之基本條件。

3. 收益法（income approach）

依據企業利用智慧財產在剩餘壽命期間，每年或每月所獲得之現

---

[52] IRS財務規則1.482-3條。

金流入，以「折算現金流量法」（discount cash flow method）來計算現值。其優點為考量成本與收益及時間因素，Gordon V. Smith & Russell L. Parr認為成本法無法表現智慧財產權的價值，而智慧財產權缺乏靈活的市場，市場法並不實用，收益法是最值得信賴的[53]。我國遺贈稅法所採依「賸餘年數」以所定「額外利益額」倍數，為礦業權、漁業權與無形資產之估計價值規定，亦屬收益法之一種。其缺點為很難估計出未來期間內的現金流入量。

以著作財產權來看，依著作權法規定可知著作之存續期間，惟其僅是擬制之最長賸餘年數，並不等同著作財產權之剩餘壽命期間。著作財產權以授權利用為主，其能產生現金流入之期間與各期間所產生現金流入量之估算，並不容易掌握。

（二）著作財產權使用價值的計算

一般著作財產權之使用，依契約自由原則，由當事人以契約約定使用授權範圍及權利金或版稅數額。權利金對於授權者而言，可收回投資成本，以維持繼續創作之活力；對於被授權者而言，可節省時間、成本、風險及迴避爭執之訴訟費用。權利金一般係考慮：1.授權所得之合理利潤：所得金額是否能彌補授權者的機會成本損失？是否應採排他性之專屬授權（exclusive license），以獲得單一來源高金額授權，或是採非排他性之一般授權，多項來源但較低金額授權，何種較有利？2.發明標的物的生命週期：如生命週期短者採一次付款方式為宜。3.發明標的物的市場分析：是否具有市場潛力，以及競爭對手的投資。4.授權對手是誰：對方是否具有優勢？是否為競爭者？等因素修正調整後所決定。

至於權利金支付時間與方式，又可分為三種：1.定額權利金：

---

[53] Gordon V. Smith & Russell L. Parr, Valuation of Intellectual Property and Intangible Assets (2000), P108.

支付一固定金額，可一次（lump sum）或分期付款（installment）方式。2.營運權利金：依產品產出或銷售的金額在契約期間持續支付。3.保障權利金：被授權人保證將支付一定最低金額之權利金，縱使未生產或銷售該產品，亦有支付權利金之義務。

　　經濟部智慧財產局依著作權法第47條第4項規定，編製教科用書及教學輔助用品之使用報酬率[54]，係依重製、編輯或改作與著作類型分別規定；而同法第69條第2項規定音樂著作強制授權許可，申請人應給付之使用報酬，則以預定發行之錄音著作批發價格一定百分比計算[55]。另依同法第69條所成立之著作權仲介團體，採集中管理授權，則依不同之利用人或場所訂定不同之使用報酬費率。

（三）著作財產權賠償責任的計算

　　學者孫遠釗研究指出[56]，一件著作物其著作權之金錢價值幾何，向為爭論之焦點。不同的計算方式，會產生迥然不同的計算結果；越新穎的著作物，其著作權價值也越不容易證明。依照傳統的侵權行為法，原告若就侵害著作權之行為起訴請求損害賠償，除須證明確有侵權行為外，尚須證明其實際所受損害，而損害之計算依據，自然涉及其著作權之價值。

　　原告往往因為價值之不易證明，或實際受損金額微薄，而放棄法律上之追訴權利，使著作權法所設之救濟制度淪為虛設。惟在法定損

---

[54] 參考經濟部智慧財產局1998年1月23日（87）台內著字第8702053號公告修正「發布著作權法第47條第4項之使用報酬率」。

[55] 依音樂著作強制授權申請許可及使用報酬辦法第12條第2項規定，申請人應給付之使用報酬，其計算公式為：

$$使用報酬 = \frac{預定發行之錄音著作批發價格 \times 5.4\% \times 預定發行之錄音著作數量}{預定發行之錄音著作所利用之音樂著作數量}$$

[56] 孫遠釗，美國著作權法令暨判決之研究（民國97年度：法令暨最近判例）期末報告，經濟部智慧財產局（殷博智財產管理公司執行），2008年11月，初版，頁715。

害賠償之制度下，原告在證明侵權行為成立後，即可不請求實際之損害賠償，而選擇請求法定之損害賠償，雖然金額限定在法律規定之範圍內，但對原告而言，可避免舉證責任之煩，既可更有效率地保障其權利，亦可收警示侵權行為人之效。

　　一般在和解或民事訴訟程序中，被侵害之一方得請求侵害人應負之賠償責任，可依下列方法計算：

1. 依被侵害人所受損失及所失利益

　　按侵權行為之損害賠償原以恢復原狀為原則，例外則採金錢賠償[57]，在著作財產權之侵害，恢復原狀已不可能，故被侵害之一方所受之具體損失及所失經濟利益，得依民法第216條之規定，提出損害賠償之請求。此請求賠償之方法雖符合公平原則，但在訴訟實務上，將面臨因果關係舉證之困難問題[58]。

　　至於其損失求償之額度，除可依前述交易價值的計算方式，以成本法、市場法或收益法加以計算外[59]，如被侵害人不能證明其損失額度時，依著作權法第88條第2項第1款但書規定，亦得以其行使權利依通常情形可得預期之利益，減除被侵害後行使同一權利所得利益之差額，為其所受損害。以此種方法計算損害賠償，在理論上合理，但實務上如市場飽和、經濟不景氣或有數位侵權行為人時，均使計算變為困難[60]。

---

[57] 參見民法第213條規定。

[58] 許忠信，著作權侵害之損害賠償責任，政治大學法律研究所碩士論文，1994年6月，頁160。

[59] 實務上法院大多採成本法評估，最高法院89年台上字第908號民事判決。

[60] 此計算方式係採差額說，羅明通，著作權法論【Ⅱ】，三民書局，2005年10月，6版，頁435。

2. 依侵害人因侵害行為所得之利益

此為著作權法第88條第2項第2款本文規定之計算方法，被侵害人不須證明自己之損失及所失利益，只需司法或警察機關搜索時，查扣侵害人之帳冊，或於訴訟中要求被告提出相關帳冊，為計算之依據，依其販售之價格與銷售量計算銷售收入，再扣除其成本後之淨利益為其所得之利益。如侵害人不能證明其成本或必要費用時，則依同法條同項同款但書之規定，將以其侵害行為所得之全部收入，為其所得之利益。

此種計算方式，免去被侵害人自行計算與舉證之困擾，改由侵害人負舉證之責，並賦予其成本或必要費用舉證不能時，逕以總所得額為賠償。雖然對侵害人不甚公平，亦有逾越填補損失之精神，惟其本款採以淨利益為賠償之總額，課予侵害人負成本或必要費用舉證之責，僅當不能舉證時，始依總所得額為賠償，尚不失衡平。但如侵害人尚未出售或獲利甚少時，被害人即不宜以此計算方式為請求。

3. 由法院酌定損害賠償額

此種計算方式原則上係為彌補前述計算方式之不足，當被侵害人不易證明其實際損害額，得請求法院依侵害情節，在法定賠償額度範圍內酌定損害賠償額[61]。在實務上，法院認為因相互拷貝電腦軟體只需幾分鐘內即可完成，具有不特定之流通性，原告所受損害顯難以估計，自屬不易證明其實際損害額[62]，而引此規定酌定損害賠償額。

又著作權法第88條第3項除採此法定賠償外，亦對損害行為屬故

---

[61] 現行規定為新臺幣一萬元以上一百萬元以下，如損害行為屬故意且情節重大者，賠償額得增至新臺幣五百萬元。本項規定係1985年修正著作權法時，仿美國著作權法第504條規定，並以著作之零售價格500倍計算，缺乏彈性，於1992年修正時，改由法院依侵害情節酌定，以符實際。

[62] 臺灣板橋地方法院96年度重智字第12號民事判決。

意且情節重大者[63]，得增加賠償額，而此類似懲罰性賠償金，並不能
代表著作財產權之價值。

三、著作財產權評價制度之建立

著作財產權評價之方法，無論在學術上或法律規範上，有各種不
同之計算方法，以配合各種使用目的或各種不同著作類型評價所需。
易言之，著作財產權評價在技術上並不困難，而現今著作財產權評價
並未受重視，亦未普及，實因尚未建立評價制度。基於此，本文則認
為著作財產權評價制度之建立，則須經由著作財產權交易市場平台之
建立、鑑價師之導入與著作財產權鑑價制度之立法等三方面之配合，
始能建立評價制度，活絡市場。

（一）著作財產權交易市場平台之建立

市場之產生須有供需雙方之參與，著作之產生與使用，在日常生
活中自然發生，因此著作財產權交易市場，並無專利權或商標等無形
資產，有待政府強化供給面之問題[64]，而現階段政府則需加強輔導著
作財產權交易平台之設置。

國際上仲介團體所管理的權利中，最普遍的有公開演出權、公

---

[63] 臺灣板橋地方法院96年度重智字第13號民事判決。法院認定被告既以經營資訊軟體服
務等項目為業，自有其不特定之消費客源，事實上自難以估計其非法拷貝之數量，
其侵害原告軟體著作權範圍，絕對遠超過已有之證物，其行為業已嚴重擠壓原告之該
等軟體市場，自可謂情節重大，且被告以資訊軟體服務為業，竟非法重製於其公司內
部使用之電腦或銷售、維修之電腦中，被告侵害原告著作權乃屬故意。惟雖認為被告
之損害行為屬故意且情節重大，但僅以法定賠償之上標100萬元論處，並未增加賠償
額。

[64] 相關討論請參考黃鋒榮，無形資產的評價與鑑價師之評估，嶺東財經法學，創刊號，
2008年6月，頁115-116。

開播送權、音樂著作的機械重製權、劇本或戲劇舞蹈著作的公開演出權，以及文字著述和音樂著作的影印重製權等類型[65]。而國內以經濟部智慧財產局許可之七個著作權仲介團體為主，所建立之著作財產權交易市場平台，其所管理之著作財產權之類型亦相似，詳如表7-2所示，除社團法人中華語文著作權仲介協會（COLCIA）外，其餘六個著作權仲介團體，大多採線上申請或授權管理。惟其因係非營利組織，大多由著作權人或其被授權人所組成，其著作之來源有限，規模有待整合擴大。

表7-2　經許可之「著作權仲介團體之相關資料」

	團體名稱	負責人	類別	管理權能	地址／電子信箱／網站電話／傳真	備註
1	社團法人台灣音樂著作權人聯合總會（MCAT）	蔡清忠	音樂著作	公開播送權、公開演出權、公開傳輸權	台北市松山區105南京東路4段130號9樓http://www.mcat.org.tw 電話：（02）2570-1680 傳真：（02）2570-1681	88.01.20許可88.06.22法人登記
2	社團法人中華音樂著作權仲介協會（MUST）	吳楚楚	音樂著作	公開播送權、公開演出權、公開傳輸權	台北市松山區105南京東路4段1號7樓http://www.must.org.tw 電話：（02）2717-7557 傳真：（02）2717-7556	88.01.20許可88.05.17法人登記

---

[65] 陳麗桂，著作權仲介團體的性質和功能簡介，亞信國際專利商標事務所網站http://www.mission.com.tw/news-view.asp?idno=218（上網日期：2009年10月13日）。

	團體名稱	負責人	類別	管理權能	地址／電子信箱／網站電話／傳真	備註
3	社團法人台灣音樂著作權協會（TMCS）	黃銘得	音樂著作	公開傳輸權、公開播送權、公開演出權	台北市基隆路1段8號5樓之1http://www.tmcs.org.tw 電話：（02）2769-8088 傳真：（02）2769-9788	91.02.27許可91.04.30法人登記
4	社團法人中華民國錄音著作權人協會（ARCO）	張松輝	錄音著作	公開播送權、公開演出報酬請求	台北市松山區105八德路4段85號4樓http://www.arco.org.tw 電話：（02）2718-8818 傳真：（02）2742-0621	88.01.20許可88.05.31法人登記
5	社團法人中華有聲出版錄音著作權管理協會（RPAT）	楊碧村	錄音著作	公開播送權、公開演出報酬請求權	台北市復興南路1段1號13樓之5http://www.rpat.org.tw 電話：（02）8772-3060 傳真：（02）8772-2973	90.10.22許可91.02.07法人登記
6	社團法人中華音樂視聽著作仲介協會（AMCO）	張松輝	視聽著作	公開播送權、公開上映權	台北市松山區105八德路4段85號4樓http://www.amco.org.tw 電話：（02）2718-8818 傳真：（02）2742-0621	88.01.20許可88.05.26法人登記
7	社團法人中華語文著作權仲介協會（COLCIA）	符兆祥	語文著作	重製權	台北市重慶南路2段21號2樓之3 電話：（02）2396-2089 傳真：（02）2341-0661	95.08.08許可95.11.20法人登記

資料來源：經濟部智慧財產局網頁（網頁更新日期：2008/6/24）http://oldweb.tipo.gov.tw/copyright/copyright_book/copyright_book_24.asp（上網日期：2009年10月13日）。

　　在美國為加速著作權電子化授權，由著作人、出版商（或內容提供者）與利用者共同建立之著作權清算中心（copyright clearance center，簡稱CCC）[66]，建立一終端對終端（end-to-end）連結系統，利用者直接在網頁上點選所需之著作及其系統所設定之各種授權條款、利用方式與授權金後，著作人或內容提供者在線上立即授權，並傳送該著作之電子內容，利用者以即時下載方式，取得該著作。

　　國內亦有如法源法律網[67]、月旦法學知識庫[68]等提供法律相關期刊或電子書等文獻複製授權，提供線上傳輸服務，均略具市場規模。本文以為，政府可在現有基礎上，輔導並鼓勵民間業者以購併或策略聯盟方式，擴大其經營規模，並與國際相關機構合作，讓著作財產權市場之交易平台更多樣，以提高著作之使用價值。

（二）鑑價師制度之導入

　　就著作財產權而言，它是一個異質性高、交易量少，又存在著價值差距的市場，必須要有專業之鑑價師提供服務，來協助評估著作財產權之價值，以促進供需雙方覓得合理的交易價格，來達成交易，活絡市場的流通性。因此，在著作財產權市場之發展中，導入鑑價師制度，有其必要性。

　　由於著作財產權為無形資產之一種，其鑑價雖有其獨特之處，但

---

[66] CCC由一群著作人、出版商於1978年成立，目前已代表幾乎全世界每一個國家數萬名著作人、出版商與發明者，並可授權數百萬的書籍、期刊、報紙、網頁（websites）、電子書（ebooks）、影像、布落格（blogs）及其他著作，是IFRRO的創會會員，亦是重製權組織（reproduction rights organizations, RROs）的一個國際網站，與全世界RROs姐妹網站簽訂共同協議，並在180多個國中註冊。CCC網站http://www.copyright.com/ccc/viewPage.do?pageCode=au1-n（上網日期：2009年4月14日）。

[67] 法源法律網站http://www.lawbank.com.tw/logoutok.php（上網日期：2009年10月13日）。

[68] 月旦法學知識庫網站http://www.lawdata.com.tw/anglekmc/ttswebx?@0:0:1:lawkm@@0.08079348787382962（上網日期：2009年10月13日）。

其鑑價之原理與方法，與其他無形資產相近，故本文以為，其鑑價師制度之建立，仍宜在無形資產鑑價師體制下運作，較為簡便可行。以下僅就無形資產鑑價師制度之建立，究由民間抑或由政府主導，以及鑑價師執業與道德規範問題，作初步探討。

1. 無形資產鑑價師制度之建立

我國現行法律並無有關無形資產鑑價師之法源，但是在企業合併、股東以技術或其他無形資產入股時，董事會需針對有關的無形資產作評價，以供合併價格之擬定與股東股本之計算；在相關無形資產侵權之民事訴訟中，法官對於被侵害人所受損害或所失利益之金額，必須予以核計。諸如此類情形，目前大多由會計師負責估算價值，亦有部份則委由民間機構或個人辦理。惟此種依個案選任專家方式，缺乏體制的支持，不但無法發揮專業之公信力，亦難以應付未來市場成長的需求。

在美國企業鑑價之專業認證，係由民間組織之「美國全國企業鑑價分析師協會」（NACVA）[69]或類似團體所辦理。目前國際間唯一之國際性鑑價專業機構係「國際顧問鑑價師與分析師協會」（IACVA）[70]，旨在對全球企業鑑價與無形資產鑑價之專業人員提供服務與支援。而在我國則有中華無形資產暨企業評價協會與財團法人中華科技經濟鑑測中心已辦理企業評價之相關認證訓練，而中華企業評價學會更已辦理二屆企業評價師培訓[71]。可見民間團體對於鑑價師之需求殷切，亦有能力與意願辦理相關教育訓練工作。至於專業證照

---

[69] The National Association of Certified Valuation Analysts (NACVA) Website http://www.nacva.com/（上網日期：2009年10月13日）。

[70] International Association of Consultants, Valuers and Analysts (IACVA) Website http://www.iacva.org/（上網日期：2009年10月13日）。

[71] 參考中華企業評價學會網站http://www.valuation.org.tw/（上網日期：2009年10月13日）。

之考試工作，由於缺乏法源，目前仍無一套制度可依循。

　　本文認為政府在此制度發展之初，宜著重在相關法律之修正或訂定，賦予無形資產鑑價師之法源；同時，亦可輔導公會或財團法人（仿保險公會或中華民國證券暨期貨市場發展基金會模式）先對從業人員之專業能力予以認證，俟辦理一段期間，且市場日趨成熟時，可循不動產鑑價制度模式，研訂無形資產鑑定師法與鑑價技術規則，再由政府舉辦無形資產鑑定師高等考試，以維持其素質。

2. 鑑價師執業與道德之規範

　　無形資產之鑑價，常需涉及委託人之營業秘密，第三人欲進行鑑價時，將造成侵入性損害，鑑價師專業與自律的形象尤其重要。經濟部工業局於2005年「台灣技術交易機制發展計畫」中，委由中華無形資產暨企業評價協會等單位研究，擬定「智慧財產評價執業規範」、「智慧財產評價道德規範」與「智慧財產評價準則」等範本[72]，提供現行從業之機構或人員參考，雖無約束力，但已呈現政府與民間對執業與道德之重視。另財團法人中華民國會計研究發展基金會繼「財務會計準則公報」與「審計準則公報」之制定外，亦著手「評價準則公報」[73]研訂。相信在各專業團體努力下，無形資產之鑑價制度，將更臻健全，與世界先進國家並駕齊驅。

---

[72] 範本公佈在台灣技術交易市場資訊網站，係提供有關學會或機構擬定其會員或從事智慧財產評價人員之內部規範參考，屬於自發性規範，並無拘束力。網址：http://www.twtm.com.tw/resource/project.aspx?tsfsg=4bcf1f7cc45054e8ba7bec93799b84f6（上網日期：2009年10月13日）。

[73] 目前該基金會已發布評價準則公報第一號「一般公認評價準則總綱」（於2007年12月26日發布）第二號「職業道德準則」（於2008年8月13日發布）及第三號「評價報告準則」（於2009年8月21日發布）；另進行評價準則公報第四號「評價流程準則」（2009年6月5日開始三讀）制定作業。參考財團法人中華民國會計研究發展基金會網站http://www.ardf.org.tw/（上網日期：2009年10月13日）。

3. 著作財產權鑑價制度之立法

　　社會、經濟、政治等制度之建立有賴法律規範，其發展亦藉由法律調整之，惟如法律沒有事先妥善計畫，則無法適應社會發展所需求[74]。進入21世紀知識經濟的時代，著作財產權將越形重要，藉由鑑價制度之法制化，將使當事人有所依循，可相當程度節省交易成本，對社會福祉更有所助益。

　　著作財產權鑑價制度之立法，究採取何種方式，並非易事。有主張以正式的法律規範為當[75]，亦即採取單獨立法，並為符合經濟環境迅速變遷之需要，依憲法要求之授權明確性，以委任立法方式，授權行政機關發布法規命令，迅速參酌國內外之發展趨勢即時修訂，以為法律之補充。而以不動產鑑價制度為基礎，將其鑑價標的擴充至著作財產權等無形資產之鑑價，乃不失為簡便可行之途徑。

　　至於鑑價方法之選擇、鑑價師執業與道德之規範與鑑價技術規則等事項，本文以為宜由鑑價師公會或財團法人機構研究擬定發布。政府部門雖具有公信力，但仍不宜直接介入鑑價工作，以免過度干預民間經濟活動。鑑價制度中，亦應導入鑑價協議制度，經由當事人間機密協議、測試協議、篩選協議與選擇協議之合意，得以解決彼此間對標的價值認知之衝突[76]。

　　最後，鑑價結果之效力，固然取決當事人對鑑價者專業之信賴程度，但基於誠信原則及禁反言原則，對於合意送交鑑價之結果，除非鑑價結果顯有悖常情或二次以上之鑑價差距超過一定百分比以上，須重新另覓鑑價機構重新鑑價外，鑑價之結果對當事人，具有約束力，則是修訂各相關法規之重點。

---

[74]　羅傳賢，立法程序與技術，五南書局，2002年7月，3版，頁93。

[75]　詹炳耀，同前註26，頁334。

[76]　詹炳耀，同前註26，頁335-336。

伍、結　論

　　被繼承人死亡時所擁有之著作財產權,則與一般財產同樣列入遺產,除遺贈外,由繼承人依民法規定繼承,同時,亦面臨遺產稅之申報與核課問題。由於著作財產權內容繁雜,辨識本不容易,遺產稅之納稅義務人於申報限期內對繼承財產負有完整申報之責任,亦不得以稽徵機關未提供遺產資料為由而免其短、漏報之責;著作權法第88條與遺贈稅法施行細則第34條已規範可供評價之方式,本文以為若能提高對著作權重視程度,則著作權亦能如商標權或專利權般具市場價值,智慧財產權終會取代傳統有形資產,而成為國家社會經濟活動或財富衡量的指標。

　　民間團體對於鑑價師之需求殷切,亦有能力與意願辦理相關教育訓練工作,本文建議參考不動產鑑價制度模式,研訂無形資產鑑定師法與鑑價技術規則,再由政府舉辦無形資產鑑定師高等考試,以維持其素質。鑑價師執業與道德之規範,係屬道德範疇之自律行為,宜採較高之要求;修訂或制定相關法律時,建議對於違背專業精神或舞弊之行為,訂立相當之罰責。以不動產鑑價制度為基礎,將其鑑價標的擴充至著作財產權等無形資產之鑑價,乃不失為簡便可行之途徑,有關鑑價相關事項宜由鑑價師公會或財團法人機構研究擬定發布,以維繫專業之水準。

參考文獻

中文部分

江敏雄(1995),「現行遺產稅科徵問題淺論」,《中國稅務旬刊》,第1574期,頁7-9。

林大容譯（2001），Leif Edvinsson & Michael S. Malone著，《智慧資本—如何衡量資訊時代無形資產的價值（Intellectual capital-realizing your company's true value by finding its hidden roots）》，台北：麥田出版社。

邱永和（1999），「國有智慧財產鑑價之研究」，收錄於《財團法人工業資訊促進會88年度委託學術機構研究計畫期末報告》。

周玉津（1995），「實物抵繳遺產稅似開倒車」，《中國稅務旬刊》，第1559期，頁20。

周林（1999），「版權價值評估」，收錄於《知識產權價值評估中的法律問題》，大陸：法律出版社。

孫遠釗（2008），《美國著作權法令暨判決之研究（民國97年度：法令暨最近判例）期末報告》，經濟部智慧財產局（殷博智慧財產管理公司執行）。

張孟元、劉江彬（2005），《無形資產評估鑑價之理論與實務》，台北：華泰書局。

陳棋炎、黃宗樂、郭振恭合著（2009），《民法繼承新論》，台北：三民書局。

陳麗桂（2009），「著作權仲介團體的性質和功能簡介」，亞信國際專利商標事務所網站http://www.mission.com.tw/news-view. asp?idno=218。

郭振恭（2003），「論歸扣之標的及效力」，收錄於林秀雄主編《民法親屬繼承實例問題分析》，台北：三民書局。

許忠信（1994），《著作權侵害之損害賠償責任》，政治大學法律研究所碩士論文。

黃鋒榮（2008），「無形資產的評價與鑑價師之評估」，《嶺東財經法學》，創刊號，頁115-116。

詹炳耀（2003），《智慧財產估價的法制化研究》，台北大學法律研究所博士論文。

楊建成（2002），「智慧財產權審判中專家鑑定問題研究」，收錄於《兩岸智慧財產權保護與運用》，台北：政治科技政策與法律研究中心。

戴至中譯（2005），約翰‧貝瑞（John Berry）著，《最無形的、最核心─有效衡量並管理企業六大無形資產、讓競爭優勢極大化的具體策略》，台北：美商麥格羅希爾公司台灣分公司。

戴東雄（2003），《繼承法實例解說》，自版。

鍾鳳娥（2003），《以公共設施保留地及未上市（櫃）股票抵繳遺產及贈與稅問題之研究》，淡江大學會計學系研究所碩士論文。

謝釗益（1997），「遺產及贈與稅實物抵繳之研究」，《財稅研究》，第29卷第2期，頁43。

劉江彬、黃俊英（2004），《智慧財產管理總論》，台北：華泰書局。

劉博文（2002），《智慧財產權之保護與管理》，台北：揚智出版社。

羅友三（1995），「新修訂遺贈稅法評析」，《中國稅務旬刊》，第1560期，頁9。

羅明通（2005），《著作權法論【Ⅱ】》，台北：三民書局。

羅傳賢（2002），《立法程序與技術》，台北：五南書局。

英文部分

Gordon V. Smith & Russell L. Parr (2000), "Valuation of Intellectual Property and Intangible Assets".

Joshua M. Daniels (2008), "Lost in Translation: Anime, Moral Rights, and Market Failure", Boston University Law Review,June 2008：709-742.

Robert F. Reilly & Robert P. Schweihs(1999), "Valuing Intellangible Assets".

第八章　一「門」學問
——動態商標之研析

曾勝珍[*]　許淑閔[**]

目次

[*]　本文作者係嶺東科技大學財務金融所專任教授、教育部保護校園智慧財產權跨部會諮詢小組委員、加拿大英屬哥倫比亞大學法學院訪問學者暨博士後研究員

[**]　本文作者係嶺東科技大學財經法律研究所碩士

摘要 SUMMARY

　　商標申請案分為形式審查與實體審查，動作商標雖為非傳統商標之一種，審查上亦無傳統商標審查嚴格，惟仍適用商標法之一般原則與商標註冊要件。科技進步使代表商品來源的商標設計越趨多元化，目前國際社會承認動態商標有WIPO之新加坡商標法、歐盟共同體商標規則、美國以及台灣商標法修正草案。

　　本文以一「門」學問為題，除引起讀者閱讀興趣外，係指藍寶堅尼車門開啟方式為向上升起，與車體呈現平行狀，有別一般車門設計，正為動態商標之範例，又動態商標發展歷史甚短且未見訴訟案，本文將介紹歐美動態商標註冊案，希冀對動態商標之介紹達拋磚引玉之功能。

壹、前　言

　　商標申請案分為形式審查與實體審查，前者指申請人對申請案的描述，必須符合台灣商標法施行細則等規定，後者指商標本身設計符台商標註冊要件，商標申請案的准駁意見，必須經商標專責機關先行審查申請案是否符合形式要件,若符合形式要件,商標專責機關再進而審查實體要件,動作商標雖為非傳統商標之一種,審查上亦無傳統商標審查嚴格,惟仍適用商標法之一般原則。標識欲申請為註冊商標時,須符合商標法中註冊積極要件與消極要件,包括識別性、第二意義、功能性最為重要。

　　科技進步使代表商品來源的商標設計越趨多元化,目前台灣商標法保障擴及氣味商標、雷射商標、位置商標與動態商標,國際社會承認動態商標有WIPO之新加坡商標法、歐盟共同體商標規則、美國以及台灣商標法修正草案,動態商標發展歷史甚短且未見訴訟案,本文將利用歐盟商標線上查詢服務系統【CTM－Online (Community Trade Mark Consulltation Service)】及美國商標檢索系統(Trademark Electronic Search System,簡稱TESS)介紹歐美動態商標註冊案,希冀本文對動態商標之介紹能達拋磚引玉之功能。

貳、商標審查要件

一、概　說

　　商標專責機關須先審查申請案是否符合形式要件[1]。再審查實體要件,動作商標雖為非傳統商標之一種,審查條件亦無傳統商標審查嚴格,一般消費者可能不習慣以非傳統商標作為表彰的商品或服務來源,因此建議經過市場調查取得商標識別性[2],標識欲申請為註

---

[1] 本文僅說明申請動態商標時具備圖樣格式。

[2] 洪淑敏,〈國外非傳統商標之審查〉,《商標法制與實務論文集》,經濟部智慧財產局,2006年6月,164頁;曾淑婷,《氣味商標問題之研究》,台灣大學法律研究

冊商標時，須符合商標法中註冊積極要件與消極要件，積極要件指識別性、第二意義，消極要件如台灣商標法第23條第1項列舉之18款事由，以下亦將介紹美國與歐洲司法實務在非傳統商標部分之發展。

二、形式審查

美國商標法施行細則[3]規定標章申請註冊時，申請人必須清楚描給標章圖樣，要件如下所述；台灣部分亦同。

（一）美　國

動作商標圖樣須描繪獨特動作含5張以上的解析圖[4]，美國商標法施行細要求商標圖樣上傳至TEAS（Trademark Electronic Application System簡稱商標電子申請系統），申請書與樣本圖的規定整理如下[5]。

申請表格內容	樣本表格內容
1.申請表格紙張格式：寬21.6公分、長29.7公分（A4規格）、上下邊界3.8公分。	1.紙張格式：寬21.6公分、長29.7公分（A4規格），邊界2.5公分。

所碩士論文，2006年6月，44頁；WIPO Secretariat, *Standing Committee on the Law of Trademark, Industiial Designs and Geograpilical Indications*, SCT 17th Session, WIPO Doc. SCT/17/3 (March 30, 2007), at6.

[3] U.S. Trademark Law Rules of Practice & Federal Statute U.S. Patent &Trademark Office, November 1, 2007 (37 C.F.R. Part 2-Rules of Practice in Trademark Cases)，參考經濟部智慧財產局美國商標法施行細則之譯文。

[4] U.S. Trademark Law Rules of Practice & Federal Statutes U.S. Patent & Trademark Office, Novembel 1, 2007 (37 C.F.R. Part 2-Rules of Practicem Trademark Cases) §2.53?

[5] 美國商標施行細則第2.51條至第2.59條。

申請表格內容	樣本表格內容
2.申請人簽署申請書及宣誓或檢視聲明書。	2.表格紙張為具彈性、堅韌、平滑、不反光、潔白且耐用之紙張製作。
3.申請人姓名、國籍、住居所及郵件地址、主張優先權。	3.圖樣樣本長寬為8公分,文字敘述與圖樣樣本間矩至少有2.5公分。
4.是否依據商標法第1條規定提出申請。	4.在特殊情況時,主管機關接受錄音帶、錄影帶、CD-ROM等。
5.商品或服務的類別	5.交付於TEAS需交付JPG檔

　　申請案必須附上數位影像檔,格式為JPG[6]檔,西元2006年9月8日,美國專利商標局(United States Patent and Trademark Office,簡稱USPTO)發佈一則關於「TEAS影像申請檔[7]」格式,首次申請案如為格式化或設計標誌,申請人須附上一個黑白影像檔,當主管機關要求附上實際使用於商業上的樣品時,申請人須提供已被掃瞄的圖樣或數位相片,其檔案不可以超過二百萬位元,突顯商品是使用中。隨即,2006年10月25日公告「聲音/動作商標和電子歸檔[8]」的例外程序要求,聲音或動作商標樣本,由WAV、MP3或MPEG組成[9],美國商標審查程序手冊[10](以下稱商標審查手冊)規定特別圖樣特點,標章以黏貼、錄音方式或修改過將不會被接受[11]。

---

[6] U.S. Trademark Law Rules of Practice & Federal Statutes U.S. Patent & Trademark Office, Novembel 1, 2007 (37 C.F.R. Part 2-Rules of Practicem Trademark Cases) §2.53。每一吋裡的粒子介於300～350個間,長寬度皆在250～944畫素間。線條須勻稱、輪廓明顯、連續,除官方文件接受JPG和PDF圖像外,其他文件格式為JPG格式。

[7] 『美國專利商標局新聞卷,「Image files for TEAS」,發布日期:2006/9/8』,http//www.uspto.gov/teas/index.html,最後瀏覽日: 2008/3/27。

[8] 『美國專利商標局新聞稿,「Sound/Motion Marks and Electronic Filing」,發布日期:2006/11/27』,同前揭註,最後瀏覽日:2008/3/27。

[9] 申請人可透過電子郵件方式夾帶JPG檔寄給TEAS。

[10] Trademark Manual of Examination Procedures-5th edition,2007年9月修正第5版,於同月施行。美國商標審查程序手冊,自第八篇起規定商標申請要求,第807條以下有關商標描繪規定,動態商標屬非傳統商標,格式較特別。

[11] 特別圖示指包含全部或部份標識的圖樣,有特殊形式,圖樣有特色且可成為令人滿意

　　標識申請案使用標準格式時[12]，審查代理人評估標識在樣品上的使用方法且決定是否有包含不能用標準格式展現的必要要件或特色，如標誌的組成是描述標誌的解決辦法，基本格式的要求可能是不適當的。審查代理人確定圖樣在基本格式裡表現出一個特別形式，如果修正案留於標章的審查結果沒有重大的變更，申請者應該提出另一個有特別形式的圖樣，假設專業審查人對標章圖樣審查結果有另一個標準時，則應將把該圖樣用另一個形式向商標專利局申請[13]。

　　基本格式要求，商標名稱組成，包含空格以不超過26個字母為原則。如果超過26個字母，美國商標專利局的系統會自動駁回申請案而被納入公報；申請人可使用特殊格式，並附上一張數位影像圖，如選擇特殊格式，申請案不必符合基本格式要求[14]。

　　紙本格式規定，USPTO接受申請案以電子郵件或信封郵寄，但不接受傳真。標識圖樣以不超過正8公分寬為準，主管機關建立數位影像檔，審查代理人員須用內部網路的複審程序檢視標識，如商標是清楚準確，審查代理人員推定圖樣符合尺寸規格[15]。所有基本格式會儲存於USPTO系統裡，如影像圖樣須以正8公分寬為準，商標影像超過尺寸，USPTO調整影像符合要求，不符合要求，申請人須重提交

的複製品，反之，重新交付一張新圖樣，如仍有疑問將討論之，TMEP§807.04(a)。

[12] 標識須在紙張的上下紙角處、闡述者或在其他特色顯示出標章，USPTO鼓勵使用標準格式。

[13] 電子圖樣基本格式：如申請案以標準描繪格式填寫，申請案會進到TEAS裡的合適資料區域並附上一張影像圖擋。當申請案透過TEAS歸類，主管機關會透過TEAS的自動回覆系統再次確認格式。如格式符合要求，主管機關將建立一張數位影像圖，和自動產生商標特徵的說明。TMEP§807.05(a). TMEP§807.04(b).

[14] 為確定標識在自動記錄系統裡有清楚影像，審查代理人和合法檢查人員須在內部網路上公佈有利的複審程序。TMEP§807.05(a)(i), TMEP§807.05(b), TMEP§807.04(c).

[15] 圖樣在非亮面的白紙上畫出解析圖，紙張20.3-21.6公分寬、27.9-29.7公分長，以窄的一邊為頂端，紙張上方留有2.5公分寬，用黑色描繪商標，倘為顏色商標則用彩色，以平版印刷、列印或其他方法呈現圖樣，TMEP§807.06。

一個影像，USPTO建議申請人使用14號字，讓商標在公報和註冊證明書上更易於辨認[16]。

　　倘只有附上說明圖樣的文字申請表或國外註冊證明書將不被認定為圖樣，申請人不提供標章解析圖，審查代理人員必須再次審查申請案再為決定是否為商標。紙本的資訊與申請案中主要部分資訊間有不一致，審查代理人要求申請人提交一個標章解析圖樣，且決定准駁意見[17]。動作商標基本格式規定，標章含有動作（例如：短時間內的反覆動作）特微，申請人提交的圖樣是描述單一動作特點，或5張解析圖，申請人也須提交一份有詳細說明商標的申請書[18]。

（二）歐　盟

　　歐洲共同體商標法實施規則（COMMISSION REGULATION (EC) No 2868/95 of 13 December 1995 implementing Council Regulation (EC) No 40/94 on the Community trade mark）第3條[19]指出，欲申請的標章無任何特別的特色或外觀則須依正常格式將標章呈現在紙張，字母的大小寫型態是沒有限制的。申請案將以電子檔的方式儲存，標章再次複製後而成為標章分解圖，複製後的標章以不超過A4紙張的大小為基準且標章的說明及圖樣所占篇幅不超過26.2公分×17公分，紙張左邊最少要留2.5公分寬，而標章能夠清楚呈現在8公分寬與16公分長的限制篇幅裡，且該申請案會被公開在歐盟商標公報裡。

---

[16] TMEP§807.06(b), TMEP§807.06(c).

[17] TMEP§807.04(c).

[18] TMEP§807.11.

[19] 歐洲共同體商標法實施規則Rule 3。

（三）台　灣

台灣目前尚無動作商標，惟參考歐美文獻後，動作商標形式審查要件與聲音商標形式審查要件有雷同處，未來商標法修正草案通過後可以以聲音商標形式審查要件為參考之一，台灣商標法施行細則第10條關於聲音商標規定，申請註冊聲音商標者，應於申請書中聲明，並以五線譜、簡譜或描述說明表示，同時檢附存載該聲音之光碟片，以五線譜或簡譜表示者，應為相關說明；「立體、顏色及聲音商標審查基準」第4條第2項第1款對聲音商標亦有相關規定。

二、實體審查

我國商標法對於商標申請案實體審查要件分為積極要件與消極要件，前者指識別性與第二意義，後者為無商標法第23條第1項各款情形，態樣繁多，中以「功能性」最為重要。

（一）識別性

商標得以表彰業者商品，使消費者藉以區別商品或服務來源，商標必須具有識別性特點，如缺乏識別性，將無法使消費者想起商標圖案而得以降低消費者搜尋商品成本及業者賺取較高利潤，如賦予保護法律會阻礙市場的有效競爭，提供的產品商標越明顯，消費者搜尋成本將最小化，企業主潛在生產率將越大，利潤相對提高，此原則下，商標識別性強弱度成為主管機關准駁依據[20]。

台灣商標法第5條、美國商標法第45條及歐共體商標條例第4條均提及可以成為專利商標專責機關所認可的註冊商標，識別性是為註

---

[20] William M. Landes & Richard A. Posner著，金海軍譯，《知識產權法的經濟結構》，北京大學，2005年5月，頁226、240-241。

冊商標首要要件，美國聯邦第二巡迴上訴法院在1976年*Abercrombie & Fitch CO. v. Huntion World, Inc.*及1986年*Mcgraw-Edison Co. v. Walt Production & Bally Maunfacturing*兩案例中，建立識別性的判別標準，亦為台灣「商標識別性審查要點」第三點的判斷標準，依照識別性的強弱，將商標態樣分為五類，由弱至強分序為[21]：

一、通用性名稱商標：指大多數相關大眾用以稱呼該類商品或服務名稱，不具有註冊性；

二、描述性商標：直接描述商品或服務之性質、功能、品質、用途或其他特點上，不具有註冊性；

三、暗示性商標：以間接方式描述商品或服務之性質，功能、品質、用途或其他特點上，識別性較弱，屬弱勢商標，具有註冊性；

四、隨意性商標：所使用文字、圖形為一般社會大眾所熟悉，用於特定商品或服務上做為商標使用，與該商品或服務無關聯性，具有註冊性；

五、創造性商標：商標為刻意設計標章，商標文字、圖案或用語是過去所沒有，識別性最強。

　　本文挑選三個由最高行政法院做出的代表性判決，即BP英國石油代理商服務標章案[22]、美商棕欖公司牙膏案[23]、義商巴山尼狄仙諾有限公司機械器具案[24]，以及「BLACK SILICA寶石註冊案[25]」、

---

[21] 林洲富，〈顏色、立體及聲音商標於法律上保護──兼論台灣商標法相關修正規定〉，月旦法學雜誌，120期，2005年5月，頁112-114；陳文吟，《商標法論》，三民書局，2005年2月，頁53。

[22] 最高行政法院94年判字第128號。

[23] 最高行政法院92年度判字第1066號。

[24] 最高行政法院74年判字第347號。

[25] 經濟部(96)年經訴字第09606080670號。

「天明石及圖寶石註冊案[26]」、「睡眠科技有限公司案[27]」、「德商里滋菸草廠股份有限公司案[28]」等訴願案，均再再指出業者在設計商標圖案時除能表現自身產品或服務的主要特色，使商標圖樣深深地烙印相關消費者的心中外、更應注意商標本身的獨特性，才能獲准註冊登記或為訴訟勝訴關鍵之一。

（二）第二意義

　　第二意義指對於原本不具識別性之圖樣，經由申請人反覆地使用，因此產生聲譽，而具有識別性之功能時，其使用之圖樣便取得第二意義即得以註冊為商標[29]。業者取得第二意義為註冊商標時，須向消費者大眾證明該單詞主要將作為品牌名稱，才會給予商標保護，而成為吸引消資者購買的特徵，例如一個新產品上市需要一個描述性名稱，以便向消費大眾介紹，一旦產品流行後，該名稱可能貼上了最流行品牌，其他產品又會創出另一個詞語描述該產品，如「隨身碟」已在84年由精威科技股份有限公司取得註冊，嗣後生產其產品的廠商，如創見資訊股份有限公司，則必須以快閃記憶體（Flash Disk）取得註冊登記[30]。

　　第二意義的規定在台灣商標法第23條第4項、美國商標法第2條

[26] 經濟部(96)年經訴字第09606080330號。
[27] 經濟部(95)年經訴字第09506169570號。
[28] 經濟部(95)年經訴字第09506168600號。
[29] 陳文吟，前揭註20，頁51、56。
[30] 金海軍譯，前揭註20，頁242、243。

(f)款[31]、歐共體商標條例第7條[32]，而台灣「商標識別性審查要點」第10點與「行政院公平交易委員會對於公平交易法第20條案件之處理原則第10點」亦有類似規定。第二意義是否產生、何時產生，其舉證責任則由主張取得第二意義者來承擔，並無判別標準，則需個案作判定，通常係爭商品或服務的消費者一般性的認定標準，亦是係爭標章與一定商品或服務之關聯性[33]。證據可分為：

一、直接證據[34]：為隨機取樣之消費以法庭上之證言，陳述對該標章的認識，而最直接的有力證據為消費者調查或為市場報告，但不論用哪一種方法都需要花費很多時間與成本，因此舉證責任人可以不必用二此方法來證明是否有第二意義，可用間接證據來證明即可。

二、間接證據[35]：美國聯邦第七巡迴上訴法院1989年之*Echo Travel, Inc. Travel Associates, Inc*指出法院認定第二意義時，有三項考

---

[31] 第2條(f)款：「除本條第(a)、(b)、(c)、(d)及(e)項第(3)款明文規定不符註冊外，經申請人使用且已成為申請人營業上商品之識別標識，得准予註冊。申請人如能提出證據，證明於主張其標章其顯著性當日前之五年期間即有獨占且持續使用該標章之事實，局長得採納為該標章於申請人營業上使用於商品而成為其識別之表面證據。」參考前揭註3。

[32] 第7條：「1.(b)商標不具顯著之特性；(c)商標為商品之生產或勞務之提供之標章或標示：惟其僅在交易中顯示種類，品質，數量，用途，目的，價值，原產地、生產時間或其他商品或勞務之特性者；(d)商標已成為習慣上之日常用語或交易上善意或既成之實踐之標章或標示者。3.所表彰商品或勞務之商標已經使用而且具顯著性者，如經申請註冊不適用第1項(b)，(c)及(d)款。」

[33] 王敏銓，美國商標法上識別性之研究，商標法制與實務論文集，經濟部智慧財產局，2006年6月，頁246；曾勝珍，《台灣新修正商標法草案中註冊要件之評析》，智慧財產權法專題研究，2004年6月，自版，頁66。

[34] 王敏銓，同前揭註，頁246；黃堅真，《氣味商標之研究——以實務申請探討為中心》，清華大學科技法律研究所碩士論文，2007年2月，頁43。

[35] 林洲富，前揭註21，頁114-115；黃堅真，同前揭註，頁43；王敏銓，前揭註33，頁246。本文為尊重判決原文，以維持原義，認為翻譯成「惡意抄襲」為妥。

慮因素：（一）調查消費者之認知程度，換言之，證明消費者已
公認該商標以為特定商品或服務之標識。（二）商標使用人長期
間持續使用該商標，並排除他人使用。（三）商標使用人投入大
量廣告經費，擁有大量銷售量及廣大消費者，成功建立起消費市
場地位；（四）競爭者是否惡意抄襲。USPTO當局認定其商品
或服務已具備上述之判別標準，則應許為註冊商標。

　　本文茲舉開泰管股份有限公司檢舉他事業案[36]、台灣迪生股份有
限公司檢舉他事業違反公平交易法事件[37]、台灣禮來股份有限公司檢
舉中國化學製藥股份有限公司案[38]三案例，說明要取得第二意義（公
平交易法稱次要意義），事業主必須提出相關重要證據資料證明自身
產品具有表徵意義，如業主所提之證據資料無法證明使相關事業或消
費者辨視商品來源為何處，即公平交易委員會決議其無法取得第二意
義。

（三）功能性

　　功能性理論是美國實務上發展出來的概念，從經濟學與公共政
策角度，一個非具有功能性的商標，特徵具有替代品，賦予商標權
不造成市場壟斷。如缺乏替代品、使產品價值大減或使產品生產更
便宜，將拒絕給予商標保護[39]，係指一個具有功效性、實用性的商品
或營業表徵之特徵就不能成為商標或營業表徵而受到保護，即使該
特徵已取得第二意義，也不能成為註冊商標。一般來說，功能性可

---

[36] 公平會(91)年公參字第0910008507號處分書。
[37] 公平會(85)年公訴字第03975號訴願決定書。
[38] 公平會(85)年公訴字第01978號訴願決定書。
[39] 金海軍譯，前揭註20，頁254。

分為兩種[40]：一為實用功能性[41]；二為美感功能性[42]。商標審查手冊第1202.02(a)(Ⅲ)(A)指出「商標或營業表徵之功能性如為產品之使用或目的上所必要或影響生產成本、品質，是不受商標註冊要件之保護」[43]。

在歐洲方面，歐共體商標條例第7條(1)為規定：「有下列情形之一者，不得註冊：(e)標章包括有下列情形之一者：(i)為源於商品本身之性質之形狀；(ii)為用以達致某種技術上結果所必要之商品之形狀；(iii)為賦予商品重大價值之形狀」。其實，歐洲法院對於功能性審查的個案，是鮮少的，唯一著名案例是飛利浦電動刮鬍刀案，歐洲法院針對英國上訴法院審理之*Koninklijke Philips Electronics NV v. Remington Consuner Products Ltd*[44]案，認為飛利浦三個旋轉圓形刀頭電動刮鬍刀設計，是「為了達到某種技術效果所必要之形狀」是不能取得識別性，此案與美國Traffix案中對於功能性的認定方法是一致的。然而台灣商標法第23條第1項第4款有相同規定並在「立體、顏色及聲音商標審查基準」第2條第5項第2款中亦提出功能性判斷考量因素。

本文挑選瑞士商依利好公司檢舉進聯工業公司及昌凱電器公司

---

[40] 洪淑敏，前揭註2，頁157；林洲富，前揭註71，頁116。

[41] 係指商品或其包裝容器的形狀或設計，具有實用上之效力或製造上的經濟效益，使在消費市場上有競爭優勢；*Inwood, Laboratoires Inc. v. lves Labratries, Inc*案、*Traffix Devices, Inc. v. Marketing Displays, Inc.*案、*Quaalitex Co. v. Jacobson Products Co, Inc.*案三案例為TMEP第1202.02(a)(Ⅲ)(A)款的修正依據。參考洪淑敏，前揭註2，157-159頁；黃堅貞，前揭註34，頁48。

[42] 指商品或其包裝容器的形狀或設計，藉由美的創作，吸引消費者購買，提升商品價值；最早有關美學功能性案例為1952年*Pagliero v. Wallace China Co.*案，此該判決沒有得到其他法院認同，參洪淑敏，前揭註2，頁159。

[43] 洪淑敏，前揭註2，頁163。

[44] 內容詳見宋紅松，〈商品外型與立體商標——飛利浦VS雷明頓案述評〉，智慧財產權月刊，54期，2003年6月，頁46-59。

案[45]、正烽實業公司檢舉仿冒事件案[46]、日常皮飾開發有限公司檢舉他事業違反公平交易法事件[47]三個案例事實說明為維護市場之公平競爭、防止廠商壟斷行為與獨惠業者事由，商標具有功能性者不可能為商品之表徵，故無法取得市場之佔有率。

參、動態商標註冊案

一、概　說

　　有鑑於動態商標的設計技術多涉及目前時下新興技術，例如電腦軟體的運用，而電腦被世人廣泛的運用亦是近一二十年來的時間，在國際上承認動態商標之類型僅限於WIPO之新加坡商標法、歐盟共同體商標規則、美國以及台灣商標法修正草案，以致動態商標案例至今仍不多見，因此本文利用歐盟商標線上查詢服務系統與美國商標檢索系統，介紹歐美動態商標註冊案。

二、歐洲地區

（一）Reckitt Benckiser之個人清潔用品申請案[48]

　　指定用於個人清潔或洗衣用品等清潔用品。商標（圖8-1）係指食指與拇指拿著一個骯髒硬幣放進清潔劑後，可以清除硬幣污漬。商

---

[45]　行政院(84)年台訴字第34130號、公平會(84)年公訴決字第014號。

[46]　公平會(82)年公訴字第50456號訴願決定書。

[47]　公平會(87)年公訴字第01734號訴願決定書。

[48]　Reg. 005952999。

標的顏色由紅、粉紅、黑白、青銅色、棕色與膚色組成。

圖8-1

（二）Jonathan Giles Cameron Hawkes 註冊案[49]

指定用於貴金屬、計時儀器、遊戲器具、企業管理經營等服務。商標（圖8-2）為兩個螺旋物結合成球體形狀，球體直徑一致，以軸線為中心平穩旋轉，再經由軸線使球體以緩慢方式分開並反轉直到螺旋體再次結合為球體狀。

（三）Bayer Consumer Care AG 註冊案[50]

商品指定用於醫用藥劑、嬰兒食品、殺蟲劑等。商標（圖8-3）有三張照片可參，一個波浪顏色變化，顏色從左下角開始至右上角結束，從紅色變到綠色。商標顏色由綠、黃、紅色組成。

---

[49] Reg. 004623039。

[50] Reg. 002421667。

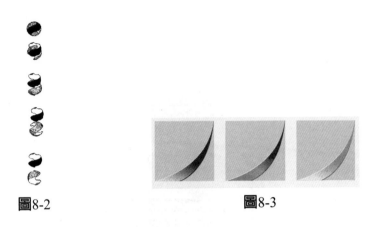

圖8-2　　　　　　　　　　　　　圖8-3

（四）IKK-Direkt之申請案[51]

　　商標主要是用於出版品、文具、廣告、保險、通訊、文化與醫療服務等。商標（圖8-4）六張圖片構成並以藍、灰色為主，商標是循序漸進出現「IKK-direkt」字樣，第四張圖片出現「e」之變形，最後將「IKK-direkt」「e」包圍。

圖8-4

（五）Fragies Vertriebsgesellschaft mbH & Co. KG之甜品註冊案[52]

商標主要是用於甜點製作材料、企業管理或提供食物、住宿之服務。商標（圖8-5）係指出在水中或液體，如咖啡、茶，放進一個像「小船」的固體，當「小船」下沈的同時轉變成糖。

圖8-5

（六）Deutsche Telekom AG註冊案[53]

商標指定用於資訊產品、紙品、企業管理、通訊或工業設計。商標（圖8-6）描述為由兩隻手構成「T」字，從觀眾角度而言，左右手掌伸直，指尖朝上；從觀眾角度可以看見右手的指尖碰觸左手掌心；最後右指尖停留在左掌心，就可辨識出「T」字。

---

[52] Reg. 004087193。
[53] Reg. 002818334。

圖8-6

（七）HENEL KGaA之申請清潔用品註冊案[54]

　　商標指定用於家庭清潔用品、個人美妝用品、清潔用品等。商標（圖8-7）顏色由黃、綠、棕、黑、白、藍色組成。黃布上有個凶猛的綠妖怪和棕妖怪；在棕妖怪的布上使用洗滌媒介凝膠，綠妖怪不受影響；凝膠淹沒棕妖怪且閉上眼睛，綠妖怪也是；棕妖怪吃下凝膠並閉著眼睛，綠妖怪則目瞪口呆；棕妖怪慢慢消失溶解，綠妖怪也很緊張；最後棕妖怪消失，凝膠到處濺散，也波及到綠妖怪。

圖8-7

---

[54] Reg. 002395473。

（八）Hans Schwarzkopf & Hekel GmbH & Co. KG個人清潔用品註冊案[55]

商標指定用於家庭清潔用品、個人美妝用品、清潔用品、廚具用具。商標（圖8-8）短片呈現出一隻手撫摸一個女人的頭髮，顏色是由黑、棕、白與膚色組成；女生的頭轉向左邊，一隻手停在她的頭髮髮線上；手摸著頭髮，髮線地方的頭髮有光澤；手摸頭髮，並順著頭髮往下，光澤隨著手的移動；手繼續摸著頭髮，白色小點出現在髮線旁，下方出現光澤；白點和頭髮上的光澤順著頭髮向下移動，手逐漸消失；手已不在頭髮上，白點與光澤隨著移動，最後停在髮尾。

圖8-8

[55] Reg. 00276813。

（九）Reckitt Benckiser (Switzerland) AG之清潔用品註冊案[56]

　　商標指定用於家庭、個人、工業、醫藥等各類清潔用品，或照明、烹飪、冷凍等設備用品。商標（圖8-9）以連續動作影像組成，「回家是一件多美好的事物！」

圖8-9

（十）Vattenfall AB之科技設計註冊案[57]

　　指定於科技、不動產業務、通訊、科學及技術性服務與研究之相關設計等商品，商標隨著光線移動，如圖8-10、圖8-11。

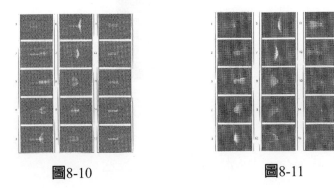

圖8-10　　　　　　　　　圖8-11

---

[56] Reg. 004799318。

[57] Reg. 001779412, 001772615。

三、美　國

（一）Univision Communications公司之影音註冊案[58]

商標指定用於事先錄製的影片、卡帶，或喜劇、動作片、卡通等動作片。商標（圖8-12）描述為，藍黑白三色為商標特色，標章以捲筒式軟片為背景由「UNICINE」組成，藍色的「UNI」，白色的「CINE」並用藍框框住。慢慢出現「UNICINE」時，有閃爍的白光，背景為藍黑色的捲筒軟片，捲筒以逆時針方向旋轉鬆開再出現E-N-I-C-U-N-I。

圖8-12

（十三）Spark數位媒體公司申請案[59]

用於電影的製作與配製服務，商標（如圖8-13）由連續動作影像組成，「SPARK DIGITAL MEDIA」已格式化。「SPARK」以較大的字並在「DIGITAL MEDIA」之上。

---

[58] Reg. 3241528。
[59] Reg. 3428105。

圖8-13

（十四）ELFENWORKS PRODUCTIONS之影音註冊案[60]

指定用於影音業與DVD製作，商標（8-14）描述以動畫為特色，標章是個有翅磅的女小精靈且可感覺小精靈享受旋轉樂趣，透過她的手後可變成「ELFENWORKS」。動畫開始時有小精靈身體上半部的特寫鏡頭，當小精靈放開手時，會呈現出「ELFENWORKS」，此字出現在螢幕中間和小精靈面前，最後小精靈手臂慢慢伸到她的頭並往上抬。

圖8-14

---

[60] Reg. 3319030。

（十五）RKO電影公司註冊案[61]

指定用於CD、DVD、錄影帶、卡帶等商品，商標（圖8-15）由「RKO PICTURES」組成，以雲與氣壓為背景，有個像地球球體的頂端上有個無線電塔台，塔台傳出由七個同心圓組成的廣播聲波，配合優美旋律及有節奏音調，令人想起一個怪異的摩斯電報號碼（Morse code）訊號。

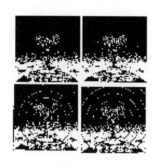

圖8-15

（十六）二十世紀幅克斯電影公司之電影業註冊案[62]

商標指定用於生產和配製影集，事先預錄的錄影帶，卡帶和光碟等服務。商標（圖8-16）藉由電腦展現不同角度的連續短暫的影像。

---

[61] Reg. 2690376。
[62] Reg. 2092752。

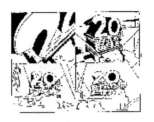

圖8-16

（十七）哥倫比亞影業公司之影音業註冊案[63]

商標指定用於動畫影集，販售影片膠捲、影碟片或電腦的IC晶片記憶體等。商標（圖8-17）是會移動的發亮燈光影像組成，背景為天空與白雲。影像是位女神拿著一把放在檯柱上的火把，「COLUMBIA」的字通過火把後，天空出現一道彩虹圍繞女神。

圖8-17

（十八）Broadway影像公司提供娛樂服務註冊案[64]

商標指定用於提供娛樂服務，商標（圖8-18）描述都市天空的輪廓為背景，兩個同心圓裡包圍著「BROADWAY VIDEO」，當都市

---

[63] Reg. 1975999。
[64] Reg. 2092415。

天空的輪廓進入「BROADWAY VIDEO」裡，其字以順時針方向圍繞城市。圓圈包含一條紅色閃電且成「V」字。

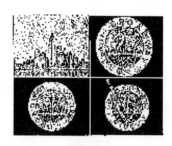

圖8-18

（十九）華納公司之卡通播放註冊案[65]

　　指定透過電視節目播送卡通節目提供娛樂服務，商標（圖8-19）由星星的連續動作組成。

圖8-19

---

[65] Reg. 1339596。

（二十）微軟股份有限公司之電腦科技業註冊案[66]

商標指定用於電腦遊戲和系統軟體設計的商品，商標（圖8-20）由長方形和彎曲線及小圓組成，十六個小黑點圍繞著長方形。位於最上面的黑點第一個發亮，以三個發亮的小圓為一組以順時針方向連續繞著長方形；結束時，最頂端的小圓和長方形裡的小圓會同時發亮。

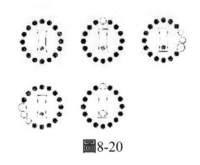

圖8-20

（二一）VIDIGREET卡片申請案[67]

商標指定用於提供賀卡、電子賀卡、或從電腦螢幕等其他傳輸系統下載電子賀卡。商標（圖8-21）描述以黑色畫出「VID」，「GREET」和一個人帶著帽子的樣子，用綠色畫出「I」字夾在「VID」、「GREET」間。標誌有個特色即「VIDIGREET」的「D」字，當虛擬人物戴著帽子或頭巾，站在靜物（「D」）上，頭向上抬並揮揮他的右手臂。當螢幕靜止時，人物即張口言之，之後人物會回到螢幕裡消失，人物全部消失後，靜物以垂直狀與水平狀消失，令人聯想到是螢幕關掉電源。

---

[66] Reg. 3252687。

[67] Reg. 3431730。

圖8-21

（二二）數位整合公司註冊案[68]

商標指定用於廣告與電腦服務，商標（圖8-22）的描述為「Ｃ」的小圓點以逆時針方向畫出且從最高點到左邊，小圓點分裂成兩個小圓點，一個在上一個在下。

圖8-22

（二三）ZixIt公司註冊案[69]

指定用於電信服務，商標（圖8-23）描述為利用四張解析圖說明一雙眼睛在同一水平線上來回轉動。

---

[68] Reg. 2645188。

[69] Jerome Gilson; Anne Gilson LaLonde, Cinnarnoon Buns, Marching Docks and Cherry. Scented Racecar Exhaust: Protecting nontraditional Tradezarks, 95 Trademark Rep. 773 (July-August 2005), p807; Reg. 2490649.

圖8-23

（二四）Target Health股份有限公司的病歷電腦連線系統 註冊案[70]

指定用於經由全球網路系統匯整與提供病歷記錄，商標（圖 8-24）由連續影像組成，一個圓形圖章是關於「TARGET HEALTH INC」且以順時針方向旋轉並了解其側面圖。

圖8-24

（二五）ChatSpace股份有限公司註冊案[71]

商標指定用於電腦軟體系統，提供線上討論室，商標（圖8-25）的描述是由連續動作影像組成，傳達出軟體的使用操作與用戶之間的

聯繫。描繪圖中間有個具3D立體形狀的「C」附屬在一個只有半球體的垂直軸徑上並以360度的順時針方向旋轉。

圖8-25

（二六）BALLANTYNE OF OMAHA之搜尋服務系統註冊案[72]

用於強大搜尋系統搜尋知識、出租與租賃服務，商標由一個程式寫成，以一條強光圓柱線為基準，再投射到空中輪流旋轉。

（二七）EBS有限公司註冊案[73]

商標指定用於拍賣、籌措慈善基金、金融服務等，商標（圖8-26）描述四種體育項目的主要動作。

---

[72] Jerome Gilson; Anne Gilson LaLande. supra note 69, p807; Reg.2323892 。

[73] Reg. 3272038。

圖8-26

（二八）國家城市股份有限公司之註冊案[74]

商標指定用於銀行服務，商標（圖8-27）由數字「0」組成，
「0」為完整結構，「0」先縮成與銀行支票的尺寸一樣後再慢慢充
滿整個畫面。

圖8-27

（二九）友邦投資信託股份有限公司自動付款註冊案[75]

商標指定用於電子匯款、說明與交付系統服務，商標（圖8-28）
由「Diect Pay」和「Convenient Payment Program」交叉排列和一個

---

[74]　Jerome Gilson; Anne Gilson LaLonde, supra note 68, p807; Reg. 2756210。

[75]　Reg. 2809748。

帶有連續動作的箭頭組成。

圖8-28

（三十）美國郵局註冊案[76]

商品指定用於信用卡交易、電子匯款、電子郵件傳送等服務，商標（圖8-29）的描述是個像鷹狀的旗子隨噴射器尾端移動。

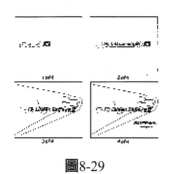

圖8-29

---

[76] Reg. 2600363。

（三一）Timberline Venture Management Corporation註冊案[77]

商標指定用於提供金融、投資風險、有價證券管理的分析與諮詢等，商標（圖8-30）藉由電腦顯現出連續短暫閃亮元素，在一個自由空間的小方形裡出現星星且逐漸變大，而三角形沿著有弧度的空間分散。

圖8-30

（三二）美國口吃治療與訓練協會註冊案[78]

指定用於治療口吃的臨床實驗與關心有口吃的小孩、青年人與成年人及家人之服務商標，商標（圖8-31）以自由（free hand）的方式畫出以黑色為底的手勢側面輪廓，描述圖下方有「American Institute for Stuttering」（美國口吃協會）的字樣。

---

[77] Reg. 2438246。
[78] Reg. 3019740。

圖8-31

（三三）維吉尼亞州香菸社會福利基金會之註冊案[79]

指定用於推廣民眾公開吸菸的負面影響之商標服務，商標（圖8-32）由一個類似字母「Y」組成，「Y」在一秒鐘內以順時針方向形成一個鬆散形狀，並由另一較小的鬆垮圓圈框住「？」。

圖8-32

（三四）紐約豐田汽車聯合代理商申請案[80]

指定用於代理汽車商品的商標，商標（圖8-33）由五張析解圖組成，標章開始於臉或頭，手輕敲著頭且面帶笑容，當手輕點太陽穴，頭上會有興奮的線條，隨後，手遠離頭部。

[79] Jerome Gilsom: Anne Gilson LaLonde, supra note 69, p807; Reg. 2709214。
[80] Reg. 3442655。

圖8-33

（三五）藍寶堅尼汽車註冊案[81]

指定用於汽車商品的註冊案，商標（圖8-34）有個獨特的車門開啟動作。車門的開啟方式與車體呈現平行，逐漸升到一個平行位置。

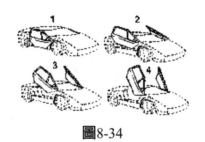

圖8-34

肆、結　論

商標申請案之審查，可分為形式審查與實體審查，動作商標雖為非傳統商標之一種，審查也無傳統商標審查嚴格，但仍有適用商標法之一般原則。未來台灣商標法修正草案通過後，商標的保護型態將

---

[81] 該案亦在1999年11月26日向CTM申請註冊，申請結果駁回：Reg. 2793439。

不受限制，因此可參考歐美文獻，將動態商標的申請圖檔格式可為單一動作的特點或有五張以上的解析圖呈現，其格式為JPG檔，檔案最大為2M，如為影片方式者，影像檔以WAV.、MP3.檔為主並儲存於CD或DVD中。更認為現行「立體、顏色及聲音商標審查基準」改為「非傳統商標審查基準」以符合商標法保護之客體。

商標的註冊要件在商標法中均有明文規定，除需注意商標本身的獨特性外，第二意義具有識別性之功能時便可註冊商標，但有學者認為第二意義為識別性之例外[82]。而功能性理論的功能主要是維護市場上公平競爭。行政院公平交易委員會對於公平交易法第20條之案件處理原則」第9條與商標法的規定有異曲同工之妙，且公平交易法已於88年將功能性納入規範，復公平交易法為商標法之普通法，本文以為商標法已把功能性納入規範，爾後如遇有商標功能性之疑慮，認為商標權人或第三人應籲請經濟部依商標法規定，似為較妥。

歐美兩大商標查詢系統資料庫裡的商標說明書上能夠正確記載說明與其圖案，能有效率的搜尋到申請案[83]，從案例可以得知，動態商標主要使用與電腦相關之產業上。而動態商標對國內外之產官學而言，仍為一個新名詞，在中英文的用語亦尚未明確，雖然歐盟的CTMONLINE系統將動態商標歸類為「other」，可供使用者搜尋相關資料，或利用TESS系統時須花費過多的搜尋及過濾時間，於此，建議台灣或他國未來能對動態商標定下專用語，本文以為可為動態商標（motion mark），以符合經濟成本。另有學者建議，針對動態商標制定一個商標設計法規，如繪圖法規，以有別於其他商標種類[84]。

---

[82] 陳文吟，前揭註21，頁58。

[83] Lesley Matty, *Rock, Paper, Scissors, Trademark? A Comparative, Analysis of Motion Mark as a feature of Trademark in the United Sta tes and Europe*, 14 Cardozo J. Intl & Comp. L. 557(2006). at 582.

[84] Lesley Matty, *Id*, at584.

參考文獻

中文

William M. Landes & Richard A. Posner著，金海軍譯，知識產權法的經濟結構，北京大學，2005年5月。

王敏銓，美國商標法上識別性之研究，商標法制與實務論文集，經濟部智慧財產局，2006年6月。

宋紅松，商品外型與立體商標─飛利浦VS雷明頓案述評，智慧財產權月刊，54期，2003年6月。

林洲富，顏色、立體及聲音商標於法律上保護─兼論台灣商標法相關修正規定，月旦法學雜誌，120期，2005年5月。

洪淑敏，國外非傳統商標之審查，商標法制與實務論文集，經濟部智慧財產局，2006年6月。

陳文吟，商標法論，三民書局，2005年2月。

曾淑婷，氣味商標問題之研究，台灣大學法律研究所碩士論文，2006年6月。

曾勝珍，台灣新修正商標法草案中註冊要件之評析，智慧財產權法專題研究，2004年6月，自版。

黃堅真，氣味商標之研究─以實務申請探討為中心，清華大學科技法律研究所碩士論文，2007年2月。

英文

Jerome Gilson; Anne Gilson LaLonde, *Cinnamon Buns, Marching Docks and Cherry-Scented Racecar Exhaust: Protecting nontraditional Trademarks*, 95 Trademark Rep. 773 (July-August 2005).

Lesley Matty, *Rock, Paper, Scissors, Trademark? A Comparative,*

Analysis of Motion Mark as a feature of Trademark in the United States and Europe, 14 Cardozo J. Int'l & Comp. L. 557 (2006).

WIPO Secretariat, *Standing Committee on the Law of Trademark, Industiial Designs and Geograpilical Indications*, SCT 17th Session, WIPO Doc. SCT/17/3 (March 30, 2007), at6.

網路資源

『美國專利商標局新聞稿，「Image files for TEAS」，發布日期：2006/9/8』，http://www.uspto.gov/teas/index.html，最後瀏覽日：2008/3/27。

『美國專利商標局新聞稿，「Sound/Motion Marks and Electronic Filing，發布日期：2006/11/27』，http://www.uspto.gov/teas/index.html，最後瀏覽日：2008/3/27。

CTM-ONLINE-Trade mark consultation service-Basic, http://oami europa.eu/CTMOnline/RequestManager/en_SearchBasic_NoReg

Trademark Electronic Search System (TESS), http://tess2.uspto.gov/bin/gate.exe?f=search&state=bliqfi.1.1

國家圖書館出版品預行編目資料

智慧財產權法專論：科技時代新思維／曾勝珍
著.--初版--.--臺北市：五南,2011.08
　面；　公分.
部分內容為英文
ISBN 978-957-11-6340-6（平裝）
1.智慧財產權 2.著作權法 3.專利法規
553.433　　　　　　　　　100012970

1T42

智慧財產權法專論——
科技時代新思維

作　　者 — 曾勝珍

發 行 人 — 楊榮川

總 編 輯 — 龐君豪

主　　編 — 劉靜芬　林振煌

責任編輯 — 李奇蓁　王政軒

封面設計 — P.Design視覺企劃

出 版 者 — 五南圖書出版股份有限公司

地　　址：106台北市大安區和平東路二段339號4樓

電　　話：(02)2705-5066　傳　真：(02)2706-6100

網　　址：http://www.wunan.com.tw

電子郵件：wunan@wunan.com.tw

劃撥帳號：01068953

戶　　名：五南圖書出版股份有限公司

台中市駐區辦公室/台中市中區中山路6號

電　　話：(04)2223-0891　傳　真：(04)2223-3549

高雄市駐區辦公室/高雄市新興區中山一路290號

電　　話：(07)2358-702　傳　真：(07)2350-236

法律顧問　元貞聯合法律事務所　張澤平律師

出版日期　2011年 8 月初版一刷

定　　價　新臺幣400元